RENEWING MORAL THEOLOGY

CHRISTIAN ETHICS AS ACTION, CHARACTER AND GRACE

DANIEL A. WESTBERG

IVP Academic

An imprint of InterVarsity Press
Downers Grove, Illinois

InterVarsity Press
P.O. Box 1400, Downers Grove, IL 60515-1426
ivpress.com
email@ivpress.com

InterVarsity Press® is the book-publishing division of InterVarsity Christian Fellowship/USA®, a movement of students and faculty active on campus at hundreds of universities, colleges and schools of nursing in the United States of America, and a member movement of the International Fellowship of Evangelical Students. For information about local and regional activities, visit intervarsity.org.

Scripture quotations, unless otherwise noted, are from the New Revised Standard Version of the Bible, *copyright 1989 by the Division of Christian Education of the National Council of the Churches of Christ in the USA. Used by permission. All rights reserved.*

Cover design: Cindy Kiple
Interior design: Beth McGill

Images: compass illustration: ©Christopher Brewer/iStockphoto
        antique compass: Barry Rosenthal/Getty Images

ISBN 978-0-8308-2460-1 (print)
ISBN 978-0-8308-9770-4 (digital)

Printed in the United States of America ♾

g green press **INITIATIVE** *As a member of the Green Press Initiative, InterVarsity Press is committed to protecting the environment and to the responsible use of natural resources. To learn more, visit greenpressinitiative.org.*

Library of Congress Cataloging-in-Publication Data
A catalog record for this book is available from the Library of Congress.

P	23	22	21	20	19	18	17	16	15	14	13	12	11	10	9	8	7	6	5	4	3	2	1
Y	34	33	32	31	30	29	28	27	26	25	24	23	22	21	20	19	18	17	16	15			

This book is dedicated to

Harry Edwin Westberg 1924–

Gladys Rudine Westberg 1924–2008

Dorothy Nelson Westberg 1922–

As missionaries, church workers and parents,

they have been disciples of the Lord,

witnesses to God's grace and

examples of Christian character.

Contents

PREFACE

W HEN I BEGAN TEACHING Anglican moral theology to seminary students about fifteen years ago, I realized that we had few, if any, current textbooks to choose from. Anglican theologians have, of course, produced important and sometimes brilliant work on ethical topics in recent years, but the systematic approach to moral theology represented by Kenneth Kirk, R. C. Mortimer and Lindsay Dewar was swept away a couple of generations ago by the shifting and seductive winds of the 1960s. Though I see the publication of Joseph Fletcher's *Situation Ethics* in 1966 as a kind of boundary marker for the end of that phase of Anglican ethical thought, the older style of moral theology certainly would have come to an end from the social, theological and philosophical pressures of the time without any direct influence from Fletcher.

Renewing Moral Theology is my attempt to breathe new life into this Anglican tradition, with the immediate aim of providing a systematic presentation of Christian ethics that builds on the Thomistic foundation shared with Catholic moral theology. This foundation is not as clear as it used to be, however, since after the Second Vatican Council the deficiencies of the standard understanding of Aquinas were exposed, resulting in a widespread revisionism, conservative reactions and a spectrum of positions, a condition long familiar to Protestants. Thomas Aquinas still retains for Catholics a certain preeminence, which can often be more of a stumbling block than a help, because strange new ways of approaching ethics often are presented as interpretations of Aquinas, resulting in a sometimes bewildering array of moral theologies all claiming to be "Thomistic."[1]

---

[1]For a fine guide to the interpretations and misinterpretations of Aquinas on a variety of topics see Fergus Kerr, *After Aquinas: Versions of Thomism* (Oxford: Blackwell, 2002).

The wider and more important purpose of this book is to provide for the general Christian public a blending of the strengths of the Catholic tradition with evangelical emphases and convictions. Catholics and Protestants have realized that they have much to profit from each other's strengths, and this book has been written to further the possibility of mutual enrichment in the area of ethics. This blending has been a feature of the best Anglican tradition of moral theology, long before the rather recent rise of seminaries and the need of theological colleges for textbooks. We find in Richard Hooker and Jeremy Taylor, for example, the helpful combination and harmonizing of Catholic moral philosophy of the Thomistic tradition with Reformed theological principles and Christ-centered spirituality, a tradition in which this book aims to follow.

One purpose of this project is to provide for contemporary Christians renewed confidence in the area of moral convictions. The trustworthiness of Scripture, especially for evangelicals, has been and still should provide a strong foundation; but the incorporation of the approach of Thomas Aquinas, which is a Christian modification of Aristotle, should provide further confidence in a philosophical and psychological soundness that academic ethicists are continuing to appreciate: when cleansed of Neo-Scholastic accretions, the theology of Aquinas provides integrity and consistency that, like the music of J. S. Bach or the architecture of Chartres Cathedral, can stand as a perennial monument in Christian culture.

Some readers may wonder at the lack of emphasis on natural law in a work meant to represent Thomistic ethics. I understand that in a postmodern relativistic society in which moral standards are considered to be opinions and matters of taste, the notion of objective moral norms has strong appeal to traditionalists and conservatives as the needed corrective to subjective individualism. However, there are dangers associated with a natural law approach that I would avoid, among which are, for example, the ease with which cultural norms are assumed to be equivalent to eternally valid moral principles, and the appeal to "common sense" or natural law in justifying social policies that sometimes conflict with ethics of the gospel, such as the focus on retributive views of punishment.

Another reason for resisting natural law comes from my study of its position and role in the ethical section of the *Summa Theologiae* (hereafter abbreviated *ST* in citations). Natural law is dealt with in one question only (*ST* I-II, q. 94). It is brilliant and important, but it is far removed from the section on ethical reasoning where Aquinas demonstrates how intellect, will and emotion combine to choose our actions, a description that has little or nothing to do with natural law, or law in general, for that matter. This leads to a more general theme in this book, which is the relation of law to moral reasoning. Until recently, the only alternative to an ethic based on consequences (such as utilitarianism) was an ethic based on obedience to the commands of God or obedience to the dictates of the reasoned conscience. Many interpretations of the ethics of Aquinas were forced into this template so that the dominant themes became the roles of conscience and obedient will. The very different model of practical reasoning actually developed by Aquinas (and followed by Richard Hooker, for example) needs to be highlighted, as this book does, while explaining the proper role of law in the Christian life (see especially chapter eight).

Since this book was written as a seminary text, I want to acknowledge the help of students at Nashotah House, who in successive years of gradual production and trial of the text in the classroom have given helpful suggestions for improvements, among whom are Jake Dell and Kreigh Knerr. John Trenum has my thanks for some of the more tedious tasks such as checking references and producing a portion of the index. The book has also been used recently in the ethics course of the distance-learning program at Nashotah House under the teaching of Kent Anderson, who has given me helpful advice and encouragement.

Some of my present and former colleagues at Nashotah House have seen various sections and given useful feedback, including Tom Holtzen, Garwood Anderson, Steve Schlossberg and Jack Gabig. Professors at other seminaries and institutions also have read some of the chapters, such as William Witt at Trinity School for Ministry, Jeff Greenman of Regent College and Kent Dunnington of Greenville college. I'm also grateful to Paul Reasoner and a group of students at Bethel University who engaged with some of this material, as well as to Victor Austin and other members of the Anglican interest group at the Society of Christian Ethics who have made helpful suggestions.

I want to thank my editor at InterVarsity Press, Daniel Reid, for taking an interest in this project. If I look at the work as a kind of challenging voyage by sailboat, Dan has encouraged me to grip the boat's tiller firmly, to ignore the tantalizing vagaries of fresh breezes and unexplored coves, and guide the craft, tacking and even reversing course as needed, to reach the safe haven of satisfactory completion.

Finally, my wife, Lisa, is my closest partner in the larger navigation through the uncertainties of life. Through calm passages and threatening squalls she has patiently provided encouragement and practical support. I am happy that together we can share life's challenges, mysteries and opportunities to grow in grace—and also the promised blessings to come.

PART ONE

1

MORAL THEOLOGY

Tradition and Prospects

M ORAL THEOLOGY is the term often used in Catholic and Anglican circles for what other traditions call *Christian ethics* or *theological ethics*. Sometimes these terms are distinguished by defining Christian ethics as the more general approach to the elements of Christian character and behavior, while moral theology deals with the application to economics, medicine, sexuality and other areas of life where difficult decisions must be made. Thus Christian ethics could be said to deal largely with foundational questions: the human person, moral psychology, general principles, and norms, while moral theology focuses on applying those principles to specific cases.[1]

In this book *Christian ethics* and *moral theology* are used more or less interchangeably, as is common elsewhere. This is not so much because of contemporary slackness, but because the methods of approaching the field have changed so considerably in the last fifty years that the starting points, assumptions and methodology no longer fit the traditional terminology.

Anglican moral theology developed as a method of handling the inherited Catholic model but from a perspective influenced by key insights of the Protestant Reformation. There were benefits in the continued use of Roman Catholic sources in ethics: the scholastic method offered clear definitions; a philosophical psychology for understanding the nature of persons, actions and agency; a theoretical basis for analyzing the moral character of

---

[1]Herbert Waddams, *A New Introduction to Moral Theology*, rev. ed. (London: SCM Press, 1972), p. 29.

actions; and a methodology for handling and resolving difficult cases (known as casuistry). But with this inheritance came also the danger of the flaws of the Roman approach: a philosophical rather than biblical character, scholastic technical vocabulary, a somewhat rigid framework and a spirit of legalism.

In the 1950s, shortly before major changes in the following decade in both Protestant and Roman Catholic ethics, Lindsay Dewar gave a short series of lectures on moral theology to clergy in the Church of England, with three topics: the place of law, the doctrine of conscience and Christian casuistry. Dewar's approach reflected the Catholic tradition in which the moral difficulties of the Christian life were to be analyzed in terms of cases of conscience and the correct application of rules and laws. There is a certain quaint unreality in Dewar's concern to avoid rigorism and an overly scrupulous conscience, which shows the different atmosphere in which Christian people now think and live as well as the extent to which the older moral theology (even outside of Roman Catholic circles) conveyed a legalistic mentality. This is one of Dewar's chief examples of a moral difficulty to be resolved:

> Here is a young man who is invited to play a game of tennis on a Sunday afternoon with some friends with whom he is spending what is commonly . . . called "the week-end." We may suppose that he has been brought up in such a way that he has never done this, and has been taught to think that this is wrong. But now he becomes genuinely doubtful. If he refuses to make a fourth, the game will be spoiled for his friends. What is he to do?[2]

There is no doubt that the church in the modern world would do well to abandon its increasingly secular indifference to the Sabbath principle and recover a renewed emphasis on properly honoring the Lord's Day, but that is not really what concerns Dewar. He sees the problem only in terms of the young man having proper authority (which he might get from his vicar) for his conscience to allow him to play tennis on Sunday afternoon. The young man has been brought up to consider that sports and certain activities are to be avoided on Sundays (the story of Eric Liddell in the film *Chariots of Fire* reminds us how strong these convictions used to be), and yet he would be disappointing his friends and host for the weekend if he declined to play.

---

[2]Lindsay Dewar, *A Short Introduction to Moral Theology* (London: A. R. Mowbray, 1956), p. 37.

For many of us it is hard, however, not to be reminded of the tithing of mint, dill and cumin (Mt 23:23).

Lindsay Dewar's style of ethical reasoning was not atypical of the Catholic-based moral theology used by American and British theological colleges and parish priests in the nineteenth and twentieth centuries. Contemporary with Dewar was R. C. Mortimer, bishop of Exeter and Regius Professor of Moral and Pastoral Theology at Oxford, who contributed an introduction still used for training priests in moral theology in some parts of the Anglican communion.[3] Although he provided an extensive coverage of the virtues that has some connection to the Thomistic tradition, he gave prudence very slight treatment; he also changed its position from the first to the last of the moral virtues, giving it an entirely different coloring from Aquinas's treatment. It is clear from the first half of the book that Mortimer understood human action within the context of law and conscience, and he even admitted in his preface that he had relied heavily on Roman Catholic sources of moral theology.[4]

Also common in Anglican seminaries in the first half of the twentieth century for use in ethics were the works of Kenneth Kirk (Regius Professor of Moral and Pastoral Theology at Oxford and later bishop of that diocese). One of his chief contributions was to stress the link between moral, ascetical and mystical theology, especially in *The Vision of God*, but also in *Some Principles of Moral Theology*. Kirk's stress on beatitude as the goal of the moral life and on the importance of the Holy Spirit contrasts favorably with much of the traditional Roman Catholic treatment in the moral handbooks. But Kirk was not able to make a break with the prevailing theoretical structure of action constituted by conscience and obedience to law (see *Conscience and Its Problems: An Introduction to Casuistry*).

Some readers may want to defend and preserve this classical type of moral theology and welcome the older emphasis on conscience and obedience to law, because they take the view that Christian people in modern Western societies have compromised too much with the spirit of the age, have become too undisciplined, abandoned important Christian principles and weakened the application of scriptural norms to Christian discipleship.

---

[3]R. C. Mortimer, *The Elements of Moral Theology*, rev. ed. (London: Adam & Charles Black, 1953).
[4]Ibid., p. v.

That position may be an important part of the moral framework of those Anglicans who have left the standard jurisdictions in North America, and of those in other parts of the world who feel alienated from the liberalism of the modern Western church.

That reactionary view may be correct in its judgment that the church in modern Western countries is in need of moral revitalization, and that we should pray for the correction and leading of the Holy Spirit. The point for us here, however, is not so much that moral standards have slipped, but that Christians are now realizing that a whole new moral framework is needed: a new way of explaining Christian discipleship, of understanding the motivation of our actions and of incorporating the concerns that laws and commandments point to without developing a checklist mentality and legalistic attitudes.

The example of playing tennis on Sunday given by Lindsay Dewar shows that fresh thinking and approaches in Christian ethics were indeed required. What we got in the 1960s, however, was "situation ethics," an impossibly reductionist attempt to clear away all the clutter of moral theology except for the single principle of doing the most loving thing.[5] The severe defects in the method of Joseph Fletcher (who was an Episcopal moral theology professor at the time) certainly were noted. A professor of philosophical ethics in a secular university called it "a very bad book, poorly written, weakly argued, astonishingly ignorant, and incredibly inaccurate,"[6] and many theologians and ethicists pointed out numerous flaws and weak points.[7] But Fletcher's simplistic approach, implying that moral norms are not absolute and should be regarded as merely vague rules of thumb, and that we would do best by obeying only the "rule of love," was immensely persuasive. Many Christian people at that time, and many more since who have never heard of Joseph Fletcher, probably think about ethical problems in the antiauthoritarian, individualistic and impatient way that Fletcher recommended, and they resolve morally difficult situations with their own bottom-line confidence that their intentions are loving. Nevertheless, we

---

[5]Joseph Fletcher, *Situation Ethics: The New Morality* (Philadelphia: Westminster, 1966).

[6]Marcus Singer, *Morals and Values: Readings in Theoretical and Practical Ethics* (New York: Scribner, 1977), p. 452.

[7]See, for example, Harvey Cox, ed., *The Situation Ethics Debate* (Philadelphia: Westminster, 1968).

may say that Fletcher grasped two points that the traditional moral theology had obscured: (1) the primacy of Christian love (setting aside the problem of his reductionism); (2) the impoverishment of an ethic that conceives moral decisions primarily in terms of fulfilling an obligation to obey the law, or otherwise securing proper authority to set the rule aside, characteristic of the approach known as casuistry.

The rigidity and legalism of the moral theology taught in Roman Catholic seminaries had been under attack for some time. Even before the Second Vatican Council (1962–1965) moral theologians had expressed dissatisfaction with the classical model. Some of these critics were attacked for promoting their own kind of situation ethics,[8] but some also produced positive studies that looked back to Thomas Aquinas for an ethics based on virtue and grace—with charity central—rather than on law and casuistry.[9]

Vatican II tackled a wide range of issues and reforms, of course, but in the area of moral theology the challenge was to draw more richly on Scripture and recover a Christ-centered emphasis: "Special care should be given to the perfecting of moral theology. Its scientific presentation should draw more fully on the teaching of Holy Scripture and should throw light upon the exalted vocation of the faithful in Christ and their obligation to bring forth fruit in charity for the life of the world."[10] In many programs in Catholic universities and seminaries there was an inevitable period of confusion and experimentation; but very few have argued for a return to the former era of the scholastic handbooks of moral theology. Even the most conservative ethicists loyal to the magisterium see the need to articulate a moral theology that is more biblical, christocentric and conducive to Christian discipleship.

---

[8]Papal pronouncements on the dangers of *situationis ethica* were made in 1952 and 1956. See John Mahoney, *The Making of Moral Theology: A Study of the Roman Catholic Tradition* (Oxford: Clarendon, 1987), pp. 202-10. For a recent helpful survey, see James Keenan, *A History of Catholic Moral Theology in the Twentieth Century: From Confessing Sins to Liberating Consciences* (New York: Continuum, 2010).

[9]See Gérard Gilleman, *The Primacy of Charity in Moral Theology* (Westminster, MD: Newman Press, 1959).

[10]"Decree on the Training of Priests," paragraph 16, in *Vatican Council II: The Conciliar and Post Conciliar Documents*, ed. Austin Flannery, rev. ed. (Collegeville, MN: Liturgical Press, 1984), p. 720.

Recent Favorable Developments

The recovery of Aristotle and the rise of virtue ethics. The rejection of classic moral theology in the 1960s was due not just to impatience with legalism, but also to the fact that the Thomistic and Scholastic traditions were so different from the ethical systems of the day: utilitarianism, Kantianism, emotivism and linguistic analysis prevailed and were unsympathetic to the world of premodern moral philosophy. But the impoverishment and restrictions of the Enlightenment-inspired ethical methods became obvious. Aristotle's teleological ethics, with its account of intellect, choice, friendship and the virtues became relevant again. Especially after the publication in the early 1980s of Alasdair MacIntyre's *After Virtue*,[11] a large volume of work on virtue has been produced in both philosophical and theological ethics.

The contribution of Aristotelian ethics to a biblically based Christian morality is not obvious at first, and there has been a strong tradition of suspicion of the applicability of Aristotle's moral philosophy to the understanding of Christian morality not only in Protestantism but also in Roman Catholic thought from the time of the reintroduction of Aristotle's works in the thirteenth century. Some think that there is a fundamental problem with a humanistic ethical system that developed without reference to original sin and God's revelation. In the following chapters we will consider some of these points more closely, but here we can assert that there has been a strong interest in moving away from the act-centered moral systems of Immanuel Kant's deontological ethics and from utilitarianism to the broader view of character and virtue.[12]

A richer view of biblical ethics. When Christian ethics was conceived principally as obedience to the will of God expressed through law, it followed that the reading of the Bible would concentrate on the Decalogue, the relevance of other Jewish law and the passages in the Gospels and Epistles in the form of commands and norms. In the work of biblical scholars such as Richard Hays we are led to pay attention to the moral implications of Scripture in a much more comprehensive way: one can discern principles that should govern our

---

[11]Alasdair MacIntyre, *After Virtue: A Study in Moral Theory* (London: Duckworth, 1981).

[12]A helpful resource for Protestants skeptical of virtue ethics is the treatment by the Mennonite Joseph Kotva Jr., *The Christian Case for Virtue Ethics* (Washington, DC: Georgetown University Press, 1996).

decisions; the many stories and accounts of people's actions provide paradigms for conduct (both positive and negative); and the "symbolic world" created by different authors presents us with attitudes and frameworks for understanding our relationship to God, to the created order and to each other.[13] Interest in virtue ethics has led to more fruitful explorations of biblical perspectives on character formation and moral development.[14]

We should also note Stanley Hauerwas, who has been an advocate for the narrative mode of reading Scripture. He made an early contribution to a sympathetic reading of Thomas Aquinas's ethics,[15] but he has moved on to a more determinedly anti–natural law type of narrative ethics that centers on the importance of forming Christian communal identity, shaped by a common understanding and practical expression of the gospel, following especially the pattern of the life of Christ. Some have noted a measure of reductionism and selective use of Scripture in his approach,[16] but Hauerwas clearly has been helpful in expressing fundamental features of the outlook and motivation of a contemporary Christian virtue ethics.

Reassessment of the history of moral theology. For centuries it was assumed that the moral theology of the Neo-Scholastic manuals was basically the same system developed by Thomas Aquinas, with further developments and applications to new cases. It was natural for Anglican and other non–Roman Catholic theologians to assume that they could be aided in their study of Aquinas by consulting contemporary Roman Catholic handbooks of moral theology. The true character of Thomistic ethics was not represented well—in some respects greatly distorted—in spite of the many citations from the *Summa Theologiae*. This is similar to the many distortions of the message of sections of the Bible itself by some fundamentalist Protestants (and other types, too, of course) who in spite of the quotation of numerous biblical proof texts end up falsifying biblical teaching with false assumptions and alien patterns of thought.

---

[13]Richard Hays, *The Moral Vision of the New Testament: A Contemporary Introduction to New Testament Ethics* (San Francisco: HarperSanFrancisco, 1996), summary on p. 209.

[14]See, for example, William Brown, ed., *Character and Scripture: Moral Formation, Community, and Biblical Interpretation* (Grand Rapids: Eerdmans, 2002).

[15]Stanley Hauerwas, *Character and the Christian Life: A Study in Theological Ethics* (San Antonio: Trinity University Press, 1975).

[16]See the critical analysis in Hays, *Moral Vision*, pp. 258-66.

The discordance of the manuals of moral theology from the ethics of Thomas Aquinas certainly was apparent to a number of theologians before Vatican II, which is why there was broad acceptance by that council of the need to change course. Gérard Gilleman, arguing in the 1950s that love should be seen as the fundamental category in Thomistic ethics, wrote of the standard ethical handbooks, "Law rather than love is their dominant theme. Where there should be a spiritual impulse, we find a fixed body of doctrine. Even inspiration and liberty are precisely codified."[17]

More recently Servais Pinckaers has pointed out the points where moral theology departed from authentic Thomism: the shift from practical reason to conscience, the eclipse of virtues, a false view of freedom, the atomization of human action into individual cases needing resolution, the tendency to define the minimal fulfilling of the law and, above all, the development of an ethics of obligation.[18]

Although many of the factors behind the departures from Thomas Aquinas are complex and (because they reflect changes and shifts in Western philosophy) call for further reflection, this conclusion for our purposes is eminently valid: most of the faults associated with classic Roman Catholic moral theology (and that we also find in Anglicans such as Dewar, Mortimer and Kirk) are not the faults of Thomas Aquinas but rather lie in the later distortions of the Roman Catholic manuals.[19] The way is now clearer for us to reappropriate the ethics of Aquinas in a more authentic and ecumenical way.

Roman Catholic moral theology since Vatican II. The Roman Catholic Church experienced a major reassessment, not to say dismantling, of its traditional approach to moral theology after Vatican II. The approach of the old handbooks had been criticized for some time as legalistic, scholastic and excessively dependent upon a natural-law view asserting that the basic norms of morality were accessible to people by use of reason.

Many Catholic moral theologians responded to the call for a more Scripture-based and Christ-centered ethics. The influential Irish theologian

[17]Gérard Gilleman, *The Primacy of Charity in Moral Theology* (Westminster, MD: Newman Press, 1959), pp. xxviii-xxix.
[18]Servais Pinckaers, *The Sources of Christian Ethics*, trans. Mary Thomas Noble (Washington, DC: Catholic University of America Press, 1995).
[19]This is clearly and compellingly described by Pinckaers, *Sources of Christian Ethics*.

Enda McDonagh, in his essay "The Quest for Moral Theology," wrote, "Where the manuals of almost four centuries treated Jesus as at best an authority for the occasional moral pronouncement such as that on divorce, recent works of renewal sought to establish him at the source and centre of moral life and thought for Christians."[20]

A generation after Vatican II, when John Paul II issued the encyclical *Veritatis Splendor,* in an attempt to point out some of the errors of contemporary Roman Catholic moral theology, it was evident that no single approach to ethics had secured acceptance as the proper alternative to the old handbook approach. In spite of disagreement about what should replace the moral theology manual, there was wide agreement about the need to move away from the legalistic nature of Catholic ethics from Trent to Vatican II, well expressed by Joseph DiNoia:

> The reasons for the powerful hold of legalism in moral theology since the Council of Trent are complex and could be the subject of a lengthy discussion . . . legalistic moral theology tended to put matters not in terms of good and evil but in terms of the permitted and the forbidden. In this style of moral theology, moral norms were viewed more as laws to be enforced and obeyed than as principles for a good life, lived in view of God's invitation to ultimate communion. In a legalistic perspective, happiness is a kind of extrinsic reward for a life lived in conformity to an arduous code of conduct. The framework is contractual rather than virtue-centered and personalist.[21]

Not surprisingly, there is now within Catholic moral thought a spectrum or even a potpourri of various schools of liberal, revisionist and conservative approaches resulting from the abandonment of the old moral handbooks.[22] But it should be noted that there is a certain lingering momentum to the traditional subject matter, and that treatments of newer, more liberal approaches to Catholic moral theology still deal with human action, mortal and venial sin, conscience, natural law, and so on, even if their starting

---

[20]Enda McDonagh, *Doing the Truth: The Quest for Moral Theology* (Notre Dame, IN: University of Notre Dame Press, 1979), p. 32.

[21]J. A. DiNoia, "*Veritatis Splendor*: Moral Life as Transfigured Life," in *"Veritatis Splendor" and the Renewal of Moral Theology: Studies by Ten Outstanding Scholars,* ed. J. A. DiNoia and Romanus Cessario (Princeton, NJ: Scepter Publishers, 1994), pp. 3-4.

[22]See Thomas Hibbs, "Interpretations of Aquinas's Ethics Since Vatican II," in *The Ethics of Aquinas,* ed. Stephen Pope (Washington, DC: Georgetown University Press, 2002), pp. 412-25.

points and conclusions are at variance from the tradition.[23]

Two interesting approaches are worthy of note for our purposes because they represent more thorough and respectful attempts to reappropriate Thomistic ethics for contemporary Christian ethics. There is the "new natural law" approach, represented by John Finnis and Germain Grisez, substituting a phenomenological view of human nature for the old Scholastic metaphysics and terminology, usually arriving at positions supporting the magisterium, but with a completely reorganized methodology.[24] How faithful this approach is to Aquinas has been a topic for lively debate.[25]

The second approach, represented by Servais Pinckaers, Romanus Cessario, Livio Melina and others, is centered on recapturing the "realist" moral theology of Aquinas, locating it within sacred doctrine as a whole, stressing the virtues and the role of the Spirit in the Christian moral life. Human action and natural law certainly are part of this description, but put in a theological context of the human being as the image of God.[26] This way of reading Aquinas preserves the necessary elements of moral reasoning and gives them the proper theological and spiritual context.

THE ELEMENTS OF A RENEWED MORAL THEOLOGY

It is clear that a new systematic moral theology not only for Anglicans but also for the wider church will need to be very different from the classical versions. Yet what is required cannot be so radical that it dispenses entirely with the matters of the theory of action, law, the nature of sin, virtues and vices, and casuistry. In other words, the ethics developed by Thomas Aquinas in the *Summa Theologiae,* properly understood, still can furnish us with the

---

[23]See, for example, Timothy O'Connell, *Principles for a Catholic Morality*, rev. ed. (San Francisco: Harper & Row, 1990).

[24]An impressive production is Germain Grisez, *The Way of the Lord Jesus*, 3 vols. (Chicago: Franciscan Herald Press, 1983–1997).

[25]See Russell Hittinger, *A Critique of the New Natural Law* (Notre Dame, IN: University of Notre Dame Press, 1989).

[26]See Romanus Cessario, *The Moral Virtues and Theological Ethics*, 2nd ed. (Notre Dame, IN: University of Notre Dame Press, 2009); idem, *Introduction to Moral Theology* (Washington, DC: Catholic University of America Press, 2001); Livio Melina, *Sharing in Christ's Virtues: For a Renewal of Moral Theology in Light of "Veritatis Splendor,"* trans. William May (Washington, DC: Catholic University of America Press, 2001); Michael Sherwin, *By Knowledge and by Love: Charity and Knowledge in the Moral Theology of St. Thomas Aquinas* (Washington, DC: Catholic University of America Press, 2005).

foundation for a moral theology based on truth, reality and the grace of God—one that is psychologically and philosophically rich, and both instructive and suggestive for contemporary Christian people.

At the same time, the Thomistic basis needs to be treated as merely that, the best starting point in our moral theological tradition for describing certain key aspects of moral theory, but not sufficient. The historical pattern was to focus on the "ethical midsection" of the *Summa Theologiae* (i.e., I-II and II-II, the entire *secunda pars*), which in its extensive treatment is extremely hard to digest. It is understandable that certain sections were left unread, and other sections excerpted and focused on, with the tendency to distort and misunderstand.[27] Thus the theology and anthropology of part I (*prima pars*) and the Christology and soteriology of part III (*tertia pars*) were commonly not integrated with the ethical treatment.[28]

Even with that said, however, we can note certain unfortunate impressions arising from the decisions that Aquinas made in constructing the *Summa Theologiae*. With the doctrine of Christ postponed to the final section (on the grounds that salvation in Christ is the basis for our final return to God), there is little sense of Christian identity directly connected to the discussion of ethics. It may be the case that Aquinas assumed this as foundational at the outset, just as he assumed a basic acceptance of the truth of revelation at the very beginning of the work. But a vital and evangelical moral theology cannot be content with Christ's importance implied as a "hidden center" and made explicit later on.

We can now articulate what should be the main distinctive elements of a new moral theology:

1. **A renewed biblical basis.** The many contributions to our reading of the biblical texts and the different modes in which Scripture communicates topics for ethical reflection provide an opportunity to enrich moral theology. New understandings of the role of law in Judaism and in Pauline

---

[27]See Leonard Boyle, *The Setting of the Summa Theologiae of Saint Thomas* (Toronto: Pontifical Institute of Mediaeval Studies, 1982); see also Mark Jordan, "The *Summa's* Reform of Moral Teaching—and Its Failures," in *Contemplating Aquinas: On the Varieties of Interpretation*, ed. Fergus Kerr (London: SCM Press, 2003), pp. 41-54.

[28]See the persuasive argument urging us to understand the theological context of the ethics of Aquinas in Fergus Kerr, "Doctrine of God and Theological Ethics According to Thomas Aquinas," in *The Doctrine of God and Theological Ethics*, ed. Alan Torrance and Michael Banner (London: T & T Clark, 2006), pp. 71-84.

theology and new appreciation for the themes of virtue and character in the Scriptures will enable us to make clear that a proper moral theology for the church is only an explication of what is implied by reflection on the biblical witness.

2. **A sound moral psychology**. The vocabulary of Scripture includes terms such as *mind, heart, will* and *conscience,* but not in a systematic way. Moral theology requires definitions and theories of how thoughts and desires become actions and behavior. Because of the renewed and widespread conviction today of the value of Aristotle's treatment of ethics and moral reasoning, we can be more confident of the soundness of its Christian appropriation by Aquinas in his account of action and practical reason. Further, the role that emotions play in relation to intellect and will was highly developed by Aquinas, and it not only supplies a more complete moral psychology but also illuminates the nature of virtue and character and the connection to spirituality.

3. **The proper place for law in ethics.** Law is a central aspect of Scripture and must figure in any account of our relationships to God, to society and to each other. The concept of law is often affected by prevailing social, political and philosophical views, which partly explains the distortions of law, freedom and conscience that arose in the classic Catholic moral theology described above. Among the challenges for any new moral theology are these: how to do justice to the biblical revelation of law; how to incorporate law into an Aristotelian account of moral reasoning that had little need for it; and how to understand the traditional Lutheran separation of law and gospel with its resistance to a positive role for law in Christian discipleship.

4. **Spirituality**. Like some other aspects of the ethics of Aquinas, this is a feature that was either developed completely separate from moral theology or simply neglected in the centuries following Aquinas, especially as moral theology centered on law, obedience or disobedience, and scholastic casuistry. The retrieval and incorporation of human emotion within moral psychology and the discussion of virtues will demonstrate the importance of the handling of emotion and of the role of the Holy Spirit in the formation of Christian character.

CATHOLIC AND EVANGELICAL

Part of the contribution of Anglicanism within the wider church has been its ability to inhabit two worlds (not to say parallel universes): to bring together and sometimes successfully harmonize Catholic and Protestant traditions and convictions in a helpful way—for example, in matters of liturgy and sacramental theology. Moral theology too has had a tradition of combining key doctrines and approaches associated with the Protestant Reformation with a philosophical and doctrinal base inherited from the Roman Catholic tradition. We see this in Richard Hooker and Jeremy Taylor, for instance, where the former preserved major ethical sections of Thomas Aquinas along with a confidence in justification by faith, and the latter combined casuistic discussions from the Catholic tradition with a more Christ-centered spirituality.

In the twentieth century there is a wider ecumenical range of examples of cross-pollination and mutual influence between the Catholic and Protestant ethical traditions. Although much of Helmut Thielicke's consideration of the Catholic tradition took the form of disagreement and challenge, it is fair to say that Karl Barth, while somewhat idiosyncratic in his account of moral reasoning, represents a wise blending in many of his discussions of concrete ethical problems in the *Church Dogmatics*.[29] Paul Ramsey's work on the morality of war and medical ethics shows how Protestant moral thought was greatly enriched by making use of the analytical tools developed by Catholic moral theology.[30] Stanley Hauerwas, already mentioned in connection with the rise of virtue ethics, represents a valuable interaction between Catholic and Protestant tradition in the understanding of moral agency and Christian character, in emphasizing the communal aspect of Christian morality, and in approaches to specific issues. Oliver O'Donovan, as an Anglican, provides a clear model (and challenge) in keeping before us

---

[29]See Helmuth Thielicke, *Theological Ethics*, ed. William Lazareth, 3 vols. (Philadelphia: Fortress, 1964–1969), abridged somewhat from the German edition of the late 1950s. In the *Church Dogmatics* Karl Barth placed his ethical discussions as part of the larger sectional themes of God, creation and reconciliation, and he drew on a wide range of Reformed and Catholic theology. We should also note the appreciation of Barth by Catholics such as Hans Urs von Balthasar, *The Theology of Karl Barth: Exposition and Interpretation* (San Francisco: Ignatius Press, 1992).

[30]See Paul Ramsey, *War and the Christian Conscience: How Shall Modern War Be Conducted Justly?* (Durham, NC: Duke University Press, 1961); idem, *The Patient as Person: Explorations in Medical Ethics* (New Haven: Yale University Press, 1970).

the call to be evangelical and christocentric, but at the same time to have the patience to work through the details of practical reasoning and analysis of action associated with Roman Catholic ethics.

I am aiming in this introductory work to construct a moral theology in this vein, by using the moral philosophy and psychology provided by Thomas Aquinas (much of it derived from Aristotle), combined with an evangelical concern for the centrality of the gospel of Christ and confidence in Scripture. Following the example of the *Summa Theologiae* itself, I will attempt to draw deeply from the wells of both Scripture and the best moral philosophy.

My hope is that the reader will see the combined Catholic and evangelical emphasis in respect for the richness of tradition, some suspicion of modern assumptions in ethics derived from the Enlightenment, as well as care for the challenge of contemporary Christian discipleship. The evangelical view (to speak in a general way) of discipleship involves personal commitment to following the will of God with its strengths in emphasizing conversion and devotional life; and this can only be strengthened by the corresponding concern from Catholic ethics for accurate knowledge, philosophical system and the analytical tools for understanding the nature of moral problems and appropriate responses.

Readers from both Catholic and evangelical backgrounds should feel that they are on familiar territory much of the time, and also find themselves challenged at times by material that may well seem new and somewhat alien. Protestant readers will need to pay attention to the explanations of practical reason and action in chapters two through five, and to the later emphasis on moral virtues; and some Catholic readers might be surprised by the focus on sin, conversion and the will of God in chapters six through eight.

Part of the purpose of *Renewing Moral Theology* is to help evangelical and Catholic readers feel more at home in each other's territory and to respect the strengths offered by each tradition. To that end, the content is presented as being mutually enriching, and this is illustrated by citing examples and quotations, historical and contemporary, that may be unfamiliar to readers from a different tradition. Francis de Sales and Josef Pieper, for example, are not well known to Protestant evangelicals, while Catholics (and even Anglicans who are not evangelical) may not be very familiar with John Stott or

J. I. Packer. Happily, there are figures such as C. S. Lewis who command respect across the Christian spectrum and represent that wise blending of Catholic and evangelical that this book aspires to.[31]

Readers should note that at the end of each chapter are a few suggestions for further reading, which in some cases represent further detail and in other cases alternate or complementary views. In nearly every chapter there is a section from the *Summa Theologiae* (abbreviated *ST*) with the roman numerals indicating the major part, and the arabic numerals the question and article. The recommended translation is known as the "Blackfriars edition," published with the Latin text facing a more modern and dynamic English translation.

FOR FURTHER READING

Joseph Kotva, *The Christian Case for Virtue Ethics* (Washington, DC: Georgetown University Press, 1996), chaps. 1, 2, 6.

Servais Pinckaers, *The Sources of Christian Morality*, trans. Mary Thomas Noble (Washington, DC: Catholic University of America Press, 1995), especially chaps. 11-12, on the Roman Catholic "manuals" or handbooks of moral theology and a Catholic view of Protestant ethics.

Stephen Pope, ed., *The Ethics of Aquinas* (Washington, DC: Georgetown University Press, 2002), part III, pp. 355-425, on the interpretation of Aquinas's ethics in the twentieth century.

---

[31]A recent Roman Catholic introduction to ethics features a number of references to C. S. Lewis; see William Mattison III, *Introducing Moral Theology: True Happiness and the Virtues* (Grand Rapids: Brazos Press, 2008).

2

Purpose, Reason
and Action

WE TEND TO SEPARATE the ordinary "everyday" actions of our lives from the difficult choices and from what we consider to be the more genuinely "moral" decisions that occasionally need to be made. Thus brushing one's teeth, writing an email, going for a walk, washing the dishes and so on are not seen as ethical decisions or part of moral theology, whereas the decision to report to your superior someone at work whom you suspect of misusing funds would be an ethical or moral decision, as, of course, would thinking about whether or not to get a divorce.

There are several reasons for this. First, the everyday, mundane decisions are usually quick and easy. These decisions often are made with little reflection, and with no moral agonizing or pondering. There is no need to "figure out" what to do. Occasionally, one may not "feel like" doing the dishes or getting exercise, but that seems to be a matter of mood rather than of morality. Second, in many mundane decisions there are no major moral rules or principles at stake, such as telling the truth or the duty to protect life. If there is no moral problem to be solved, no conflict between duty and inclination, it does not seem to belong to ethics.

This sense of what moral actions are has been reinforced by the traditions of both moral theology and philosophical ethics that focused on "cases of conscience" (the *dubitantium* or matters of doubt) or on crisis situations. Should I let myself starve, or should I save my life by becoming a cannibal? Would it be possible and ethical to find a way for one or two on this overcrowded lifeboat to volunteer (or be selected at random) as sacrificial victims so that the rest of the group could have a chance to make it back to land?

HUMAN ACTION IS MORAL ACTION

In reality, all of our genuine actions (setting aside unconscious actions such as doodling while on the telephone or drumming your fingers while thinking of something else) have moral import and are moral actions.[1] That is, they are expressions of purpose, desires and attitudes revealed in a decision to do something. Brushing your teeth is not just a mechanical habit or piece of learned behavior; it reflects a well-founded concern for hygiene and good health, which has a social dimension as well as individual benefit. Having a meal with friends or family can serve a number of different purposes besides simple nourishment. It might be the occasion for trying new cuisine, honoring someone's birthday or retirement, or sharing joys and disappointments.

Motivation. Many students of ethics in the twentieth century were taught to distinguish between schools of ethics based on a sense of duty (*deontological* ethics) and those based on producing good results (*teleological* or *consequentialist* ethics). There are purely philosophical (or secular) versions of these systems of ethics, with long-standing discussions about the assumptions, claims and procedures. For many Christians, an ethical system based on duty seems more obviously compatible with the Christian life that is taught to us from an early age as involving commands given to us by God and obedience to the Lord's will. An ethical system that is looking primarily for good results seems inevitably misguided and unspiritual, betraying an inherent element of selfishness and presumption. Better to do what is right and leave the results to God.

The ethical system presented in this book is unabashedly teleological (from the Greek word *telos*, "end" or "result"), but it has little in common with utilitarianism or consequentialist ethics that attempt to generate the best outcome. That is because the ultimate end or purpose in Thomistic ethics is based on acting for a purpose that can be described as the supreme good, sheer joy and complete fulfillment. The term that Thomas Aquinas used is *beatitudo*, and this is really the guiding principle of human action.

---

[1]For further discussion, see Charles Pinches, "Human Acts Are Moral Acts," in *Theology and Action: After Theory in Christian Ethics* (Grand Rapids: Eerdmans, 2002), pp. 87-110.

As Fergus Kerr puts it, "We need to notice that the a priori condition of moral agency is Thomas' characterization of God as 'object' of the bliss of all the blessed—*objectum* in the mediaeval sense, not of something inertly over against us, waiting for our subjectivity to impose a significance; but as something which provokes and evokes response from us."[2] We find agreement in the Westminster Catechism: "What is the chief end of man? The chief end of man is to love God and enjoy him forever." With some conceptual dexterity one can possibly turn loving God into a duty; but it is more than a little contradictory to conceive of a God-given duty to enjoy him.

The French philosopher Henri Bergson (1859–1941) divided morality and religion into two basic groups: those that operate from "pressure" and those that are based on "attraction."[3] Moralities and religions that specialize in pressure describe morality in terms of duty and obligation, while a morality or a religion of attraction or aspiration points to a fundamental motivation of growth, fulfillment and happiness.

The Christian life presented in the Scriptures, in the life of Christ and described in sermons and saints' lives is obviously a combination of duty and joy, of obligation and fulfillment. But which is more fundamental? Jesus in the garden of Gethsemane prayed that the cup of suffering might be avoided, but he accepted that God's will and not his own was to be done. On the other hand, the Epistle to the Hebrews says that our Lord, "who for the sake of the joy that was set before him endured the cross, disregarding its shame" (Heb 12:2), speaking of an ultimate joyful purpose.

The assumption that an ethics based on duty is more "ethical" or more Christian is understandable when we think of morality in the restricted sense of special decisions where we sense difficulty, confusion and especially conflict. It is especially in times of temptation when inclination and desire lead to a course of action more attractive to us, but if we are honest, we know that the right thing to do is what we ought to do—that is our "duty." But if we expand morality from these special situations of doubt, conflict and temptation, and we accept that all of our conscious actions reflect our mo-

[2]Fergus Kerr, "Doctrine of God and Theological Ethics According to Thomas Aquinas," in *The Doctrine of God and Theological Ethics*, ed. Alan Torrance and Michael Banner (London: T & T Clark, 2006), p. 82.

[3]Henri Bergson, *The Two Sources of Morality and Religion*, trans. R. Ashley Audra and Cloudesley Brereton (New York: Doubleday, 1935), pp. 41-42.

rality, then it is easier to see that the more fundamental picture of being attracted to good things (such as marriage, friends and career) and through them to the good itself is sounder philosophically, psychologically and biblically. The sense of duty is secondary to overall purpose. Laws and lists of duties, job descriptions, and responsibilities are important and essential, but they do not furnish fundamental motivation, except at certain stages of immaturity or training.

In an Aristotelian-Thomist view of human action the motivation prompting action is a desire for fulfillment—to achieve a more complete level of being. The ultimate goal, that final purpose that exists as the remote purpose behind all other actions, is perfect well-being and happiness.[4]

The classical and medieval model of action in nature included a metaphysics in which natural objects were described as "desiring" or "seeking" a form corresponding to their natures. Fire would "seek" to rise to its proper sphere; acorns would "seek" the form of an oak tree, the completion of their nature.

Modern physics and biology no longer allow us to describe the operations of nature in this fashion, except metaphorically. And there are alternatives to metaphysics of the desire for the good, based more on empirical study of the behavior of human beings. Abraham Maslow's hierarchy of human needs is an outline of the varying types and levels of human needs that provide the basis for human motivation. At the bottom level are physiological needs for food, warmth, activity, sex and so on. The next level is safety and security needs, which a person can focus on when the basic survival is no longer problematic. Once security needs are met, one may turn to the need for belonging in groups or relationships, then for esteem (both from others and from one's self), and finally for self-actualization.

Another alternative to an Aristotelian scheme, developed within conservative Roman Catholic circles, is to take a phenomenological approach and simply identify, from observation, certain "basic human goods" that describe what all people make fundamental to their behavior. According to this school, these basic goods are life (including health), knowledge, play, aesthetic experience, friendship, practical reasonableness (living with freedom and reason and integrity) and religion.[5] The advantage of a system

---

[4]Aristotle, *Nicomachean Ethics* I.6-7; Thomas Aquinas, *ST* I-II, q. 3, a. 1.
[5]See John Finnis, *Natural Law and Natural Rights* (Oxford: Clarendon, 1980), pp. 85-90; Germain

of goods like this is that while universal claims about human nature are made, the starting point is observable reality with no dependence on an underlying metaphysical explanation. As fixed characteristics of human beings, without a hierarchy of value, these basic goods become the foundation for a new "natural law" furnishing binding moral axioms, based on not violating any of the basic human goods.

We need not give up the Aristotelian-Thomist picture completely, however. If one takes a *theological* starting point with a doctrine of creation as expressive of God's will, then there is a certain truth in speaking of the "desire" of the acorn to become an oak tree, of stars to shine and of cats to hunt. This language is not explanatory in a strictly scientific sense, but it is descriptive of creatures' actions in that they are living in accordance with purposes immanent in the created world.

Actions and purpose. Animals and plants fulfill their natures by responding to the world around them in a fairly predictable stimulus-response pattern. Squirrels build nests, bees construct hives and cats chase mice because they are preprogrammed to respond to certain objects. The ability of higher animals to be trained indicates a certain flexibility and openness, so that "instinct" should not be made too rigid; but there remains a basic stimulus-response pattern behind natural movement or the actions of animals.

Human action follows patterns partly shared with other animals, but also on a completely different level. Instinct and biological urges still operate, of course, but a much larger range of possibilities is opened up by the use of the mind. This is not to deny that a few animals have some capacity for using elements of language and tools. But the difference between animal actions and human action is analogous to the difference between the song of a nightingale (which is programmed to perform a sequence of sounds) or a parrot (which is able to mimic a variety of sound patterns), and the human voice capable of describing a vast range of experiences, observations and emotions through language and music.

Human beings are able to put their actions into a means-end structure that expresses purpose. Actions are pointless without some kind of purpose, and we may ask someone *why* they are doing something such as digging a

Grisez, *The Way of the Lord Jesus*, vol. 1, *Christian Moral Principles* (Chicago: Franciscan Herald Press, 1983).

hole in the backyard when we cannot discern the reason. Why are you decorating your house with bunting? Why have you joined this political organization? The question "What are you doing, and why?" can even be asked of someone who is just lying down: that person might reply that she is meditating, or nursing a sore back or simply resting.[6]

Human beings give shape and structure to their lives by purposeful action. It makes no sense to ask an animal (even if communication were possible), "What are you hoping to achieve this year?" or "What is the purpose of your life?" Human beings can have plans and projects, and then figure out the best way to achieve their goals. That is basically what is meant by practical reasoning: directing one's mind to concrete action in the service of the goals of one's life, both immediate and long-term.

Actions make sense, have meaning, and can be freely chosen in the context of a means-end pattern of reasoning. If the purpose is clear and desirable, the actions required to achieve that purpose are intelligible. We understand why someone might get up before dawn in order to run and train for a marathon race, even if we disagreed (privately) about the desirability of the goal.

Actions are the result of desire guided by reason. Some desires are felt strongly and urgently, but many are not. The task of practical reasoning is to identify the particular action to be undertaken in order to accomplish the desired goal.

Practical reasoning: means-end deliberation and choice of action. Practical reason is thought leading to action, or the reasoning process that leads to *doing something*. Practical reasoning ends up not with an item of knowledge, but with an action. As Aristotle described the process of deliberation and choice, deliberation ends with a choice (*prohairesis*), and the decision is an action. As we will consider below, this is a bit too succinct; however, the conclusion of the process of reasoning is an action, and that is what makes the process "practical" reasoning.

We distinguish this process leading to genuine action from hypothetical reasoning, which remains an item of reasoning. What would you do in such a situation? Would it be correct to tell a lie in this situation? This requires a

---

[6]See G. E. M. Anscombe's classic work *Intention* (Ithaca, NY: Cornell University Press, 1969), pp. 34-35.

consideration of principles, circumstances and so on, and good ethical analysis may yield a conclusion one concludes is the "right one"—but this is not practical reasoning. It is the kind of moral reasoning that the authors of moral handbooks were trained to do. It involves deliberation (about options available) and judgments about what is the best line of reasoning, but it was not practical reasoning either at the beginning or at the end.

Practical reasoning starts with the desire to achieve something, an intention to *do* something. We then set the process of practical reasoning in motion, and the perception that the time and the occasion are right produces a choice and an action. This has been diagramed for us as Aristotle's outline of practical reasoning:[7]

Figure 2.1

This is too simple for complex actions that require deliberation and direction, but it does characterize a certain basic kind of everyday action such as getting up in the morning, eating lunch, answering the telephone and so on.

We may suppose a pretty basic kind of "reasoning" pattern that includes these elements:

> Desire: "I feel hungry; I want some food."
>
> Perception: Awareness that a suitable gap of time has occurred since the last meal; that lunch is being served downstairs; that you have an appointment for lunch and the clock indicates it is time to go; etc.
>
> Conclusion: The **action** follows the conjoining of desire and perception.

Figure 2.2

We can see that the hinge element is the perception that one brings to the situation that then generates the action. In the example of eating, we may be biologically driven and share with Pavlov's dogs an automatic arousal of in-

---

[7]William Prior, *Virtue and Knowledge: An Introduction to Ancient Greek Ethics* (London: Routledge, 1991), p. 176.

terest in food when encountering the smell of freshly baked bread, or sizzling steaks or hearing the lunch bell ring. But the perception of the situation includes not only our own feelings of hunger and interest in food, but also the time and circumstances (for example: too short an interval since the last meal; we are on a diet and trying to cut back; food will be waiting at home later on). Thus the awareness of the various relevant factors to apply to the situation leads to the judgment "Go ahead and buy that doughnut or hotdog" or "Don't eat now; wait for a proper meal later on." It is a mixture of understanding the reality of the situation (perhaps the awareness that our calorie intake does not really need a big boost right now) and the reasons for taking one course over another, plus control over one's emotional disposition.

The perception also includes the recognition of the means-end structure of the action, the purpose for which it serves. Thus both the circumstances of the agent and occasion, but also the purpose for which one is doing the action are involved. (In the case of eating, this hardly applies, because the reason for eating is so self-evident.) Further, the action chosen is in accordance with our desires.

Let us consider an action that is chosen purely because we can understand the reason for it and not because we are inclined to it.

> Principle: People need to go to the dentist when their teeth need repairing.
> Perception: I am a person with a bad tooth (and have the means and opportunity to visit the dentist, etc.).
> Conclusion: I need to go to the dentist.

Figure 2.3

The decision to go to the dentist is contrary to the inclinations of most people because it costs money and might be painful (or at least represents that possibility), not to mention that many people may have irrational fears about dentists. Nevertheless, there is a kind of desire to go the dentist, which we might call a "rational desire." It is that aspect of our minds that can desire to do certain actions in accordance with the reasons for them and takes long-term results into account. It is the desire for the end, in this case a set of attractive, healthy teeth, which carries over to choose willingly the means to achieve the end, a visit to the dentist.

We can note here that what Thomas Aquinas calls the "will" (*voluntas*) is exactly this notion of a rational desire for reaching or accomplishing an end. There are other kinds of desire based on our sense appetites (such as the desire to eat and sleep), but the will is the desire that is formed by having a structure of reasoning based on means to an end (*ST* I, q. 80, a. 2, ad 2).

Aristotle identified (but not very clearly) both types of practical reason in his brief discussion in the work *De Motu Animalium* (*On the Movement of Animals*). In the first case, of taking a walk, Aristotle is describing the decision to act. In the second instance, about a cloak, there are two parts: the conclusion of the first line of reasoning is a speculative proposition, specifying the need for a cloak; while in the second part, "the conclusion which results from the two premises is the action."[8] Here is the somewhat cryptic fashion in which Aristotle described it:

> For example, whenever someone thinks that every man should take walks, and that he is a man, at once he takes a walk. Or if he thinks that no man should take a walk now, and that he is a man, at once he remains at rest. And he does both these things, if nothing prevents or compels him. I should make something good; a house is something good. At once he makes a house. I need covering; a cloak is a covering. I need a cloak. What I need I have to make; I need a cloak. I have to make a cloak. And the conclusion, the "I have to make a cloak," is an action.[9]

This passage is indeed confusing, but Aristotle was able to distinguish two different types of reasoning, which he named (1) "through the good" and (2) "through the possible."[10] What he meant was that the first type of reasoning is a decision to act in accordance with a general principle reflecting a vision of what is good (e.g., it is good for people to walk or to live in houses), while the second type of reasoning deals with possibility—that is, to *figure out* how to achieve a desired goal. Though he was certainly not completely clear, Aristotle identified the difference between the first type of reasoning, which involves combining a principle with perception of the circumstances and which then results in an action, and the second type, which looks at an

---

[8]See Martha Nussbaum, *Aristotle's De Motu Animalium: Text with Translation, Commentary, and Interpretive Essays* (Princeton, NJ: Princeton University Press, 1985), p. 40.

[9]Ibid., lines 14-20.

[10]*Dia tou agathou* and *dia tou dynatou* (Aristotle, *De Motu Animalium* 701a24-25).

end to achieve (e.g., bodily warmth) and then reasons back to a specific means to achieve it, concluding with the decision to start making a cloak.

Both types of reasoning are features of practical reasoning, and how to distinguish them has been a challenge to scholars of Aristotle;[11] it is one of the contributions of Thomas Aquinas (in his reading of Aristotle) that this difference between the reasoning about actions in accordance with a principle is more clearly distinguished from deliberating about the best means to achieve a given end, and this insight enabled Aquinas greater refinement in the description of human action.

THE THOMISTIC PRACTICAL SYLLOGISM

The "practical syllogism" or "operative syllogism" are the terms used by Thomas Aquinas to describe the kind of decision that Aristotle meant by reasoning "through the good," such as going for a walk or building a house. It represents that confluence of desire, perception of the circumstances and judgment that results in an action or in a decision not to act. (Again, the practical syllogism should not be confused with the reasoning from end to means, the process of *figuring out* what steps to take to accomplish a certain goal.)

For Aquinas, the practical syllogism includes a major premise of the form "do this" or "avoid this," along with the judgment about a particular action here and now as an instance covered by the major premise, with the conclusion to do or to avoid following deductively. We can see in the following example that the same physical action—let us say, taking a tool from your employer—could be the subject of very different lines in a practical syllogism; in the first example the action of taking the tool is seen as something wrong:

Operative principle:	Avoid stealing.
Minor premise:	This action [taking the tool] would be an act of stealing.
	[Judgment about the action and circumstances]
Conclusion:	Avoid this action.

Figure 2.4

---

[11]See the discussion of various interpretations of the practical syllogism in Aristotle in my *Right Practical Reason: Aristotle, Action and Prudence in Aquinas* (Oxford: Clarendon, 1994), pp. 17-25.

Alternatively, one could sketch it in the following way, where the person selects a different feature of the action to combine with a different operative principle and the opposite conclusion:

Operative principle:	Get revenge on my previous employer.
Minor premise:	This action [taking the tool] would be a good way to get revenge.
Conclusion:	Perform this action.

Figure 2.5

This does not really seem to be a reasoning "process" because it is often virtually instantaneous, and we are mostly unaware that it occurs. The key is in the minor premise, the perception and judgment that the action considered is of a certain type. That perception is what guides the recognition of the major operative premise governing the action. Or one might say that the act of judgment involves the simultaneous selection of principle and judgment about the action.[12]

Further, an operative principle is simply a principle for action that one holds. By "holding" a principle such as "Honor your father and mother," we indicate that a person agrees with the principle, has some understanding of its basis and range of application, and has determined to make it operative in life—the person wants to fulfill it.

In the example above about revenge, someone might know the biblical teaching "Do not repay anyone evil for evil," and yet the emotional reaction to an injustice still produces a principle of revenge. There may well be in a person's mind a dissonance between principles that one has been taught (or thinks that one ought to have, and would claim to agree with when asked) and those that actually are operative for that person.

Note also the pivotal nature of the minor premise. It makes a big difference whether the taking of the tool (in the example above) is recognized as an instance of stealing rather than one of getting back at somebody; in

---

[12]Note the similarity to the act of "recognition" of the moral character of an action in Oliver O'Donovan, "Christian Moral Reasoning," in *New Dictionary of Christian Ethics and Pastoral Theology*, ed. David Atkinson and David Field (Downers Grove, IL: InterVarsity Press, 1995), p. 126.

other cases it may be a contrast between legitimate pleasure and self-indulgence. One does not really think about the operative principle until the mind perceives that the particular action that seems good in this situation falls under a relevant operative principle.

Aquinas also thought that one could subsume all actions under one basic principle, "Do good and avoid evil," also known as the first principle of practical reason (*ST* I-II, q. 94, a. 2). We can thus express the basic generation of all human actions in syllogistic form:

Positive		**Negative**	
Operative principle:	Do good.	Operative principle:	Avoid evil.
Premise:	This action is good.	Premise:	This action is evil.
Conclusion:	Do this.	Conclusion:	Avoid this.

Figure 2.6

This minimalistic syllogism implies that every human being has an operative principle to pursue good and avoid evil as the basic motivation for action. Its generality allows all actions to be encompassed, but naturally it provides no help for pointing to specific actions. That is the "job," as it were, of the act of judgment in the minor premise, the ability to perceive what in the present situation is "the good" action that one should do. Since we will see that the Thomistic account of sin is based on pursuing what is *apparently* good, the importance of sound judgment is paramount.

The centrality of judgment. The key to the effective integration of thought and action is the stage of the minor premise in the syllogism, the perception and judgment about the action. Everything that goes into moral instruction, experience, awareness of emotional reactions, attitude toward others, goals and desires comes into play in the perception and judgment expressed schematically as the major and minor premise of the practical syllogism.

Take, for example, a woman who works too much, what some would call a workaholic. She is someone who literally does not know when to stop working. She makes the choice in favor of work when others would have returned home to be with family or enjoyed some recreation. (Note that we are speaking not of the need to work long hours to finish a special project,

but of a habitual pattern of overwork.) We begin to see signs of unhealth-
iness—the results of lack of exercise, remoteness from family and few
hobbies or outside interests. This workaholic may pride herself in her "will
power" and stamina, or her loyalty to the firm, or her strong "work ethic."
There probably are other emotional issues involved: the avoidance of family
and intimate relationships; or various fears of not measuring up; or an exaggerated sense of importance to the firm. When other people are able to make
the judgment "It's time to stop working for today," our workaholic friend
continues to see work as a good to pursue, or leisure time as an evil to avoid.
Her attitudes, emotions and lack of self-awareness cause her to distort her
ability to judge her situation clearly.

Wisdom involves the ability to see clearly the elements of our external
circumstances and relationships, as well as an inner self-awareness, that together constitute our perception and vision, which in turn produce the judgments about what to do. The person who is wise in biblical terms is the one
who not only is well informed about the teaching of Scripture and has priorities and values in proper relation to God, but also has the self-awareness
and insight into situations in which these values are concretely expressed in
decisions and actions.

Practical reason, actions and character. Our moral vision—the way we
look at the world, others and ourselves—is what determines our judgments
and actions. This vision is made up not only of our principles and convictions and beliefs, but also attitudes and desires, our affective response to the
real world. Our goals and what we value in life—all of these go into shaping
the more specific intentions that we make judgments about and turn into
concrete actions.

The atomized view of ethics in which the moral life is seen as a series of
decisions where moral principles and criteria are sifted through is wrong on
a number of accounts. One of the major errors is the conveyance of a false
sense of freedom, as if we are neutral agents weighing options and discerning the correct moral balance. In fact, however, we bring to each situation the moral vision that we already have. The kinds of things that we
desire and are important to us, and the framework we use to interpret our
situation—all are part of our character.

When we make a judgment about some action, "This is the good I want to do here and now," the set of concerns underlying our action is something proposed by the set of qualities of character that make up who we are. This is part of the limitation of practical reason. According to Aristotle, choice is something concerned with means rather than ends.[13] Those things that are important for us to achieve are already part of our view of the world, and we use practical reason to discern how to fulfill them. As Aquinas put it in discussing prudence (practical reason when it functions well), practical reason "does not appoint the ends . . . but only to arrange our activities which serve to reach them" (*ST* II-II, q. 47, a. 6). Our total character—the outlook and attitudes of reason, will and emotions—in a sense predetermine what we are going to decide to do.

Let us imagine a middle-aged man deciding to buy a Harley-Davidson motorcycle. He may do research on comparative resale values, the savings in money for fuel compared to his truck and so on, but the decision is probably actually being made in terms of the need for a little excitement, the fulfillment of a boyhood fantasy, a desire to look cool in the neighborhood. His practical reasoning is done about the object that has already deeply captured his vision.

We can make this more explicit in reference to an action that is of greater moral import: a decision to break up a marriage. Since the divorce rate among Protestant Christians is virtually the same as in society at large, we can assume that these decisions to divorce are being made in spite of knowing the church's teaching on the permanence of marriage, the importance of sacred vows and the often disastrous consequences of broken marriages on children and society at large. In the case of a marital breakup where the husband finally decides to leave his wife, let us say, such a decision is obviously not made by a rational weighing of the pros and cons, but is a product of the vision and character he has developed up to that point. As a Catholic Thomist philosopher puts it,

> It is an unsettling thought that decisions of an important kind, the kind we tend to concentrate on in doing ethics, are not simply a matter of assessing a situation in the light of principles and then deciding, but are in some mysterious way made before we make them. Does it not seem reasonable to assume

---

[13]See Aristotle, *Nicomachean Ethics* III.3 at 1113a9-14.

that, when a man leaves his wife, or vice versa, the decision is the cumulative effect of a whole series of minor decisions, each of them, when taken singly, of little moment—what the moralist would call indifferent acts—which yet, in the aggregate, in unforeseen and also unintended combinations, constitute the person we are when the momentous decision is to be made? Our dreams, our fantasies, our unspoken way of seeing ourselves and others, the shifting furniture of imagination, all those innocent reveries . . . are, in the view of the moral life which emerges, important because they are elements of our vision of ourselves and others. That is, the moral life is a continuum, not episodic as if it were composed of discontinuous puncta or moments.[14]

What McInerny helps us to see is that there is a relationship between the overall direction of a person's life and the large series of individual decisions and reactions. The moral life should not be restricted to the isolated decisions, but instead must be seen in the context of the development of character and the pattern of actions.

Both the qualities of character and the individual actions themselves are integral to the moral life. The ethical system of Thomas Aquinas provides that balance between emphasis on character that underlies the treatment of the moral life within the framework of the virtues, and analysis of the morality of individual actions, whether they are right or wrong. In the next few chapters we will consider in more detail the process of practical reasoning, the moral evaluation of individual actions and the mutual influence of actions and dispositions. This will provide the foundation for the correct analysis of actions and for the development of the virtues.

FOR FURTHER READING

Thomas Aquinas, *ST* I-II, qq. 1-11.

David M. Gallagher, "The Will and Its Acts," in *The Ethics of Aquinas*, ed. Stephen Pope (Washington, DC: Georgetown University Press, 2002), pp. 69-89.

Ralph McInerny, *Ethica Thomistica: The Moral Philosophy of Thomas Aquinas*, rev. ed. (Washington, DC: Catholic University of America Press, 1997), chaps. 1-3.

Charles Pinches, *Theology and Action: After Theory in Christian Ethics* (Grand Rapids: Eerdmans, 2002), ch. 4.

---

[14]Ralph McInerny, *Ethica Thomistica: The Moral Philosophy of Thomas Aquinas* (Washington, DC: Catholic University of America Press, 1982), pp. 93-94.

3

THE PROCESS OF PRACTICAL REASONING

H OW OFTEN DO WE NEED to make decisions? How much decision making or practical reasoning is there when one's daily routine is repetitive and predictable? Take, for example, Jimmy, who is a worker at a Ford assembly plant in Oakville, Ontario. He hears the clock radio go off, gets up and dresses and shaves, has a bite to eat, jumps in the car, drives on the expressway to the Ford plant. He goes in and gets his new assignment from the foreman: work on mounting tires. And so that is what he does all day, except for lunch and a couple of other breaks. Where is the practical reasoning involved in this? For the most part, all of Jimmy's actions are predetermined—not by any cosmic determinism, but by himself and the nature of his job. He has already determined by experience what type of clothes to wear, the route to drive, perhaps the radio station to listen to. When he is ready to work, he is given instructions, and there is a technique worked out to mount tires in the quickest and most efficient way. There is very little to deliberate about, except perhaps whether to wear work boots or running shoes, to listen to hard rock or golden oldies.

Since human beings, whether they work on an assembly line or not, and even if they often eat the same food and experience the same daily routine, are not robots, there is a level at which attitude, will and choice continually operate. Aristotle, in his *Nicomachean Ethics* (hereafter abbreviated *NE* in citations), which Thomas Aquinas used as the basis for his account of human action, provided a brilliant analysis of the elements of action: desire, purpose, perception and decision, which are aspects of all human action even if there is no obvious deliberation. We will make use of the paradigms in Aristotle when we consider the problem of sin in human nature (see chapter six), and especially how to explain how a person may know in one sense (on the level of principle) that an action is wrong and yet act against his or her better judgment.

First we need to articulate more clearly the flow of human action in order to accommodate the complex range and variety of actions, but also bring out the ways in which reason, volition and emotion interact with each other. Here we essentially follow the guidance of Thomas Aquinas and his modifications of Aristotle in the *Summa Theologiae* and other works.[1]

Thomistic Refinements to Action Theory

Deliberation and decision. Aristotle made clear that deliberation was an essential part of action guided by reason (*NE* III.3), and that good deliberation was the mark of the person who has the excellence of practical wisdom (*NE* VII.5). But what is not so clear in Aristotle's account is the rationality of action that does not require deliberation. For example, when Aristotle tells us that choice is "a deliberate desire for things that are within our power: we arrive at a decision on the basis of deliberation" (*NE* III.3), many readers have drawn the conclusion that it is deliberation that supplies the rationality of our choices. The implication, then, is that actions that are not deliberated are less than rational, and that quick or spontaneous decisions are made on the basis of emotion or habit and lack rationality. But if we take the distinction between "means-end" reasoning and the practical syllogism (from the previous chapter), then all actions chosen by us under the framework of the operative syllogism ("This is the good thing to do") have rational force because of the mind's judgment, even when there is no apparent deliberation involved.

If we consider the routine of Jimmy in the example above, it would not be right to say that this is all at a submoral level on the grounds that he has little need to think about his actions. By making use of the distinction be-

---

[1]Because of the length of the *Summa Theologiae*, readers often forget its purpose as a handbook and summary, and that many of the topics are expanded on elsewhere in more detail. The practical syllogism is only briefly summarized in the *Summa Theologiae*, and the reader needs to consult the more detailed works of Aquinas, *De Veritate* and *De Malo*, for a full picture. See Daniel Westberg, *Right Practical Reason: Aristotle, Action, and Prudence in Aquinas* (New York: Oxford University Press, 1994), pp. 149-64.

tween deliberation and decision, we can see that Jimmy does not have to deliberate in order to figure out what he is going to do or how to do it. That is already mostly obvious. But he does have to decide to do these things, with a series of reaffirmations based on perceiving "This is what is good for me to do right now." There can be a mixture of motives behind his daily decisions for doing what he does: the decent paycheck, commitment to his family, the satisfaction of providing good performance, or even honoring God. It is this possible variability in the way that these daily decisions are made that makes human actions rational and moral, even when they seem to be extremely limited in terms of flexibility, creativity, or even possible alternatives. Thus we may say that *all human actions require a decision based on the judgment that this is the good thing to do now*, but also maintain that many actions do not require much deliberation.

Aquinas made this point by treating decision or choice first (*ST* I-II, q. 13) in the section on practical reasoning, followed by deliberation (which is q. 14). This has confused and misled readers ever since, and they complain that he is giving us a confused or different kind of scheme for understanding action (even though he clearly describes deliberation as preceding choice).[2] But if one considers that the role of deliberation is to be an *aid* to reason in making a decision, then there is a logical order of treatment. After all, deliberation does not come before a decision in the case of the many times we engage in actions where it is obvious what to do.

It is when we have an intention, a desire to do something, but are not clear about the means that we require deliberation. My wife and I have friends in New Zealand who have invited us to take part in the olive harvest, and this is something we would very much like to do, but we have to find the right opportunity for it. In order to do this, we need to sit down with calendars, check airline websites, confer with colleagues at work, calculate the costs and so on, to consider the feasibility. This all remains theoretical until we actually know that we can secure leave from work, confirm the dates with our New Zealand friends and know how much the trip will cost. The deliberation phase will be over when it becomes clear what the trip involves and what we need to do. The decision, our actual judgment "This is the right

---

[2]*ST* I-II, q. 14 has the title *De consilio quod electionem praecedit* ("on counsel or deliberating which precedes choice").

thing to do" still needs to be made, and this can be seen to involve other moral factors: Should the money be spent on some other worthy cause? Can we afford that much time away this year? And so on.

What confuses these stages of figuring out what to do (means-end reasoning), and then the decision to do it (the practical syllogism), is that there can be lack of clarity and a need for deliberation at both stages. But the kind of deliberation that one does at the stage of "This is right for me to do" is in aid of a completely different kind of uncertainty than when one needs to identify the best way to achieve a certain goal.

For an example, let us take the decision to be ordained to Christian ministry. There is the kind of deliberation involved in calculating expenses, finding the right seminary program and sponsorship, and assessing qualifications and resources. When all of that is settled to the point that there is a specific time and place to begin training, then that stage of investigation is finished, and one has a specific action to make a decision about. This, of course, may be even more difficult: Should I quit my present job and relocate my family? Is this truly my calling from God? This involves weighing these factors and selecting different points of view from which to make more clearly the judgment "This is the right thing for me to do."

Execution. Aristotle stressed the close connection between choice and action: a man chooses something; at once he goes and does it.[3] In cases where the choice is fully in line with the person's desires, there is probably that kind of direct connection, even when there may be a delay of time. You decide in the morning to go to the cinema that evening; a movie that you have been waiting for is opening. You look forward during the day to this, and there is no question that you will actually go. Your decision will become activated at the right time, without hesitation.

Suppose you make a decision in the morning to call your dentist, or to start on the research project you have been assigned or to take a forty-five-minute walk for exercise in the evening. You find later that somehow you "forgot" to telephone the clinic or did not have the number handy; or that the research materials looked too complicated and you would need further instructions; or that you ended up watching an important sports event on

---

[3]This is found in both *Nicomachean Ethics* and *De Motu Animalium*.

television instead of taking the walk. In these cases there are mixed or conflicting feelings, and when obstacles are encountered, the action you had previously decided on is abandoned or postponed.

There are other prior factors affecting poor performance. The Platonist would stress the fact that you did not sufficiently understand the *reasons* for what you did. In the case of your failed evening walk, if you really understood what lack of exercise does to your heart, you would spend less time watching television and more time working out. The defender of Aristotle would say that there was something lacking in your choice or decision; it was not "decisive" enough and remained a bit of good advice rather than a real decision. These are plausible explanations for many cases. In the complex world of human actions many theories (perhaps even sociobiology and economic choice theory) manage to capture some portion of the truth. But to do justice to our actual experience of human action (our own and others'), there is genuine value in the expansion and treatment that Aquinas gave to the stage of execution.

Aquinas focused as much as Aristotle on the importance of good deliberation, the centrality of judgment in choice of action and the close link between this decision and the action that follows. But Aquinas was sensitive to the fact that a whole range of emotional and attitudinal factors come into play in the carrying out of the decision, and that this is an area where the moral virtues (which shape attitudes and feelings) have an important role. It is important for ethics not only to make the right decision (which is essential, of course), but also to carry it out at the right time, in the right way and with the right frame of mind.

Let us say that a professor assigns a two-thousand-word essay project. Some students will treat it as a mechanical task, unpleasant but necessary, like vacuuming floors and dusting furniture when company is coming; others will not pay much attention to the guidelines; others are chronically late. Leaving aside the difference in actual abilities for the task, there is a wide variation based on attitude and character revealed in the way that assignments are dealt with.

Jesus told a short parable about a father and his two sons (Mt 21:28-31):

> "A man had two sons; he went to the first and said, 'Son, go and work in the
> vineyard today.' He answered, 'I will not'; but later he changed his mind and

went. The father went to the second and said the same; and he answered, 'I go, sir'; but he did not go. Which of the two did the will of his father?" They said, "The first."

The first son changes his mind and actually goes into the vineyard to work as his father requested or, rather, commanded. We cannot be sure whether the second son had no intention of going to the vineyard all along and merely said yes in order to temporarily appease his father, or if at breakfast he was willing to go and later never managed to get out there. But we are more likely to be in the position of the second son, to acquiesce and promise and not follow through, and so we are apt to be more lenient or charitable toward the second son.

The importance of executing the decision in the appropriate way is thus crucial, and it was one of the contributions of Thomas Aquinas to the theory of action to clarify this. We are now in a position to present the whole flow of the process of action.

The stages of practical reason. If one takes the traditional reading of Aquinas on the process of human action (following the reading of *ST* I-II, qq. 8-17, by the later scholastic commenters on the *Summa*), there are twelve stages of action, with alternating activations of reason and will.[4] This is hopelessly complex and misleading, and requires modification to be faithful to the actual thought of Aquinas.

The Aristotelian basis for Thomas Aquinas can be restored if we make two moves: (1) treat the discussion in qq. 8-11 as prolegomena, describing the dynamic character of the will in general; (2) pair off the separate acts of intellect and will into combined stages, so that each stage of action has an intellectual and a volitional component. Thus the stage of intention has input from both reason and will, deliberation involves both reason and will, and decision and execution likewise comprise both intellect and will. This is easy to see in the case of intention and decision, whose double components are discussed in single questions by Aquinas (*ST* I-II, q. 12 and q. 13, respectively), while the parts of reason and will in deliberation and execution are treated in separate questions (qq. 14-15 and qq. 16-17, respectively).

---

[4]The twelve parts of action: (1) perception; (2) wish; (3) judgment; (4) intention; (5) deliberation; (6) consent; (7) decision; (8) choice; (9) command; (10) application; (11) performance; (12) completion. See Thomas Gilby, "Structure of a Human Act," appendix 1 in vol. 17 of the Blackfriars edition of *Summa Theologiae* (London: Blackfriars, 1970), p. 211.

This makes a total of eight aspects combined into four stages of action (see fig. 3.1, "Stages of Practical Reason"). The terminology employed here basically follows Thomas Gilby's translation, and the only substantial change is the term *execution* for the stage that combines "command" and "application."

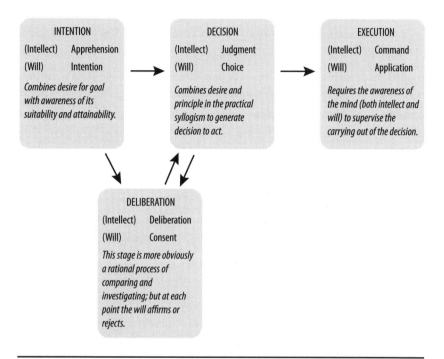

Figure 3.1. Stages of practical reason. A summary of the presentation by Thomas Aquinas in *Summa Theologiae*, I-II, qq. 12-17

Let us note the advantages of this schema for understanding the Thomistic view of human action over the traditional twelve-stage model:

1. First, there is a sensible chronological sequence to the stages of action. If one begins with intention in q. 12, Aquinas does present the process of practical reasoning and action in a coherent sequence. The reason why deliberation (q. 14) comes after decision (q. 13) is that deliberation is often not necessary, and it should be treated as an adjunct to judgment and choice, which is the heart of all human action.

2. It is much clearer that Aquinas adopted and followed the Aristotelian flow of human action without excessive complication. The only sub-

stantial addition is the stage of execution, representing an important insight and improvement on Aquinas's part, as explained above.

3. The four-stage sequence deals with a major problem in moral theology, the splitting of intellect and will. In the traditional twelve-stage model each activation of the intellect is then responded to by the will—for example, after deliberation ("consent"), and after judgment ("choice"). This fits the late Scholastic model, in which freedom is associated with the will, and the judgment of intellect is considered to be "indifferent"—just the presentation of an option that is then received or chosen by the will. There is a powerful philosophical tradition behind this,[5] but it badly distorts a properly Thomistic view of action. The harmony and unity of intellect and will are properly restored by our four-stage unified model.

4. This scheme exactly corresponds to Aquinas's understanding of prudence, the virtue of practical reason in *ST* II-II, q. 48. There are three parts to prudence, dealing with three different aspects: the aspect of *consilium* (counsel) in deliberation, the aspect of *judgment* and the aspect of *command* in execution, which Aquinas calls "the principal act."

5. The four stages with their intellectual and volitional components help us to make the links to the role of emotion, attitude and spirituality in the stages of human action. Each stage has its characteristic operation, potential pitfalls, and need for awareness, balance and spiritual insight. (This will be elucidated below.)

Is the Thomistic schema true to life? Let us consider first, however, the explanatory value of the Thomistic process of action in a hypothetical example.

Marlene is a financial adviser, the mother of two children and a faithful church member. Tom, her husband, is on a business trip to China. She has been spending time on two new accounts looking at resources and options and researching different investment possibilities. A phone call comes in.

"Marlene, can you take on another new client?" says the caller.

---

[5]See especially Servais Pinckaers, "Freedom of Indifference," in *The Sources of Christian Ethics*, trans. Mary Thomas Noble (Washington, DC: Catholic University of America Press, 1995), pp. 327-53.

"I'm pretty busy as it is," she replies. "Why don't you check with Jim?"

As she is about to return to her spreadsheets, she notices the picture of her family on the shelf and says to herself, "Oh, I'd better not forget to help Amy with her costume. Let's see . . . I think we have the materials at home, but if I'm going to be working on that, I won't have time to make supper. I'll phone the pizza place when I'm leaving the office and pick up the food on the way home."

While they are eating supper, the phone rings, and Amy answers it. "It's for you, mom."

Marlene takes the phone, listens for about twenty seconds, and says, "That sounds like a worthwhile project, but we're already committed with our charitable giving. Thank you."

After the cleaning up from supper has been dealt with, Marlene says, "OK, Amy, no TV tonight. Come here, and we'll take some fittings for your costume, and then I'll work on it while you do your homework. You can read *Harry Potter* later on if there's any time left."

Marlene checks her email before going to bed. As she's deleting junk mail and trivial items, she spots a message from the chairperson of the finance committee at church about scheduling a planning meeting for the fall fundraising campaign. She reads the message and thinks, "I'm going to be even busier in the fall. Maybe it's time to resign from the committee." But she responds with a couple of possible dates after Tom will have returned from China. She logs off, undresses, quickly reads a very short devotional passage and climbs into bed.

We can infer some of Marlene's intentions. She wants to take good care of her family, be responsible and successful at work, do her part in the life of her church, and have a relationship with God. It is also possible that she is hoping to do too much.

She is able to make quick decisions. For example, she decided not to take on another client; she scanned her email inbox and deleted irrelevant items; she turned down another request for a charitable donation. These decisions could be described as the use of sound judgment, based on her priorities and circumstances: "This is not good for me to do now." These are sound, rational judgments, and Marlene was able to make them with very little deliberation.

Some deliberation was required when she realized that Amy's costume needed work and there was little time. She went through the evening's agenda and saw that she could have some extra time by picking up pizza.

She thought for a minute about her finance committee, filing away for future consideration, perhaps, the need for a more thorough deliberation and decision about her participation.

From this short slice of life, Marlene carries through on her decisions and acts appropriately in relation to others; but there could be the potential, if time pressure were increased, of making hasty and ill-considered decisions.

The Function of Moral Laws in the Process of Practical Reason

Strictly speaking, there is openness, or flexibility, or freedom in the two middle stages of practical reason—deliberation and decision, where options are examined, and different ways of looking at an action and judging it are possible.

For both Aristotle and Thomas Aquinas, a person's intentions come from his or her character and are not part of practical reason. One simply has certain desires and attitudes that have been adopted, shaped and instilled from past experience. One deliberates about and decides on the actions that are judged as means to the purposes that one already has.

Peter, for example, might have decided in high school that his goal was to be a millionaire by the age of forty. If this is seriously pursued, then decisions about education, savings and investments, and alertness to business opportunities are judged under the framework of this goal. This is not to say at some point in his thirties Peter might not reconsider his priorities in life and consciously relinquish that goal. But as long as he affirms that purpose, then it functions as a fixed point for his practical reasoning.

In the stage of execution there is no more openness: the action is fully specified already, and it is a matter of carrying it out. But the carrying out of a complex decision, or one that is implemented over time, such as a new policy at a business firm, involves a certain monitoring as part of implementation; that is an implication of the use of the mind and its awareness of circumstances in carrying out a decision. Unanticipated difficulties or circumstances can provide a feedback that the decision and action may need modification.

It is in the decision primarily, and in deliberation secondarily, where laws and rules have relevance. The structure of the practical syllogism is the combination of principle and an action judged to be an instance of that principle, or, to put it another way, the combination of a rule and a case or instance of that rule. The decision resulting in an action is a judgment that this action is a case that comes under this rule, or an instance covered by this principle. Knowledge of the laws of God and a desire to adhere to them will, of course, be essential for the informed Christian mind.[6]

Remember too that the basic principles for judging actions are "Do good and avoid evil." Many crucially important moral areas of our life are judged "good" for us without more specific rules or laws. Raising a family, for example, involves a large investment of time, sacrifice of other pleasures and opportunities, commitment to training, and so on, and is close to the core of our identities as members of the church and the kingdom of God. And yet I do not believe that parents do all these things under the rubric of obedience to any law of parenting. Raising a family is partly biological, one might say, almost self-evidently good (certainly universal across cultures), and is something modeled for us (with good and bad exemplars). Except when we are unusually tired or discouraged, we do not have to remind ourselves of the reasons for parenting. And even when we temporarily chafe at the confining pressures, we do not tell ourselves of our *duty* to be good parents; rather, we try to reconstruct the larger picture—the previous joys, the temporary nature of the difficulties, the example of other parents who persevered and so on. As a matter of fact, there *are* laws that specify what children deserve to receive from their parents, but they are applied mainly in the unusual cases to remove children from irresponsible or neglectful parents. I would say that no normal parents have ever been motivated primarily by a sense of obligation to obey the laws of parenting (whether civil or biblical). They simply see that successfully raising a family is part and parcel of their vision of what a fulfilled and good life should be.

Law, rules and regulations are primarily supplementary directions for the proper fulfillment of life's goals. They provide the instruction and insight into the ways in which things should be done and relationships conducted.

---

[6]The Thomistic structure of moral reasoning is similar to O'Donovan's notion of action being "recognized" as an instance of a rule. See O'Donovan, "Christian Moral Reasoning," p. 126.

Let us take the building of a home, for example, and assume that you are a do-it-yourselfer eager to do as much of the work on the house as you can. You plan to wire the house, and you discover that there are codes and regulations that specify types of wire and junction boxes to be used, where outlets may not be located, special requirements for the location of major appliances, and so on. You could see this set of rules as an inconvenient form of bureaucracy, especially when you are forced to redo some work in a different way to conform to the code, or you could see these regulations as a good way to promote the safe use of electricity in your home, based on the experience of problems in the past (including damaging fires), and representing a kind of "method of electrical wisdom."

Most people will see the same principle operating behind traffic laws and other regulations that affect our behavior in society. Rather than a dangerous free-for-all, we are all much better off being told to drive on a particular side of the road, not to exceed speed limits, and so on, even if we chafe under these restrictions at times.

What about situations where morality does come down to a matter of obedience or disobedience to law? Let us return to Peter and his millionaire ambitions. With some talent, hard work, good connections, favorable circumstances and so on, his goal is not an impossible one. But let us say that Peter's main business is not doing as well as he had hoped, and he realizes at the age of thirty-six that he is not going to achieve his goal in the way he thought. He is comfortable and doing well, but he is not even halfway to being a millionaire. So he is tempted to enter into some side businesses—shady real estate deals, and some investments through a storefront business with overseas links that promise a very nice return. Should Peter investigate whether he is going to be involved in deceptive advertising in the real estate deals and possibly be linked to foreign gangs and drug dealing in the investments? If he is intent on achieving his goal, Peter (and others like him) may well make the judgment "Go ahead and do this" and take the risk of immoral and illegal activity. But the laws should work to rule out the deceptive and immoral means of making money. We would hope that Peter would make the judgment "Becoming a millionaire should not be so important to me that I choose these means to achieve it."

The function of rules and laws is thus to help to specify what is right in certain situations, and to enable our judgment to filter out improper courses of action. Within the use of the practical syllogism, laws are helpful specifications of the first principle, "Do good and avoid evil," ways of spelling out what is actually good and what is evil in certain areas.

When we are not able to make a judgment with clarity, and we have to deliberate about alternative means of achieving what we want, or figure out the best way of proceeding, laws and regulations come into play in our practical reasoning to eliminate certain actions that might be appealing, more effective or cheaper, but wrong because they involve deception or injustice. The principle known as the Golden Rule will never give us any information about what our specific action should be—it is contentless—and it is pointless to set out to "obey" it. But it functions as a *regula*, a yardstick by which to measure the correctness of our actions, or as a filtering mechanism to eliminate actions that we might be tempted to take but that fail that standard.

We are conscious of the moral rules impinging on us and requiring our obedience because we are aware of those laws that address our waywardness. As we noted, most parents do not need to be aware of (or follow) laws requiring them to provide for the needs of their children. But many of us are tempted to speed when we are driving and pressed for time, or to tell a lie to get out of an awkward situation. It is when we sense the constraints of the rule on our freedom or contrary desires that we are conscious of the urge to disregard the rule.

FOR FURTHER READING

Thomas Aquinas, *ST* I-II, qq. 12-17.

Ralph McInerny, *Ethica Thomistica: The Moral Philosophy of Thomas Aquinas*, rev. ed. (Washington, DC: Catholic University of America Press, 1997), chap. 4, "The Structure of the Human Act."

Daniel Westberg, *Right Practical Reason: Aristotle, Action, and Prudence in Aquinas* (Oxford: Oxford Clarendon Press, 1994), chaps. 8-12.

4

How to Evaluate
Good and Bad Actions

To begin, I will briefly summarize the elements of an action that form the basis for assessing its moral quality—whether it can be judged good or bad. These elements are (1) the *object*, which is the directly intended action itself; (2) the *end*, or overall purpose (or combination of purposes); and (3) the *circumstances*, referring to the time, place, manner and other relevant aspects. It only takes one of these elements to be defective to render the action bad or evil, while all three must be in proper order for the action to be considered good.[1] In the pages below I will explain these aspects more thoroughly.[2]

To illustrate, consider a traditional example: almsgiving, or a charitable gift to the poor. As an action itself, this certainly should be seen as something good. However, if the funds given away were already promised for something else, or if there are more urgent claims on our resources such as unpaid bills, or if the organization receiving the donation was known to mismanage or waste funds, the rightness of the action may be called into question. Thus the circumstances or context of the action must be favorable. Likewise, the end or purpose that one had in mind might be such to distort

---

[1]In the *Summa Theologiae* the treatment is found in I-II, qq. 18-21. For modern translation with notes and commentary by Thomas Gilby, see vol. 18 of the Blackfriars edition (London: Blackfriars, 1966). See also T. J. Higgins, "Moral Good," in vol. 6 of *New Catholic Encyclopedia*, 2nd ed. (Washington, DC: Catholic University of America Press, 2003), pp. 350-54.
[2]For basic summary, see Ralph McInerny, "Good and Evil Action," in *Ethica Thomistica: The Moral Philosophy of Thomas Aquinas*, rev. ed. (Washington, DC: Catholic University of America Press, 1997), 77-89; Daniel Westberg, "Good and Evil in Human Acts," in *The Ethics of Aquinas*, ed. Stephen Pope (Washington, DC: Georgetown University Press, 2002), pp. 90-102.

the action. Instead of acting from generosity and genuine charity, one might be seeking a certain kind of reputation or influence, expecting a payback through a secret deal or perhaps be more motivated by guilt or some other kind of pressure.

There is a public or "objective" feature about the action itself and many of the circumstances that can be observed or investigated and noted. Outside observers (such as close friends and family) may question the time and place and the way the action was carried out. But there is a hiddenness about the end or purposes that we actually have, which involves our inner motivations, known ultimately only to God, and we cannot properly judge the moral characteristics underlying purpose.

A THEOLOGICAL VIEW OF DISCERNING GOOD AND EVIL ACTIONS

Let us be clear that the moral evaluation of actions is something that can properly belong to God alone, and it is only in the most limited and qualified way that moral theologians or ethicists can presume to speak about the factors that constitute good and bad actions. As the Catholic moral theologian Romanus Cessario has reminded us, moral theologians do not divide the world between good and bad objects, as if the métier of moral theology could be compared with the sorting out of black and white chess pieces.[3]

Let us recall the startling passage that opens the famous and unfinished book on ethics by Dietrich Bonhoeffer (written during the dark days of World War II):

> The knowledge of good and evil seems to be the aim of all ethical reflection.
> The first task of Christian ethics is to invalidate this knowledge. Already in
> the possibility of the knowledge of good and evil Christian ethics discerns a
> falling away from the origin. . . . It is only in the unity of his knowledge of God
> that he knows of other men, of things, and of himself. He knows all things
> only in God, and God in all things.[4]

In this powerful challenge to the claims and pretensions of standard human

---

[3]Romanus Cessario, *Introduction to Moral Theology* (Washington, DC: Catholic University of America Press, 2001), p. 157.
[4]Dietrich Bonhoeffer, *Ethics*, trans. Neville Horton Smith (New York: Simon & Schuster, 1995), p. 21.

moral systems, Bonhoeffer wanted to remind us that after the fall and our separation from God, the human attempt to develop knowledge of good and evil is really a manifestation of the separation from God.

We get a similar and powerful reminder of God as standard of the good in the opening of the ethical portion of the third section of Karl Barth's *Church Dogmatics*: the fundamental and comprehensive answer to the ethical problem is that "man's action is good in so far as it is sanctified by the Word of God," and we must look to Jesus Christ, who "is the fullness, measure and source of all goodness, and therefore of what is to be called good in human action."[5]

Neo-orthodox theologians such as Barth had a heightened suspicion of natural law and human moral standards; but there is a much more general perception among them of the natural law tradition (often associated with Thomas Aquinas) as attempting to supply a basic human morality that leads to complacency, moral distortion and, above all, independence from God. The Thomistic ethical system often is presented, incorrectly, as offering such a natural law basis for moral knowledge that forms the basis for ordinary human morality and thus has less need for God and revelation. If this were the case, then clearly the moral theology of Aquinas would be subject to the criticism of Bonhoeffer and Barth. Cessario and others, however, point to the quality of Thomistic natural law as a matter of inclination and attraction to what is good and not as a set of regulations or dictates of moral law.[6] On this basis, Cessario is able to offer a human morality that does not have positive law, human convention, public opinion or personal feelings as a standard of good and evil, but instead must, for its standard of truth, participate in the eternal law or mind of God. In considering the fundamental basis of the ethics of Aquinas, Cessario put it this way: "Within the schema of Aquinas's moral realism, all created moral goodness exists by reason of an intrinsic participation in the highest good which is God."[7] For the non-Christian, there may be indirect participation in God's eternal law through the goodness of creation, but this is not sufficient for people of faith:

---

[5]Karl Barth, *Church Dogmatics*, vol. III/4, *The Doctrine of Creation*, ed. G. W. Bromiley and T. F. Torrance (Edinburgh: T & T Clark, 1961), p. 4.

[6]Cessario, *Moral Theology*, p. 151.

[7]Ibid., p. 156.

For the Christian believer, then, the moral life implies more than that a person measures up to a standard of ethical ideals. To live the moral life means to abide with the crucified and risen Christ. Christian ethics evaluate human actions and a person's capacity to perform good ones with an eye on Christ's satisfactory death that once and for all has achieved God's promise of salvation for the human race.[8]

Then what use is this scheme to assess the goodness or badness of actions introduced at the beginning of this chapter? Principally, it is for our own use. If our calling is to be faithful Christian disciples, to glorify God in our lives and to be conformed to the image of Christ, then we need some means (with the aid of the Holy Spirit) by which we can assess our daily actions, to be aware of those aspects of our lives that are strengthening or hindering our Christian-lives.

Secondarily, this analysis will be of help to those whose ministry involves giving counsel. Many Christians will feel the need to speak to a confessor or spiritual adviser about their spiritual lives and actions, to confront the reality of their share of responsibility for the mistakes and messes that they have made, to receive the grace of forgiveness and take positive steps toward their "amendment of life."

Much of the development of Catholic moral theology, including the kind of moral analyzing of actions presented here, came from the need for priests and confessors to be able to ascertain the quality and seriousness of various sins and then assign an appropriate penance. The Roman Catholic Church went through centuries in which the practice of confession degenerated into a mechanical system wherein the chief problem to be dealt with seemed to be the breaking of certain laws of the church, and the performance of certain pro forma activities of penance would bring the person into a member in good standing again. What tended to be lost was the fundamental relationship of people to God. The process of rectifying this in the post–Vatican II Roman Catholic Church is signaled by the change from the sacrament of penance to the sacrament of reconciliation.

Many contemporary Christians are untroubled by the thought that their actions are a mixture of good and bad. The reasons for this are several: the

---

[8]Ibid., p. 149.

individualism and relativism of our culture, the easy conviction that many others are worse than we are, a confidence in the grace and love of God that may often degenerate into "cheap grace" and presumption. A key feature of this chapter, however, is how to reckon with the loss of accountability before God in modern society, the general abandonment of belief in a day of judgment and the conviction that a focus on sin and righteousness is part of an old-fashioned and morbid preoccupation that does not accord with the dominant characteristic of God as love.

To talk about goodness and badness in actions presupposes a conviction that our actions matter to God, who is our judge as well as our creator, redeemer and reconciler. What matters to God is not the number of demerit marks beside our name in some divine ledger and the amount of guilt generated by our actions (which the old penitential system often implied)—as if God becomes upset most by having his *laws* ignored or broken—but rather that our bad actions are bad for us and weaken our fellowship with him. As Aquinas put it, "We do not offend God except by doing something contrary to our own good."[9]

If we bring this perspective to the moral assessment of actions, then our interest is in developing an awareness of how to become better people: to draw closer to the kind of human beings we were created to be, to be more faithful disciples of Christ and more effective servants in God's kingdom. We can now look with more clarity and detail at the three elements of the moral assessment of actions: the object, the end, the circumstances.

THE ELEMENTS OF THE MORAL EVALUATION OF HUMAN ACTIONS

The object. The object of an action is the concrete, inherent and limited purpose of the action by which we describe or categorize the action, such as sending a letter, preparing a meal, giving an offering or writing an essay. These actions involve a number of subsidiary actions, such as, in the case of preparing dinner, finding recipes and ingredients, cutting up, preparing and cooking various items, inviting people to share in the meal, and so on; and these secondary acts receive their intelligibility from the overall action of preparing dinner.

---

[9]Thomas Aquinas, *Summa Contra Gentiles* III.122, as cited in *On the Truth of the Catholic Faith: Summa Contra Gentiles*, trans. Vernon Bourke (Garden City, NY: Hanover House, 1956), p. 143.

The reason for defining the object of an act as inherent and limited is to indicate an important principle at stake here: an action should not be given such a wide description that it hides or disguises the moral evaluation of subsidiary parts of the action. For example, a research team working to isolate and potentially correct gene defects associated with Alzheimer's disease should not furnish the description of their work merely as "finding a cure for Alzheimer's," because their research might involve debatable experimental methods, including the use and destruction of subjects such as human embryos, actions to which many would have moral objections.

Similarly, to use a contemporary political issue, "fighting the war against terrorism" or "protecting national security" ought not to be used as descriptions to cover up analysis and discussion of the means to conduct such operations, such as universal surveillance of all telephone conversations. One also thinks of the attempt to deflect concerns about the use of torture in referring to "enhanced interrogation techniques." This kind of euphemistic or favorable labeling and description is a case of importing agreement about the goodness of the end or purpose into the description of the subsidiary actions, and attempting to have the end justify the means.[10]

In the case of writing an essay as a discrete action, which will involve a number of subsidiary actions such as deciding the amount and selection of research materials, we could imagine a stressed-out student plagiarizing material, or even purchasing an essay from an online service offering a product. In this case, the student is not really trying to let the end justify the means, because the action is not "handing in an assignment" or "satisfying the course requirements." The action is writing an essay, and inherent in that description is the understanding that the student is doing his or her own research and composition, and offering a product of genuine personal thought and expression.

Let us go further in our examples with an instance of a concrete action that has a definite evil associated with it: cutting off a person's limb. If the person is healthy, this could well be an instance of torture, or in a country under older Islamic sharia law it could be an instance of punishment of a crime. But if the person has gangrene caused by diabetes, or frostbite, or has

---

[10]On the importance of correct description, and for helpful overall treatment, see Jean Porter, *Moral Action and Christian Ethics* (Cambridge: Cambridge University Press, 1995), pp. 84-124.

suffered severe and crushing injury, then the removal of the limb is the medically indicated procedure. Again, we do not say here that the end "justifies" the means, but we are giving the action of the medical professionals its proper description: surgical amputation.

The end. The end or purpose of an action is the goal to be accomplished. This is at the heart of rational human action, because we are meant to have *reasons* for our actions that distinguish us from animals (which also have a kind of freedom to make various decisions, but typically without awareness of goals or purposes, as described in chapter two). There is often not just one goal, of course, but a network of overlapping ends.

The more remote purpose of an action may sometimes be seen as the real motive factor and defining aspect of an action. Thomas Aquinas cited the example given by Aristotle in which someone who steals in order to commit adultery (by providing an attractive setting for seduction, let us imagine) is, properly speaking, more an adulterer than a thief (*ST* I-II, q. 18, a. 6).

There can be a chain of ends from the particular to the general. A seminary student performs actions in connection with a parish field work assignment in order to satisfy the requirements set out in the handbook, and this in order to earn a degree from a theological college, and this in order to become a qualified ordained minister, and this in order to serve the church. But if we ask the further question "Why do you want to do *that*?" we realize that we have shifted from the linkage of objective inherent purposes of a series of actions to the subjective and individual motives of the person.

A student might write an essay or fulfill parish responsibilities merely to satisfy the institutional requirements, when there ought to be other motivations: in the case of an essay, the recognition of the usefulness of a broader historical or theological vision in thinking about issues facing the church, or even an inherent interest in the subject. There could be a competitive urge to be superior to others. Even more important with duties in a parish, there is the hope that students see the connection to their work and their desire for effective ministry, and that they have a genuine love and concern for people and a desire to serve Christ. The goals of having a paying profession, being able to support a family, and achieving personal fulfillment are not "unspiritual," but they validly overlap with other goals. What we need is occasional reflection on the ensemble of our goals, the self-awareness that we are not deluding ourselves and the desire to have our overlapping goals reflect a balanced pattern of the right priorities.

Impure and wrong motives can make otherwise good actions morally deficient. We recognized this above with possible faulty motives in giving money. If we turn to cases of surgical procedures, the use of a cesarean section to deliver a baby may sometimes be questionable. Some surgeons are suspected of recommending unnecessary c-sections, either at the insistence of the mother, or because of personal convenience (e.g., to avoid being called in at 2:00 a.m.), or even the possibility of extra income.

The circumstances. Conditions of person, time and place, and other considerations enter into forming the context for an action. The decision to act (or refrain from acting) is based on a judgment of the object of the action in line with the purposes to be served, *in the light of the circumstances at the time.* Medical personnel arriving on the scene of a train wreck or bomb attack may make judgments about what procedures to follow and whom to help that are quite different from ones they would make in a hospital setting: time pressure and limited resources may create a triage situation in which they must ration life-saving actions.

In the more ordinary circumstances of life, all of us must make judgments about the right thing to do now in light of our goals and responsibilities and the circumstances. Time with friends, leisurely meals, favorite television programs, reading devotional books and so on, may need to be curtailed so that we can attend to work, meet unexpected demands or catch up on needed sleep.

The challenge of human life is to make concrete in real life the goals, aspirations and vision of life that we hold to and live by. We experience the succession of time during a day as presenting new circumstances in which to actualize our personalities, weak and unformed as they are. Thus there is an indeterminacy and uniqueness about each situation that calls for creative perception and judgment. Rules and principles must be applied in concrete situations in the light of the current situation. It may be necessary to judge the circumstances under principles different from the ordinary rules.

Many would argue, for example, that the circumstances of modern life affect the freedom in which we make decisions about contraception. The problems created by overpopulation and scarce resources (not a factor before the twentieth century) and by longer life span and the pressures of modern life to limit family size are, arguably, justification for coming to different conclusions about the use of artificial contraceptives. Some would argue that there is an inherent principle of the unity of the social and procreative meaning of the sex act that must be preserved, not just in general, but in each act of physical union. Others would maintain that other circumstances may affect this judgment, as reflected in the current controversy over the legitimacy of using (and making available) condoms for the prevention of AIDS in Africa and other areas where the infection rate is high and the option of abstention may not be viable.

For the most part, however, our flexibility at this point (acting correctly in a given context of circumstances) takes shape in the way we execute the decisions and judgments that we make. The way in which we execute our decisions is a key part in the Thomistic account of the circumstances governing the goodness and badness of our actions. We may make a decision to visit a friend in hospital or to begin work on a project, but laxness or procrastination on our part means that the action is not performed at the best time or with sufficient time to do it properly. We are pressed for time and preoccupied when we visit the friend; or we work on a written assignment in haste, perfunctorily or with inadequate preparation. There is a defect not in our intention and decision, but in our failure to apply ourselves with sufficient attention and time.[11] The circumstances of our performance may render an action that was otherwise good (on the basis of the object and end) into something ineffective and unfortunately defective.

Summary. For a human action to be considered good (recognizing the limitations that attach to all human action on account of the limitations of our knowledge and will) all three elements—object, end, circumstances—must be correct. An important defect in any of the three aspects is sufficient to make the action bad.

ARE ALL ETHICAL DECISIONS SITUATIONAL, OR ARE THERE ABSOLUTES?

We might push further with two lines of argument included above. First, take the example of an amputation, which can be considered something evil in

---

[11]There may not be a defect in the content or substance of the intention and decision, but there may well be a lack of clarity, firmness or wholeheartedness.

itself, since it involves the loss of a limb, but is considered good in the context of saving a person's life. Second, the example of artificial contraception, which in some circumstances, at least, could be considered legitimate.

Some Catholic moralists have taken the position that in principle all actions have a neutral action description (such as "removing a person's limb"), and they become moral actions subject to the question of whether they are good or bad only when a context is established. The object of the action (the immediate or proximate purpose that gives the action its type or nature) is neither good nor bad but neutral, and it is the end, or more general purpose, and the circumstances that give the moral contours. Having sex, for example, is neither good nor bad in the abstract; it is part of human life. It all depends on the where, why, when and how; it is the circumstances and the motivation that make the sex good or bad. There is much to be said for this position, and one could cite, perhaps, the answer that Aquinas gives to the question about stealing in a situation of need as support for this: taking what belongs to someone else, though ordinarily wrong, is morally justifiable in certain situations.

Yet we must be careful about yielding to this kind of reductionism—that is, reducing all the objects of our action, the plain and honest description of our immediate actions, to a realm of neutrality where only our overall intentions and the circumstances are morally relevant. That would imply that there are no inherently immoral actions, actions that are not to be contemplated no matter what the circumstances are, or what benevolent intentions one has.

One of the aims of Joseph Fletcher's *Situation Ethics* was precisely that: to demonstrate that all moral rules have, in principle, situations where there are exceptions that we would agree with, and that so-called moral absolutes do not exist.

One contemporary Roman Catholic moral theologian, Timothy O'Connell, reduces the category of inherently evil actions to not intentionally harming the innocent. That covers a number of actions, such as abortion, targeting civilians in warfare and knowingly putting innocent people accused of crimes to death.[12]

---

[12]Timothy O'Connell, *Principles for a Catholic Morality*, rev. ed. (San Francisco: Harper & Row, 1990), pp. 187-96.

This is insufficient. Pope John Paul II, in his encyclical on dangers in modern moral theology, quoted the Vatican II document *Gaudium et Spes*:

> Whatever is hostile to life itself, such as kind of homicide, genocide, abortion, euthanasia and voluntary suicide; whatever violates the integrity of the human person, such as mutilation, physical and mental torture and attempts to coerce the spirit; whatever is offensive to human dignity, such as subhuman living conditions, arbitrary imprisonment, deportation, slavery, prostitution and trafficking in women and children; degrading conditions of work which treat labourers as mere instruments of profit, and not as free responsible persons; all these and the like are a disgrace . . . and they are a negation of the honour due to the Creator.[13]

Added to this list through citations of Paul and Augustine are idolatry, adultery, fornication, blasphemy and other sins that we cannot affirm are no longer sins if done for a good motive. "Consequently," concludes the encyclical, "circumstances or intentions can never transform an act intrinsically evil by virtue of its object into an act 'subjectively' good or defensible as a choice."[14]

THE ROLE OF CONSEQUENCES

It is clear that classic Christian moral theology on Thomistic lines cannot be consequentialist in the sense that Joseph Fletcher's approach was; that is, that doing the "loving thing" is to produce the best outcome out of generous and benevolent motives. The inner motivation of the will, whether directed toward or away from God and his will, must be a decisive factor.

However, the consequences of an action are more than incidentally relevant. Harking back to Jesus' short parable of the two sons asked to work in the vineyard, we note that the good intentions of the one were undone by his inaction, while the defect in the initial intention of the other son was corrected by his actually going out to work.

There is no goodness in action that is merely desired and intended. Actions are concrete in this world, and their goodness is defined in part by what is accomplished. Aquinas put it this way: "Although the goodness of an action

---

[13]*Gaudium et Spes* 27, quoted in *Veritatis Splendor*, 80.
[14]*Veritatis Splendor*, 81.

is not caused by the goodness of its effect, nevertheless an action is called good because it is conducive to a good effect; in this way an action's bearing on an effect is the measure of its goodness" (*ST* I-II, q. 18, a. 2, ad 3).[15]

Consequences, when they are foreseen or are a predictable feature of a type of action, must be taken into account; they affect the goodness or badness of an action (*ST* I-II, q. 20, a. 5). Thus the possible and likely consequences are part of our analysis of both the object and the end of the act. But they do not constitute the sole *reason* for the action, nor can they be the only basis for our moral evaluation.

Let us say that a school principal must decide about disciplining a student after some serious offense, and that guidelines offer a choice between suspension and expulsion. Perhaps the more severe penalty would "send a message" and result in reform in the right direction. On the other hand, it might initiate a downward psychological spiral leading to more serious trouble. Prediction of these possible outcomes will be difficult; but there is also the effect on the student's family, on the morale of the other students and on the general regard for the authority of school policy. While all of these need to be reckoned with, there is also a central reason for acting involving justice, and punishment based on desert, clear and fair procedures, and the need to be consistent, independent of the consequences.

In sum, the desirable consequences of an anticipated action are part of the concrete good that is the attractive feature leading to a choice to act; but the many instances when achieving good results should not be the determining factor point to the essential and fundamental importance of conformity to the mind and revealed will of God.

FOR FURTHER READING

Thomas Aquinas, *ST* I-II, qq. 18-21.

Romanus Cessario, *Introduction to Moral Theology* (Washington, DC: Catholic University of America Press, 2001), 149-91.

Ralph McInerny, *Ethica Thomistica: The Moral Philosophy of Thomas Aquinas*, rev. ed. (Washington, DC: Catholic University of America Press, 1997), chap. 5, "Good and Evil Action."

---

[15]Blackfriars edition of *ST*, vol. 18, p. 13.

Charles R. Pinches, *Theology and Action: After Theory in Christian Ethics* (Grand
    Rapids: Eerdmans, 2002), chap. 5, "Naming Human Actions."

Jean Porter, *Moral Action and Christian Ethics* (Cambridge: Cambridge University
    Press, 1999), pp. 84-124.

Daniel Westberg, "Good and Evil in Human Acts," in *The Ethics of Aquinas*, ed.
    Stephen Pope (Washington, DC: Georgetown University Press, 2002), pp. 90-102.

5

ACTIONS, DISPOSITIONS
AND CHARACTER

THERE HAS BEEN A SHIFT in contemporary philosophical and theological ethics from the analysis of specific actions to the importance of character. The cultivation of character is thus seen as the foundation of good actions. No doubt this is a reaction against the atomization of human action into isolated moments of decision, and the development of the field of ethics into discussions about how to make a decision in extreme situations ("quandary ethics") where one must choose, for example, between a slow death by starvation and becoming a cannibal.

Especially for Christian ethicists interested in Christian discipleship and conformity to Christ, the shift to issues of Christian character and virtue is a helpful development. To consider the growth of Christian character over time allows us to deal with the challenge of occasional sin. A lapse into self-indulgence, sexual sin, or anger is compatible with Christian character (the very term *lapse* points to an exceptional departure from a normal, higher standard). The struggle against temptation, the recognition of sinful tendencies and the occasional lapse with subsequent repentance are experiences known to all Christians. This is solid reassurance for us. Take, for example, one of the many lists that we find in the Gospels and Epistles naming those who will not enter the kingdom of God: "Fornicators, idolaters, adulterers, male prostitutes, sodomites, thieves, the greedy, drunkards, revilers, robbers" (1 Cor 6:9-10). The description is meant to define not those who have at some time committed such offenses, but those who often behave in such ways by disposition.

At the conclusion of this chapter we will consider the important relationship between overall character and individual actions, but first we examine the role of emotion, will and the development of dispositions.

THE TRAINING AND MODERATION OF EMOTION

In the various situations where we need to make decisions and to act, the
emotional framework that we bring is important, and sometimes it becomes
dominant in those situations where we describe the agent as "carried away
by passion." We have desires and attitudes, responsive feelings, and emotional reactions to events and ideas that occur to us, all of which need development and moderation by judgments of reason. We should see this not
as intellectual suppression of emotion, but as proper guidance. The emotions are part and parcel of our moral powers, but they need the channeling
and moderation that reason provides.

In the kind of ethics that centers on a sense of duty or on the calculation
of beneficial results, emotion has been considered irrelevant at best, and
often an obstacle to correct moral analysis, especially in situations where an
inner conflict is experienced and described as tension between duty and
pleasure. In both secular and Christian versions of this approach to moral
psychology that treats emotions as irrational, the will is seen as the pivotal
mental force keeping threatening emotions in check, and moral virtue is
developed by a strong will able to suppress unruly emotions.

There has been a strong revival of interest in the connection between
emotion and morality, the reintegration of sensation and emotion with intellect and will, and the recognition of the rational basis and moral aspects
of emotion in general.[1] This difference between philosophical approaches
that are favorable toward the moral value of emotions and those that are
more suspicious goes back to ancient schools such as the Stoics.

In an Aristotelian and Thomistic moral psychology the emotions are not
irrational feelings, but reactions relating to fundamental desires and beliefs
that we have. For example, anger (one major type, at any rate) is defined by
Aristotle as a desire accompanied by pain toward the revenge of what one

---

[1]See Ronald de Sousa, *The Rationality of Emotion* (Cambridge, MA: MIT Press, 1987); Justin
Oakley, *Morality and the Emotions* (London: Routledge, 1992).

regards as a slight toward oneself (or one's friend) that is unwarranted.[2] It is not merely a feeling of irritation or hostility, but an emotion that results from an appraisal or judgment of the situation. Anger at injustice, for example, is an emotional but moral reaction dependent on specific awareness and evaluation of circumstances and events.

If we take fear, for example, we have an essential motivating emotion: the feeling surrounding the possibility of a threat. It is a good and rational thing to be aware of threats: to slow down while driving on an icy highway because of the fear of crashing; to maintain a healthy lifestyle because of the fear of having a heart attack; and so on. An awareness of the possible dangers that may occur and taking sensible precautions is part of the ensemble of motivating factors in a mature person. One of the characteristics of teenagers is an underdeveloped sense of fear that overestimates their vitality and skill and downplays threats and danger. In some cases of youthful recklessness it is in fact the *lack* of the emotion of fear that is irrational.

It is, of course, possible to be excessively fearful, to magnify threats and to limit one's life by being overly cautious. Some may avoid situations where they feel anxious and nervous, or miss out on valuable experiences and potential development because of the fears that constrict them. In extreme cases there are a range of phobias that are irrational, such as fear of taking elevators due to claustrophobia, where the emotion is a definite hindrance to living and acting well.

This illustrates an important part of the nature of emotional development and the strengthening of virtue: there is a moderate, proper amount of emotional reaction that we need in our lives, and we develop this proper amount by experience and a pattern of good judgments. The virtues relating to the emotions, especially courage and temperance and the qualities related to them, are in effect the right or proper amount of emotional response. The person who has good character and the moral virtues will have the right emotional responses to situations and events: such a person will have patience, anger, sorrow, desire for sex, need for friendship, determination to succeed and so on, in the amount appropriate to his or her situation (there will be a great difference between the appropriate amount of aggression for

---

[2]Aristotle, *Rhetoric* 1378a30-2.

a professional basketball player and for a hospital chaplain).

In the *Nicomachean Ethics* Aristotle treated at length a number of character qualities where this principle of excess and deficit apply. It is possible to have too little or too much of a good thing, such as courage. A person may be too fearful on one side of the emotional spectrum, but in the opposite direction one may easily become reckless. We can add some of the other moral qualities described by Aristotle and place them on a spectrum:[3]

Table 5.1

AREA	DEFECT	MEAN	EXCESS
fear/confidence	cowardice	courage	recklessness
pleasure/pain	insensitivity	self-control	self-indulgence
anger	apathy	gentleness	short temper
affability	grouchiness	friendliness	obsequiousness
money	stinginess	generosity	extravagance

Aristotelian and Scholastic terminology speaks of the "mean" of a virtue as the range between too little and too much of an attitude or emotional quality. This doctrine seems basically correct, but the term *mean* can imply a kind of midway point or average, and that we should aim for a sort of "happy medium" in each area of attitude or behavior. The appropriateness of the attitude will vary enormously with the situation, and the one clear thing is that it is the judgment of practical wisdom that sets the norm.

Thus the development of good character and the virtues depends fundamentally on prudence, the virtue of the practical intellect enabling a person to make an overall pattern of sound judgments about actions.

Two further points can be made here. First, it should be obvious that when we speak of prudence and good judgment, we are not talking about a character quality that can be developed by sitting in a chair reading and thinking: by definition, this virtue is developed by living properly; thinking well, yes, but then judging, deciding and performing good actions. Second, I have stressed here the importance of good practical reason and the dependence of the moral virtues on prudence. But it is also true that prudence

---

[3]Taken partially from William Prior, *Virtue and Knowledge: An Introduction to Ancient Greek Ethics* (London: Routledge, 1991), p. 165.

cannot function without the other moral virtues, so that there is a mutual dependence: the range of emotional reactions requires good judgments of reason in regard to action, and the judgment of reason in turn depends on having appropriate and moderated emotional reactions so that judgments are sound and not distorted.

EMOTION, WILL AND MORAL WEAKNESS

We have already noted the importance of a person's emotional dispositions for being able to make good choices and act well. They affect not only the ends or goals of actions through one's values and the things that one enjoys, but also the judgments and executions of actions. Now we must integrate the earlier teaching on practical reason with the function of the emotions and virtues or vices of a person's character.

We can easily see the dependence of practical reasoning on emotional dispositions in the first category of purposes and values. The pleasure (or fear, or anger) that we feel in relation to various activities, situations and people will determine decisions about our work, and other priorities, and the amount of time and money that we devote to them.

We can understand how morally corrupt people behave badly. The person who thinks nothing of cheating on an income tax return or cutting ahead of other people waiting in line has no virtue of justice, both on the level of moral principle and in feelings for other people. Sexually promiscuous persons make self-gratification a principle of life and indulge their inclinations. Similarly, there are people who seem to thrive on putting others down or gossiping maliciously about them behind their backs, people who see nothing wrong with using deception when it suits them and so on. The thing to note here is that their attitudes and behavior are determined by a *combination* of defective moral reasoning and corresponding emotions and dispositions. Discrimination and injustice are a blend of rationalizations (e.g., based on false views of race, or ideologies about the poor) and negative attitudes and feelings; and a hedonistic lifestyle is a product of unrestrained impulses guided by a self-centered frame of mind that identifies the pursuit of pleasure as a chief good. In such cases these people need to be taught moral principles as well as to acquire proper attitudes and dispositions. From a Christian point of view,

repentance (*metanoia*, a thorough change of mind on all levels) and conversion is the answer.

But what about those people who have correct moral principles, have had
good training and upbringing, have even progressed some way along a virtuous path and nevertheless find themselves—as we all do at times, since we
are all sinners—acting selfishly, cheating, deceiving, indulging themselves and so on? This all-too-human and all-too-common phenomenon
seems to contradict the model of practical reasoning offered above, where
good actions are the product of rational deliberation, judgment and execution. If one has the moral principles to recognize what is the good thing
to do in a situation, and the ability to apply them to the point that one's
conscience has identified what would be right, how is it that one can so often
act against that judgment and do the wrong thing? How can we explain bad
and sinful behavior in those who actually know better?

One answer obvious to Christians is the doctrine of original sin. There is
something—an inherent selfishness, independence and perversity—that
retains some grip on all of us. That is a global theological truth that we
accept. But what about our practical reasoning model? Are we forced to say
that it is only partially valid, and that in many situations we act without
reason, driven by emotion and irrationality?

There are three basic options here: (1) the fundamental problem is a lack
of proper knowledge; (2) the problem is not in our understanding but in our
will; and (3) the answer lies in the coordination of moral reasoning and
emotional disposition. The third is the most complex but the most realistic
and helpful paradigm.

The first, the intellectual approach, is the answer of Socrates and Plato.
There is a defect in understanding the moral features of a situation when one
behaves badly. That certainly covers many situations, where understanding
the nature of society, the other person's point of view, the basic moral
equality of human beings and so on, supports honesty, fairness in business
dealings and so on. Both the corporate criminal who manipulates stock
information or employee pension funds and the welfare scam artist have
failed to think through the implications of the basic rule that one should
treat others as one would like to be treated.

But the Socratic apologist wants to go further. In cases such as theft and adultery, the fault is one of not knowing at the proper level. It is one thing to know that adultery is considered wrong—that is, it is a basic human moral principle not to commit adultery—and another thing to know why it is wrong, with the reasons in the nature of society and of marriage itself that constitute its wrongness. The goal of training and moral education should be to help people develop a deeper understanding of the reasons that underlie our moral principles. And, further, people need to integrate these principles with their underlying rationale in their own framework of attitudes and purposes in life.

This approach of deepening the understanding, and reflecting on principles and their implications, does carry us a good deal of the way and explains the attachment to this Socratic intellectualist approach throughout history in both Western and Eastern philosophies. It underlies the emphasis that we put on ethical programs and courses, and the recent commitment to professional ethics courses in the training programs for doctors, lawyers and business leaders.

Yet there is a strong sense that this is inadequate to explain many of our wrong actions. There are times when we seem to be fully informed and actually know (in a deeper and more reflective sense) what is right and yet do something contrary to it. As Paul famously put it, "I do not understand my own actions. For I do not do what I want, but I do the very thing I hate. . . . I can will what is right, but I cannot do it. For I do not do the good I want, but the evil I do not want is what I do" (Rom 7:15-19). Paul is talking about the human inability to live perfectly according to the law, and that sin is inevitable for all of us, and that we require the transforming power of the Holy Spirit if we are to be able to live lives in accordance with God's purposes for us. There is a heightened rhetoric here; nevertheless, we sense that Paul has identified a truth about human moral reasoning: there are times when we know the good (in a Socratic sense) and want to be able to do that, and yet we find ourselves choosing to do what our better selves know is not right.

Much of the later Western theological tradition has reduced the dimensions of the problem to the second solution, one of a faulty will. The will (corrupted by original sin) simply decides to go its own way, to disobey the judgment of conscience and exert its own independence. This has seemed to provide the key, the theological answer to the Socratic fallacy of a defect in knowledge. It seems to be the answer indicated by Paul, and the quality of the will becomes the pivotal point for resolving situations of moral weakness.

Notice, however, two unwelcome implications of this simplistic answer. First, the choice of the will is made in opposition to the judgment of intellect, and thus has an irrational basis. There is no good reason to go against one's better judgment, other than not wanting to, or simply disobeying. The grounds for deciding on a course of action based on choosing an action toward a good purpose disappear, and the action becomes an expression of mood, attitude or urges.

The second implication relates to our understanding and description of wrong action and what is required to correct it. In this model the problem is the quality of the will. It is wayward, not obedient enough and not strong enough to resist temptation. The solution is to bolster one's resolve, become more obedient and strengthen the authority of conscience. When people find themselves succumbing to actions that they know are wrong, this model tells them that they are weak in will or have a spirit of disobedience.

It is true that classical philosophical ethics did not have the benefit of a theology of sin, law and the will. But the simplification of moral reasoning to the power of the will is not any more faithful to Scripture either. It is more in line with the late medieval shift in ethics to an emphasis on law, obligation, conscience and obedience, and exclusive focus on the pivotal importance of the will is a legacy of that distorted tradition. Scriptural moral psychology and spirituality have more to do with the concept of "heart," the ensemble of desires, attitudes and emotional attachments than with the concept of the will as developed in later Western thought.

More complicated, but more fruitful and true to life, is the third approach, offered by Aristotle and developed by Thomas Aquinas. It is both ironic and a revealing fact about the later Christian tradition that Aristotle's term for moral weakness, *akrasia*, is often discussed under the heading "weakness of will." This tends to predispose the discussion, especially by Christian writers, into the assumption that Aristotle's solution was inadequate, since he lacked the view of the human will of the later theological tradition. But since Thomas Aquinas found Aristotle's scheme adequate for his profound and lengthy study of evil and sin in his *De Malo*, I will offer it here as the most helpful description of the need for the combination of good practical reasoning and moral virtues.

Aristotle described four types of moral character to contrast with each other. The person of virtuous character acts well and has both good principles and corresponding good emotions. The bad or vicious person has both bad principles and badly directed emotions. In between are the "morally strong" and the "morally weak" persons: they have good principles but struggle with inconsistent desires; the strong are able to act well in spite of their desires, while the weak often succumb to an emotional choice of action inconsistent with their principles. Setting this out in the form of a chart, we can schematize the contrast:

Table 5.2

Acting Well	**Virtuous** Has good principles and appropriate emotions	**Morally Strong** Has good principles, but struggles at times to control emotions for good choices
Acting Badly	**Morally weak** Has good principles, but often gives in to contrary emotions	**Vicious** Has corrupt principles, and the emotions to match

Let us look first at the virtuous and the vicious. Both act in accordance with their moral principles and experience no conflict, because their attitudes and emotions are in line with their goals and judgments. Both are able to act freely, and they take pleasure in their actions.

The morally strong also are able to perform good actions, but often it is a struggle for them. They experience contrary emotions, and the actions that they know are right for them to perform do not always come naturally; they sometimes have to act in spite of their feelings. But notice that our moral assessment of the morally strong is to "give them credit" for the moral effort required in following their principles. In fact, the popular estimation is to think of the morally strong person as being morally superior to the virtuous person, because it takes real effort for the former to achieve these good actions, while those same good actions come more naturally to the latter, who can perform them without conflict and without so much effort. I have even heard it said that Theresa should not have been given so much praise as a "saint," because she simply did what she liked to do; she enjoyed ministering to lepers and poor dying outcasts, so what she did was not the kind of heroic self-sacrifice that it would have been for the rest of us. This reaction can be explained, I think, because it is easier for us to identify with the intermediate position of the morally strong and the morally weak, and because the emphasis on the will as the moral pivot point puts a premium on the concept of "will power" acting to fulfill the dictates of conscience. We need to realize that the goal of the moral life is to attain that state of harmony between intention, attitude and emotion, so that it will become natural and joyful for us to perform what we know is right and good.

What Is a *Habitus*, and How Are Moral Dispositions Developed?

In contemporary English the word *habit* has several different connotations, some of them not very helpful for understanding what Thomas Aquinas understood as *habitus*. Dictionaries points us in the direction of "customary practice," which directs us to behavior patterns such as the habit of walking the dog when arriving home, and watching the ten o'clock news, or having a mug of tea or hot chocolate before going to bed. Another sense is acquired patterns of behavior, such as looking in both directions before crossing a road, which become almost instinctual or involuntary. More misleading is the use of *habit* to refer to a person's idiosyncratic behavioral peculiarities and nervous tics, such as swearing at annoying drivers in traffic or unconsciously biting fingernails. This common usage depicts habits as fairly mechanical behavior and often rather trivial. The point in common among these definitions and with the notion of a *habitus* is that it involves development over a period of time and becomes, in a way, second nature to us.

A *habitus* for scholastic theologians (which translated Aristotle's *hexis*) covered a much wider range of human abilities and activities, including mastery of fields of knowledge such as geometry or physics or a foreign language, the ability to perform musical instruments, public speaking, or any number of human activities that require a combination of knowledge, skill and training.

A *habitus* is the developed skill and disposition to respond to circumstances and perform in a certain way. If we take car mechanics as an example, the important factor is training and experience, often through both theoretical courses and hands-on guided instruction. But there is also an important dispositional element of interest in the activity and the talent to visualize mechanical systems that not everyone has.

In an old joke someone asks a peasant, "Can you play the piano?" The peasant replies, "I don't really know. I've never tried." A person without a *habitus* for some activity lacks what is required to perform and finds the activity in question difficult and burdensome if not completely impossible. There are many people with "hidden talent" or the potential for doing scientific research or speaking a foreign language who never get the opportunity to develop their talent, or who begin the process but do not get beyond the initial hurdles of difficulty and discouragement.

Thus a *habitus* is a kind of disposition[4] or, better, a developed dispositional trait that shapes human activity and enables a person to perform. A developed dispositional trait can be negative as well as positive, and that is why there is the possibility of developing vices as well as the good moral qualities, which are called virtues.

Take, for example, kindness to strangers as a virtue or good character trait. This is a disposition that develops primarily on the basis of understanding the reasons for hospitality, which may include our own memories of kindness experienced and the ability to imagine what it would be like to be lost or in need of help in an unfamiliar area. Christians will have the examples of Scripture, including the parable of the good Samaritan, as guides here. The ability to show kindness, however, involves also the training of emotions, to be flexible and to set aside inconvenience. The disposition and ability to extend kindness to the stranger is not something that can be generated from theories of general benevolence ("I love humankind; it's people that I can't stand"); it develops by directing the whole personality correctly and by actually practicing deeds of kindness.

Even from an early age, human beings develop ethical principles and attitudes by a combination of reason and feelings. It is important to learn to reason about ethics, by learning to accept and give reasons for behaving in certain ways, and to be able to assess these reasons. Children start their ethical development by accepting reasons that adults give them, but they

---

[4]This is the word used by Anthony Kenny in his translation of *ST* I-II, qq. 49-54.

will need to rely on their own developing awareness of the meaning of ethical terms. In addition to reasons, however, children are also taught (and rightly so) to pay attention to their feelings in thinking about ethical matters. "How would you feel if Kelly said that to you?" For the forming of ethical beliefs is not an entirely separate process from that of forming ethical feelings and desires, and the beliefs and principles will not develop well unless feelings and desires correspond. And the formation of ethical feelings and desires is doubtless much affected by social factors, including especially the attitudes of people whom we admire and who care for us. In these ways we learn to be for and against goods and evils, and to form some of the relevant beliefs and attitudes for ourselves.[5]

Aristotle developed the analogy between the learning of a craft or skill and the acquiring of a virtue or positive moral disposition:

> We acquire the virtues by first acting just as we do in the case of acquiring crafts. For we learn a craft by making the products which we must make once we have learned the craft, for example, by building, we become builders, by playing the lyre, lyre players. And so too we become just by doing just actions, and temperate by doing temperate actions and brave by brave actions . . . and in a word states of character are formed out of corresponding acts. (*NE* 1103a31-b21)[6]

This needs some modification and qualification because of the much larger role that intention plays in moral development and the acquisition of virtuous dispositions. It is basically true that the building blocks of virtues are the patterns of repeated actions. But simple repetition of actions is not formative of moral virtue in the way that repeating basketball shots develops the ability to become an accurate shooter. There is an internal habituation that is required on the level of intellect, will and emotion that underlies the development of moral virtue. An adolescent may, under parental supervision for years, do homework assignments well, keep a tidy bedroom and do a fair share of family chores. But the behavior of this same person, upon getting older and going off to college, may well degenerate into procrastination, sloppiness and selfishness, showing that the

---

[5]See Robert Adams, *A Theory of Virtue: Excellence in Being for the Good* (Oxford: Clarendon, 2006), p. 215.
[6]Compare Aristotle, *NE* 1105a14.

earlier and better patterns of behavior were not really integrated into his or her character.

In learning to play a musical instrument, it does not matter much whether your purpose is to earn a living as a musician, to impress a person you are enamored with or merely to enjoy making music. But in moral actions, as we have seen, the structure of intentions that constitute the action must be good in order for the repetition of actions to generate the development of a virtuous disposition. Attending church every week (perhaps with an eye to checking out the young men or women, as it may be) will build up the habit (ordinary sense) of churchgoing, but it will do little to build up a *habitus* or disposition to worship God, pray or contribute to the edification of the congregation.

In her helpful study of these matters in Aristotle's ethics Nancy Sherman points out that if we take Aristotle to say that we can become just or generous by doing just or generous actions, this is to abbreviate a whole series of steps. Actions, as we know, are complex and presuppose the discrimination of a situation as requiring a response, reactive emotions that mark that response, and desires and beliefs about how and for the sake of what ends one should act. "We misconstrue Aristotle's notion of action producing character if we isolate the exterior moment of action from the interior cognitive and affective moments which characterize even the beginner's ethical behavior."[7]

Further, mere repetition of action is not going to work, because you could be reinforcing some negative traits (rather than developing the skill and proper technique required) and at best remain at a certain level, making no further progress. You must have a standard or ideal pattern to aim at in order for further practice to result in improvement. Athletes work with trainers and coaches in order to improve the quality and efficiency of their swimming or tennis stroke, to set goals and demonstrate the patterns to work on.

The greater complexity of moral actions points to the importance not only of good instruction, but also of models and examples that are provided for us in stories and literature, through people we know and admire, through mentors and, for Christians, through the lives of saints and Christian heroes in the past as well as through good models of Christian discipleship with whom we interact in our churches and fellowships. And above all, we have

---

[7]Nancy Sherman, *The Fabric of Character: Aristotle's Theory of Virtue* (Oxford: Clarendon, 1989), p. 178.

the example of Christ himself, living human life without sin, as our exemplar par excellence. His priorities, attitudes toward others and general behavior are relevant and important for us; but at the Last Supper Jesus explicitly models and instructs his disciples: "So if I, your Lord and Teacher, have washed your feet, you ought also to wash one another's feet. For I have set you an example, that you also should do as I have done to you" (Jn 13:14-15).

There is one further point to introduce here that will be expanded on in chapter nine: the difference between moral and theological virtues. Moral virtues can be developed within the framework described above, by working on attitudes, intentions, principles and so on, and then by performing repeatedly the real actions that correspond. We develop self-control by understanding the reasons for it, desiring it and actually making decisions that incorporate moderation and self-control in, for example, eating or sexual pleasure. Theological virtues, however, are based on the gift of the Holy Spirit and are not generated in the same way. Faith, hope and love are dispositions that enable us to respond and act in ways that a Christian should, but we cannot develop them ourselves.

Integrating Action and Character

One negative aspect of the newly regained emphasis on virtue and character is the relative denigration or neglect of the importance of individual actions. This probably is a result or an implication of the rejection of quandary ethics that thought of ethics as primarily the challenge of resolving moral dilemmas in extreme situations. One sometimes hears of "decisionism" in a pejorative fashion, as if virtue and character were the only really relevant moral categories, as if individual choices and decisions count for little in comparison with the development of character. This, of course, fosters the tendency to put a wedge between our own self-image, including what we think our intentions are, and the actual, specific behavior that we engage in. This is also a major factor in the attempt to justify bad actions (and especially cases of sins of omission or failure to act) by appealing to good intentions, that we meant well and so on.[8]

In both Aristotle and Thomas Aquinas we have a strong emphasis on

---

[8]See Oliver O'Donovan, *Resurrection and Moral Order: An Outline for Evangelical Ethics*, 2nd ed. (Grand Rapids: Eerdmans, 1994), especially chap. 10, "The Moral Subject."

both choice in individual actions and on virtue, the dialectic between deciding on good individual, discrete actions, and the development of good
habituated character qualities (virtues). Aristotle's description of the characteristics of virtue is that "every virtue or excellence (1) renders good the
thing itself of which it is the excellence, and (2) causes it to perform its
function well" (*NE* II.6). In other words, a moral virtue is not just a fine
human quality that improves a person's character; it is, more importantly,
the principle that enables that person to perform specific good actions.

Thomas Aquinas makes it even clearer that the purpose or rationale of a
virtue is to make a person good (so wisdom, justice and so on), but also the
principle behind actions. Virtues are positive habituations or dispositions, and
these dispositions are revealed in the actions that are associated with them.[9]
In other words, there is no virtue of hope without actions that manifest hope;
no self-control unless there is consistent evidence of actions generated by the
virtue of self-control; no genuine love without specific actions that come from
a person who loves God and neighbor. Thus benevolent intentions, projecting
an image of certain virtues, thinking oneself to be kind and patient and so on,
are counterfeit and no substitute for actions of love, kindness and patience in
circumstances that call for these qualities. Because virtues are developed by a
pattern and then a habituation of consistent right choices and actions, there
is what Oliver O'Donovan calls "the epistemological priority of act," and this
is clearly taught by Thomas Aquinas in his general principles of act and virtue.[10]

This gap between image and performance was a special target in the
teaching of Jesus. He attacked the righteous image of the Pharisees when
their zeal for observance of finer points of the law was not backed up by
concern for the weightier matters of mercy and justice; he questioned the
status of those ready to call him "Lord, Lord" but who then failed to follow
his teachings (Lk 6:46).

The view that our character traits are one thing, and that actions are the
product of discrete individual, and perhaps temporary, decisions, gives us
the illusion that we can separate who we "really" are from our sinful actions.
Even when we Christians engage in confession and repentance, the superficial recognition of our overall waywardness may limit the thoroughness of

---

[9]See Thomas Aquinas, *ST* II-II, q. 18, a. 1, on hope; *ST* I, q. 87, a. 2, on dispositions in general.
[10]O'Donovan, *Resurrection and Moral Order*, pp. 211-18. See Thomas Aquinas, *ST* I-II, q. 51, a. 2.

our repentance. We keep confession superficial by distancing ourselves from our actions: "I'm not really like that" or "I was under pressure." We nurture an illusion of ourselves as good Christians and separate our Christian identity from some of the actual decisions that we make by treating them as exceptional occurrences rather than seeing the connection between who we really are and what things we decide to do.

Surveys show that many Christians (including Roman Catholics) who affirm a general support for unborn human life are also quite often involved in procuring an abortion for convenience, allowing themselves (or a family member) an exception in an otherwise "staunch" antiabortion stance. An ethical model that sees actions as the product of individual, isolated decisions, or one that emphasizes general character traits and neglects their intrinsic connection to specific actions, is useful in sustaining such illusions. We fail to see the distorted vision of ourselves and the world that underlies the pattern of our actions. Character determines actions; actions reveal character. Karl Barth has stated this point well in a section titled "The Man of Sin in the Light of the Obedience of the Son of God":

> It is for the whole man, man in his unity of being and activity, for whom He [Christ] has died—in the ordered integrated unity in which he does what he is and is what he does. This disposes of the idea that actions are merely external and accidental and isolated. They are not, as it were derailments. A man is what he does. Their wickedness and folly counts. They are his wicked thoughts and words and works, and by them he is judged. As the one who does them, who produces these wicked thoughts and words and works, he is the man of sin who would perish if Jesus Christ had not taken his place. Nothing that he does or leaves undone is neutral or indifferent or irresponsible or outside the sphere of his accountability. He is inwardly the one who expresses himself in this way outwardly. And this disposes of the idea of an Ego which is untouched by the evil character of its actions, an Ego in which a man can remain neutral because he, too, is not touched or touched only remotely by the evil character of his actions.[11]

In the next two chapters we will turn our attention to a more thorough consideration of the nature of sin and the need for conversion to Christ.

---

[11]Karl Barth, *Church Dogmatics*, vol. IV/1, *The Doctrine of Reconciliation*, ed. G. W. Bromiley and T. F. Torrance (Edinburgh: T & T Clark, 1956), p. 405.

For Further Reading

Thomas Aquinas, *ST* I-II, qq. 49-70.

Kent Dunnington, *Addiction and Virtue: Beyond the Models of Disease and Choice* (Downers Grove, IL: IVP Academic, 2011), chap. 3, "Addiction and Habit: Resources in Aquinas," for a careful account of habit in Thomistic teaching.

Bonnie Kent, "Habits and Virtues," in *The Ethics of Aquinas*, ed. Stephen Pope (Washington, DC: Georgetown University Press, 2002), pp. 116-30.

William Mattison III, *Introducing Moral Theology: True Happiness and the Virtues* (Grand Rapids: Brazos Press, 2008), chap. 3, "Why Virtue? The Moral Life Is More Than Actions."

Oliver O'Donovan. *Resurrection and Moral Order: An Outline for Evangelical Ethics*, 2nd ed. (Grand Rapids: Eerdmans, 1994), chap. 10, "The Moral Subject."

Robert Roberts, "Character," in *New Dictionary of Christian Ethics and Pastoral Theology*, ed. David Atkinson and David Field (Downers Grove, IL: InterVarsity Press, 1995), pp. 70-76.

6

THE REALITY OF SIN

STRICTLY SPEAKING, sin has no "reality" in a metaphysical sense. Sin and evil are signs of nonbeing, of absence and failure. "A morally evil act as such is an absence of something, a failure on my part to live as humanly, as intensely as I might have done."[1] This philosophical and theological understanding (developed by Augustine) is completely removed, it must be said, from any Panglossian optimism, or a Buddhist attempt to treat evil as an illusion, because the effects of sin are very real and serious, and it is in that perspective that this chapter proceeds.

The Aristotelian account of human weakness (see chapter five), involving the conflict between principles and contrary emotions, covers many situations of human life, temptation and wrongdoing. It is a better explanation than lack of "will power" because it involves the whole psyche rather than just the will. As a pre-Christian pagan moral philosophy (however accurate it may be regarding the process of practical reasoning itself), it is defective in not dealing with the nature and extent of sin revealed in Scripture: the human heart is devious and perverse (Jer 17:9), our righteousness is like filthy rags (Is 64:6) and by nature we are estranged from and hostile to God (Col 1:21). Moral theology needs to confront the real effects of sin on thought and behavior.

Just after the 1960s, a period of preoccupation with dismantling many aspects of the traditional attitudes and human behavior in Western society, people were surprised when a book appeared by a secular psychiatrist with

---

[1]Herbert McCabe, "Evil," in *God Matters* (London: Geoffrey Chapman, 1987), p. 36.

the title *Whatever Became of Sin?*[2] Of course, the evasion of personal involvement and responsibility for sinful behavior has been a feature of human life since Adam and Eve; but the transition to a post-Christian society has changed the very way we think and speak about wrongdoing, guilt and forgiveness. Even in Christian circles and churches, in theological treatments and in popular attitudes, there has been a shift away from facing the hard facts of the corruption in our minds and hearts (and so our need for grace) to sugar-coating, self-affirmation and therapeutic approaches more or less alien to the work of the Holy Spirit.

This shift can be seen in our liturgies. For example, we can note the difference between the general confession provided by Thomas Cranmer for the service of morning prayer in the traditional (1662) Anglican prayer book, and the contemporary English and American versions printed out side by side below. We can grant to the authors of the shorter modern version a certain valid preference for the succinct over the wordy in accordance with modern English style. But beyond that, there are theological differences and a completely different emphasis revealed in these examples.

Where Cranmer had six different verbs to describe sins of commission and omission, the contemporary confession has two, short, more or less equivalent phrases to state that we have sinned against God. Cranmer has us admitting that we are "miserable offenders" and that "there is no health in us," sentiments that apparently are no longer necessary or appropriate for contemporary congregations.[3] Rather, the emphasis today is to be positive. After the merest statement that "we are sorry and repent," the confession in *Common Worship* asks God to do five things: have mercy, wash away our wrongdoings, cleanse us, renew a right spirit within us and restore us, where Cranmer had three petitions, and the Episcopal confession simply has "have mercy on us and forgive us."

The situation is not much better in more academic and theological quarters. The traditional moral theologies (both Roman Catholic and Anglican) did not handle sin very well, and the situation has become more

---

[2]Karl Menninger, *Whatever Became of Sin?* (New York: Hawthorn Books, 1973).

[3]In the 1962 revision of the *Book of Common Prayer* for the Anglican Church of Canada, a very conservative updating that left Elizabethan language and much of the material unaltered, the general confession for morning and evening prayer omitted precisely and only these two phrases about being miserable offenders and there being no health in us.

Table 6.1. Comparison of General Confessions

The Book of Common Prayer (1662) — General Confession for Morning and Evening Prayer	*Common Worship* (2000) — Order for Morning Prayer — Confession[a]	*The Book of Common Prayer* (1979)
Almighty and most merciful Father,	Lord God,	Most merciful God,
We have erred and strayed from thy ways like lost sheep.	We have sinned against you;	We confess that we have sinned against you
We have followed too much the devices and desires of our own hearts.	We have done evil in your sight.	in thought, word and deed,
We have offended against thy holy laws.	We are sorry and repent.	by what we have done,
We have left undone those things which we ought to have done;	Have mercy according to your love.	and by what we have left undone.
and we have done those things which we ought not to have done;	Wash away our wrongdoing and cleanse us	We have not loved you with our whole heart;
and there is no health in us.	from our sin.	we have not loved our neighbor as ourselves.
But thou, O Lord, have mercy upon us, miserable offenders.	Renew a right spirit within us	We are truly sorry and we humbly repent.
Spare thou them, O God, which confess their faults.	and restore us to the joy of your salvation;	For the sake of your Son Jesus Christ,
Restore thou them that are penitent; according to thy promises declared unto us in Christ Jesus our Lord.	Through Jesus Christ our Lord. Amen.	have mercy on us and forgive us; that we may delight in your will, and walk in your ways,
And grant, O most merciful Father, for His sake,		to the glory of your Name. Amen.
that we may ever hereafter live a		
godly, righteous, and sober life, to the glory of thy holy name. Amen.		

[a]*Common Worship: Services and Prayers for the Church of England* (London: Church House Publishing, 2000), p. 31.

confusing in the aftermath of Vatican II. The legalism of the Roman tradition led to preoccupation with the classification of sin, focusing on specific actions in relation to conscience. Such an approach is now widely seen as repellent, but the newer reconstructions of moral theology have trouble accommodating a view of sin that is adequate theologically, morally and spiritually. Liberal revisionists try to encourage people by pretending that real sin is something that rarely happens. Mortal sin, turning away from God, is hedged from ordinary life in the concept of a "fundamental option" (explained below in the section on mortal sin). Some more conservative moral theologians, who do take the reality of sin more seriously, share the same pastoral concern in contemporary Catholicism to get away from the older legalism, but apparently they find that sin is too difficult to incorporate into a moral theology based on virtue.[4]

The concept of sin implies both God or some superior being to whom one is responsible and a violation of a divinely authorized standard of conduct. An atheist or secular humanist can be realistic about human nature and recognize human weakness, a tendency toward selfishness, or a propensity to moral fallibility, but would not call wrong actions "sins."

We need to highlight the problem of sin for Christian ethics. This is not to return to any morbid preoccupation with sin, but to recognize the reality of human weakness and fallibility in connection with practical reasoning, and that some failures in action, whether through faulty decisions or defective execution, need to be named as sins because of their effect on our relationship with God.

This treatment of sin is all the more necessary in this work because of the erosion of the concept of sin in modern theology and church life, and in this introduction to moral theology in particular because of the fact that Aristotelian ethics lacks a category of sin as offending God, and because of the related suspicion often voiced in Reformed circles that Thomistic ethics does not treat sin seriously enough. The aim here is to fully integrate the biblical teaching on sin and either to defend the teaching of Aquinas from his attackers or to supplement it with additional insights from an evangelical point of view.

Alister McGrath, in his remarkably meager section on the nature of sin (in his volume on systematic theology), summarizes the Augustinian view of the force of sin in our lives: "The human mind has become darkened and weakened by sin. Sin makes it impossible for the sinner to think clearly, and

---

[4]Romanus Cessario, in his *Introduction to Moral Theology* (Washington, DC: Catholic University of America Press, 2001), is (properly) concerned to argue that his Thomistic "realist" moral theology must oppose certain actions as intrinsically wrong and sinful in spite of good intentions. He is relatively silent about the spiritual struggle with sin as part of Christian discipleship.

especially to understand higher spiritual truths and ideas. Similarly . . . the human will has been weakened (but not eliminated) by sin."[5]

If sin is a reality for all human beings, including Christians who are redeemed, then it has serious implications for the model of human action based on practical reasoning in terms of intention, deliberation, decision and execution. Selfishness, blindness, lack of concern and all of the attitudes and inclinations prompted by "the world, the flesh and the devil" will, of course, distort the quality of practical reasoning.

The reality of the operation of Satan should neither be minimized nor exaggerated. He may take on some form of appearance and tempt directly (as with Adam and Eve and the temptation of Jesus); more often it is by inner suggestions and persuasions, or by distortions of the truth.[6] Many in the modern world doubt the existence of a demonic world; however, reflecting on the cruel horrors generated by the monomania of leaders obsessed by sheer power and by various ideologies provides grounds for the relevance of the biblical and traditional view.[7] Nevertheless, as many patristic theologians pointed out, there are plenty of sins that can be explained simply by recognizing the force of evil societies cut off from God (the "world") and unredeemed and disordered human nature (the "flesh").

A BIBLICAL VIEW OF SIN

A concise definition of sin is provided by the Westminster Shorter Catechism: "Sin is any want of conformity unto, or transgression of, the law of God." Such a definition has a biblical basis, of course,[8] but the emphasis is put on keeping the law, with the essence of sin described as violating or not abiding by the law. The limitations of a law-based view of sin and life in Christ are well expressed by the Episcopal theologian and pastor Stephen Holmgren:

---

[5]Alister McGrath, *Christian Theology: An Introduction*, 3rd ed. (Oxford: Blackwell, 2001), p. 445.

[6]See Thomas Aquinas, *De Malo* III.3-5, in *On Evil*, trans. Richard Regan, ed. Brian Davies (New York: Oxford University Press, 2003), pp. 149-58.

[7]See Eric Mascall, "Unseen Warfare," in *The Christian Universe* (New York: Morehouse-Barlow, 1966), pp. 109-30.

[8]The footnote in the Westminster Shorter Catechism suggests Leviticus 5:17: "And if a soul sin, and commit any of these things which are forbidden to be done by the commandments of the LORD; though he wist it not, yet is he guilty, and shall bear his iniquity"; James 4:17: "Therefore to him that knoweth to do good, and doeth it not, to him it is sin"; 1 John 3:4: "Whosoever committeth sin transgresseth also the law: for sin is the transgression of the law."

One disadvantage of focusing on the identification of sins is that it encourages us to think moral theology is structured around laws, so that we see sins as infractions against these laws. . . . The moral life is not simply a matter of avoiding missteps and trying to limit the tally of notations in the great record-book of life; it is about holiness and a journey of growth into the glory of the living human person exemplified for us in Jesus Christ.[9]

Donald Bloesch, who adheres to the Reformed ethical tradition of divine command and human obedience, nevertheless emphasizes the relational and personal aspect of sin as a violation of the relationship of love and trust that a person should have with God:

In legalistic religion sin is a violation of a moral taboo or breaking of a moral code. In evangelical religion sin means wounding the heart of God. It is not so much a transgression of law as a violation of trust. It is an offense not so much against moral precepts as against love. The core of sin is not falling short of the moral ideal but the isolating and aggrandizing of the self, which the Bible calls "hardness of heart."[10]

The theme of sin in Scripture is prominent, presented to us in a wide range of examples. From the first sin in Eden, there are the elements of God's command and human disobedience, but more comprehensive is the covenantal framework: a relationship of trust and friendship with God that is disrupted because of sin. The Bible uses a wide range of terms to describe the dynamic character of sin: failure, rebellion, transgression or trespass, turning from the right path, and infidelity. Each of these images or metaphors is symbolic and illuminates some aspect of the nature of our relationship with God. Among many other Old Testament passages, Psalm 89:28-37 points to the threat of punishment for sin and transgressions, although the covenant of steadfast love remains in place.

We consider a few of the most prominent images.[11] If God is our Lord, then our covenant with him involves our allegiance; sin is like a rebellion that we initiate that breaks this covenant (see Hos 8:1), and we put ourselves

---

[9]Stephen Holmgren, *Ethics After Easter* (Cambridge, MA: Cowley, 2000), p. 108.

[10]Donald Bloesch, *Freedom for Obedience: Evangelical Ethics for Contemporary Times* (San Francisco: Harper & Row, 1987), p. 82.

[11]See John Goldingay, "Your Iniquities Have Made a Separation Between You and Your God," in *Atonement Today: A Symposium at St. John's College, Nottingham*, ed. John Goldingay (London: SPCK, 1995), pp. 39-53.

in the dangerous position of inviting God, by our actions, to "pay us a visit to put us in our place"; however, repentance can open up the possibility of pardon. This set of symbols having to do with political authority, allegiance, rebellion and pardon brings out some important aspects of sin in our relationship to God, but we need the context of other symbols to avoid overly exaggerating or being led astray (e.g., God is not a petty tyrant or anything like a "mafia godfather").[12]

Infidelity as a symbol of sin presupposes the framework of the relationship between God and his people as one of committed faithfulness that excludes other partners. Unfaithfulness is when a man or woman acts as if they had the same freedom they had before their marriage commitment, and is a violation on several different levels: the violation of promises, of course, but also of trust and of the bonds of affection, and of the integrity of the whole relationship.

The wandering of the children of Israel for forty years in the wilderness was the result of rebellion and faithlessness. Wandering from the right way is a vivid picture of sin. "God is a guide who points out the right way to go if we wish to reach a certain destination," and sin then becomes the refusal to follow the Lord's guidance and to substitute our own inclinations and judgments: "All we like sheep have gone astray" (Is 53:6).

In the New Testament we have the important word *hamartia*. The basic meaning of the word conveys the idea of "missing the mark" and falling short of what the action should be. In Aristotelian ethics, *hamartia* covers the range of wrong actions through error and through moral weakness. In the context of a virtue ethics, it carries the implication that something is lacking that ought to be there, so that there is moral failure and blameworthiness.[13] This failure to meet the expected standard is magnified into a doctrine of sin by Paul in Romans 3:23: "All have sinned and fall short of the glory of God." John Goldingay notes that in the New Testament there is still something of the Old Testament flavor of the word for rebellion, which shows that sin "involves active resistance to the destiny God sets before us."[14]

---

[12]Ibid., p. 41.
[13]See Gustav Stählin, "ἁμαρτία," in vol. 1 of *Theological Dictionary of the New Testament*, trans. and ed. Geoffrey Bromiley (Grand Rapids: Eerdmans, 1964), pp. 293-96.
[14]Goldingay, "Your Iniquities," p. 45.

Even after baptism, and with commitment to Christ and his church, the problem of sin remains a challenge. According to 1 John 1:8, "If we say that we have no sin, we deceive ourselves, and the truth is not in us." This points to the principle of sin that remains in us—the tendency to selfishness, pride, independence, despair, and the blindness and distortion that accompany these attitudes. The real challenge in dealing with sin is not to come to the point of the confession and absolution of individual sins, but to deal with the underlying attitudes and inclinations. This work of the Holy Spirit to conform us more closely to Christ is a process that we will review more fully in the following chapter on conversion.

Paul deals clearly and vividly with the ongoing reality of our sinful nature in his epistles, particularly in Romans. Our problem with sin is not that we occasionally break God's law and then need to repent and be forgiven; our problem is that we are habitual lawbreakers, living a life not merely marked by individual transgressions but characterized by inherent lawlessness (*anomia*). Our human nature (what Paul refers to as "the flesh") leads us to act against our better judgment, and to ignore what the law expects and what we ourselves really and more deeply desire (see Rom 7:14-20).[15]

The attitude of rebellion is rooted in our fallen nature. It has become second nature for us to prefer our own vision of our final end or purpose, and our own insight on how to achieve it; and though we pay lip service to serving God and acting for his kingdom, we often are far from living in a realm where it is God who exercises authority. If we take the Romans 3:23 definition of sin as falling short of the glory of God, we see that this continues to happen a lot in our lives, because that glory is often not the final end at which we are aiming. This is really what we mean by original sin—that there is an inevitability about thinking, acting and living in a human-centered rather than a God-centered way. We think ourselves as generally clean and pure, needing the occasional cleansing, when in fact we are really hopelessly and deeply stained.[16] The Cranmerian phrase "there is no health in us" (set aside by modern prayer books) points to the reality that there is no wholeness, no principle of healing in ourselves. The disorder and misdirection is permanent without the grace and healing of God.

---

[15]Ibid., p. 49.
[16]Ibid.

There is a sober warning for us in the conflict between Jesus and the Pharisees. We too take pride. We congratulate ourselves on avoiding the sinfulness of Pharisees because we are not hypocrites like they were, or we use external righteousness and holy reputation to cloak injustice and malice toward others. The warning for us, however, and what Jesus wants us to be concerned about, has more to do with the deep and hidden sinfulness in our thoughts and attitudes. There is a strong tendency to assume that our motivations are sound, well-ordered and Christ-centered, and then find that we act contrary to God's will for us; we should not be surprised by this, because we are affected by hidden self-serving and self-justifying motives. This danger is well expressed by Geoffrey Bromiley in an article on sin:

> The more one tries to track down sin, the deeper it goes and the more elusive it becomes. It is parasitic, clinging even to what is good. Yet from another angle it seems also to have a kind of independent life of its own, so that even when one has made the firmest resolves and taken all possible precautions, one still does the wrong thing that one did not will to do or fails to do the right thing that one did will. And even if one does the good or avoids the evil, how easily it is all soured by the self-righteous satisfaction that for once at least one has done a pure and blameless deed. In fact, the only possibility in the face of sin is to cast oneself wholly and utterly upon God, recognizing that even the motivation of this committal is just as much in need of the divine mercy, and that the committal cannot and must not become a new occasion for sinful pride.[17]

SIN AS UNNATURAL AND IRRATIONAL

Because God created the world, evil and sin cannot in any way be treated as part of creation, which is why they are essentially an absence of good, as stated at the opening of this chapter. They have a perverted, false kind of existence through the virulent and horrible manifestations and results often accompanying sin and evil, but fundamentally they are parasitic, corruptions of what was created good.

Thus human sin needs to be defined in relation to what human beings were created to be. In the brief indications given to us in Genesis 1-3 we

---

[17]Geoffrey Bromiley, "Sin," in vol. 4 of *The International Standard Bible Encyclopedia*, ed. Geoffrey Bromiley (Grand Rapids: Eerdmans, 1988), p. 522.

learn that men and women were created in the image of God, to thrive and experience God's blessing, to have close friendship with each other, and, above all, to experience friendship with God. The nature given to humans by God was created for those purposes. This is spelled out in some more detail by Shirley Guthrie, who depicts the characteristics of living according to the *imago Dei*:

1. Life received from God in a relationship of thankful dependence and active obedience;

2. Life with and for our fellow human beings in relationships of mutual openness and help;

3. Life that is self-affirming and self-fulfilling when we live in community with God and other people.[18]

Of course, we see an awful lot that is contrary to this picture of the image of God, both in the world in general and in ourselves: instead of thanks and obedience, bitterness and rebellion; instead of openness and help, suspicion and hatred; instead of good relationships with God and others, isolation, alienation and hostility. But the evil and sinfulness in humanity are not the basic truth about us: sin is a damaging distortion, but not a fundamental change of nature. In other words, our underlying nature, even though incapable on its own to really understand, let alone successfully live up to this fundamental creation identity, was created for this purpose, to be fulfilled in this way of a profound relationship with God and neighbor.

Evangelicals have become so used to being the party of "realists" about sin—reminding liberals, Roman Catholics and others whom they consider at best semi-Pelagian that sinfulness is endemic, that total depravity is a biblical doctrine and so on—that they have a tendency to forget that sin is something alien to our created purpose. As Guthrie puts it, "Sin may become 'second nature' to us, but it is never really 'natural.' What we are 'naturally' is what God created us to be. All of us are sinners, but our sinfulness is something *unnatural.*"[19]

This corresponds to the depiction of sin in Scripture as a departure from the true path, from what is (or ought to be) normal, to miss the true and real

---

[18]Shirley Guthrie, *Christian Doctrine*, rev. ed. (Louisville: Westminster John Knox, 2000), p. 213.
[19]Ibid.

way for us. Sin is not the truth about us; it is the distortion or denial of the truth. In the biblical worldview, writes Cornelius Plantinga, even when sin is depressingly familiar, it is never normal. It is finally unknown, irrational, alien. Sin is always a departure from the norm and is assessed accordingly. Sin is deviant and perverse, an *in*justice or *in*iquity or *in*gratitude. Sin in the Exodus literature is *dis*order and *dis*obedience.[20] From this truth of our creation in the image of God, it follows that sin and evil represent a corruption of what was originally good. Human nature becomes disordered, in relationships both toward others and toward God; and internally, in the relationships between intellect and will, and between will and the emotions.

Oliver O'Donovan provides insight here. The problem of the relation of "reason and will" in Western moral philosophy "springs out of a malfunction of the moral life" rather than from an inherent tension.[21] O'Donovan explains,

> The disjunction of hearing and doing, or of reason and will, is sin. It is the failure of man to make the response that is appropriate to him as a free rational agent. In such a failure man himself seems to disintegrate into dissociated powers, into a rational self . . . which has a cognitive relation to reality, and a voluntative self on the other, which consists of affections, emotions and decisions. This is the psychological aspect of the alienation of freedom.[22]

Such internal disorder and conflict, and the tensions and distortions generated, are sufficient to explain many of the effects of sin: the boundless self-indulgence and the multiple ways of showing malice to others. Plantinga describes the disorder and its results well: disintegration "is the main event in corruption—the breakdown of personal social integrity, the loss of shape, strength and purpose that make some entity an 'entirety' and make it *this* entirety. . . . Sin tends to disintegrate both its victims and its perpetrators. Disintegration is always deterioration, the prelude and postlude to death."[23]

MORTAL AND VENIAL SIN

Although the distinction between "mortal" or serious sins (which require

---

[20]Cornelius Plantinga Jr., *Not the Way It's Supposed to Be: A Breviary of Sin* (Grand Rapids: Eerdmans, 1995), p. 88.

[21]Oliver O'Donovan, *Resurrection and Moral Order: An Outline for Evangelical Ethics*, 2nd ed. (Grand Rapids: Eerdmans, 1994), p. 111.

[22]Ibid.

[23]Plantinga, *Not the Way*, p. 47.

confession, penance and absolution) and "venial" or less serious sins generally has been rejected by Protestants, there is instruction for us in thinking about the rationale for this differentiation.

In the pre–Vatican II Catholic moral theology, a mortal sin is an act, contrary to God's law, which "deprives the soul of sanctifying grace and makes it deserving of hell."[24] The essential evil at the heart of a mortal sin is that it opposes humankind's ultimate end and destroys the virtue of charity that orders a person to God; a venial sin does not remove the order of charity. Premeditated murder is clearly contrary to love for God and neighbor and is a mortal sin; having one drink too many might show bad judgment, and might be part of a pattern that could develop into something more serious, but in itself is not contrary to charity and thus is a venial sin.

Three conditions are required in the traditional analysis of mortal sin:

1. *Grave matter.* The action concerns a serious area of action that the person knows to be wrong (or whose conscience treats as wrong).

2. *Awareness or knowledge.* The person is aware of the moral features of the action, especially the object of the act. For example, that a deft bit of bookkeeping is really an act of theft.

3. *Deliberate consent.* In spite of awareness of the nature of the action, the person gives consent and decides, in the situation, that "this is the right thing to do now."[25]

Because all three conditions are required for a sin to be mortal, a venial sin might be an act taken without full knowledge or consent, as well as an action of a less serious kind.

It is obvious that this classification of sins into mortal and venial—sins that must be confessed and absolved, and sins that may be but do not need to be confessed—makes sense within the context of an institution with priests regularly hearing confessions. One can see the pastoral value of being able to assess degrees of culpability and to reassure a penitent in some situations that the act perhaps was not the serious sin that the person had thought it to be. The category of "mortal" sin reminds us that some sins have deadly consequences, while the "venial" category reminds those who tend

---

[24]Pietro Palazzini, ed., *Dictionary of Moral Theology* (London: Burns & Oates, 1962), p. 1134.
[25]Ibid., pp. 1134-35. See also *The Catechism of the Catholic Church*, §1857-59.

to be scrupulous that they should focus on the major issues and not the minor problems or weaknesses.

In popular understanding (which often distorts positions that require balance and nuance) mortal sins are major sins such as adultery, pride, anger, hatred and so on, while venial sins are things such as "white lies," overeating and other peccadilloes. But if we pay attention to the distinctions that matter, they are based on the degree of intention involved, and to what extent the action is out of character. A court of law distinguishes between premeditated first-degree murder and accidental homicide, for example, although the fatal consequence is the same. In a Lenten address Cardinal Manning put it this way:

> The sins which may be found even in holy men are sins of infirmity com-
> mitted through weakness; or sins of surprise committed by sudden or strong
> temptation; or sins of impetuosity, where passion carries a man for a moment
> beyond self-control; or sins of indeliberation, that is, done in haste, before as
> yet conscience and the reason have had time to deliberate and weigh what
> they are about.[26]

Thus sinful actions that are performed because of illness (such as impatience caused by the irritability of pain), or impetuosity and so on, have a lesser degree of sinfulness about them.

There is also a biblical basis for describing some sins as mortal and others as not mortal: "If you see your brother or sister committing what is not a mortal sin, you will ask, and God will give life to such a one—to those whose sin is not mortal. There is sin that is mortal [*hamartia pros thanaton*]; I do not say that you should pray about that" (1 Jn 5:16-17). One interpretation (Roman Catholic) is that mortal sin or "the sin that leads to death" (*hamartia pros thanaton*) refers to the rejection of the faith that formed the basis of the Johannine community (which would make it similar to the idea of "fundamental option" described below).[27] I. Howard Marshall takes the sin that leads to death to be "the sins that are incompatible with being a child of God" (a somewhat broader range of sins that corrupt the relationship with God).[28]

Anglican theologians of the Caroline period were wary of the distinction

---

[26]Henry Manning, *Sin and Its Consequences* (New York: D. & J. Sadlier, 1876), p. 73.
[27]See John Painter, *1, 2, and 3 John* (Collegeville, MN: Liturgical Press, 2002), p. 319.
[28]I. Howard Marshall, *The Epistles of John* (Grand Rapids: Eerdmans, 1978), p. 247.

between mortal and venial sin, primarily on spiritual grounds, in spite of their use of much of the apparatus of Roman Catholic moral theology. Jeremy Taylor, while agreeing that some sins are weightier than others (adultery worse than fornication), asserted that all sins have the formality of disobedience in the eyes of God.[29] The opposition to categorizing sins as the Roman Catholics did expressed a conviction that the mortal/venial distinction debases the conception of holiness and Christian discipleship and encourages people to continue in their course of sinning rather than to pursue holiness of life.[30] Anglican theologians have largely been opposed to this distinction, and it probably has little function outside of traditional Anglo-Catholic circles where a quasi-Roman Catholic confessional practice is the norm.[31]

Before we dismiss the distinction between mortal and venial sin as irrelevant or unhelpful, however, we should note that venial sin, though not requiring confession and absolution, is not therefore to be treated as something trivial or above concern. The more recent descriptions point to the importance of the context and direction of a person's life: venial sin may not destroy the bond of charity with God, but it does weaken it; venial sin represents a "disordered affection for created goods" and impedes the soul's progress in the exercise of the virtues.[32] An isolated sin is one thing; but as part of a pattern that develops, sin creates a greater tendency to sin again by repetition of the same acts, and deliberate, unrepented sin, even if venial, disposes us little by little to commit mortal sin.[33]

Moral theologians have developed various strategies to lessen the mechanical application of the concept of mortal sin (e.g., someone dying in a car accident just after committing a sin with no chance for repentance) and its stark legalistic features. Predictably, it is possible to interpret "full knowledge" and "deliberate consent" in such a way that very few serious sins would be mortal because of the lack of full consent in cases where there is doubt, hesitation or inner conflict.

---

[29]See H. R. McAdoo, *The Structure of Caroline Moral Theology* (London: Longmans, 1949), p. 109.

[30]See Paul Lehmann's section on Anglican moral theology in *Ethics in a Christian Context* (New York: Harper & Row, 1963), p. 314.

[31]Among the Anglicans of the last century who promoted the distinction were R. C. Mortimer and Kenneth Kirk.

[32]*Catechism of the Catholic Church*, §1863.

[33]Ibid.

Karl Rahner, Josef Fuchs and others have developed the category of "fundamental option," which has become the device favored by many Catholic revisionists or liberals. It combines a higher standard of consent of the will in action with a modern existential view of freedom, along with the conviction that in many cases of sin the offender chooses the sinful act without turning away from God. Thus the fundamental option is a choice for or against God and his grace at a very deep level, and this grace may remain operative in spite of ordinary actions, including sins, which do not express the core personality and freedom of the person. Thus many actions that would have been considered mortal sins in the old calculus are now to be considered venial, or perhaps grave, but no longer mortal, because the person has not fundamentally altered his or her choice for God.[34]

The pastoral advantages of the fundamental option are obvious, and it appears to justify a much reduced use of the confessional; but the dangers of abuse are also obvious, and this approach was one of the targets of the encyclical *Veritatis Splendor* by John Paul II.[35] The need to resort to the device of the fundamental option really derives from the legalism of the moral handbook tradition, and a richer understanding of the implications of the doctrine of charity is much more helpful theologically and spiritually.[36]

SIN AND ADDICTION

The characteristics of addictive behavior are an illuminating parallel to the pattern of sin in general.[37] There is behind every choice for sin and addiction a judgment "this is what is good for me here and now"; in a well-ordered or disciplined life, the occasional decision to indulge in a doughnut or glass of wine or some internet surfing or video game provides an opportunity to pause or relax. It is an easy process to develop a habit by re-

---

[34]A popular proponent of the fundamental option is Timothy O'Connell, *Principles for a Catholic Morality*, rev. ed. (San Francisco: Harper & Row, 1990), chap. 8.

[35]See John Paul II, *The Splendor of Truth, Veritatis Splendor: Regarding Certain Fundamental Questions of the Church's Moral Teaching* (Boston: St. Paul, 1993), §§65-70.

[36]See Jean Porter, "The Fundamental Option, Grace, and the Virtue of Charity," in *Virtue*, ed. Charles Curran and Lisa Fullam, Readings in Moral Theology 16 (Mahwah, NJ: Paulist Press, 2011), pp. 159-87.

[37]For insights on why a model of addiction based on the category of *habitus* is better because it retains the moral dimension but also accounts for the force of compulsion, see Kent Dunnington, *Addiction and Virtue: Beyond the Models of Disease and Choice* (Downers Grove, IL: IVP Academic, 2011).

peating these occasions of pleasure that are innocent and trivial in themselves, but in a life not well disciplined, the repetition of pleasurable behavior often results in escalating tolerance, desire, the attraction of stronger pleasures and exciting stimuli (e.g., sexual affairs and gambling) and then serious disorder. There then come unpleasant after-effects of such behavior: damage to the body, loss of time and money, poor performance at work, harm to family and other relationships, and accompanying self-reproach. The person may then vow to moderate or quit, but then experiences further relapses and the attendant feelings of guilt, shame and general distress.

The vicious cycle escalates as the person attempts to deal with the distress produced by engaging in new rounds of the addictive behavior, or perhaps with the first rounds of a new companion addiction. Then there is further deterioration of work and relationships, with accompanying cognitive disturbances, including denial, delusions and self-deceptions, especially about the effects of the addiction, and the degree to which one is controlled by it. The person experiences increasing preoccupation, then obsession with the addictive behavior. This factor of compulsion is evidence that one's will has become at least partly split, enfeebled and enslaved.[38]

We should note several points in this quick sketch. First, there is a strong parallel in the addictive process to the way in which sin develops a hold on our lives: the ease with which we choose sinful behavior and repeat it frequently, generating a pattern that becomes impossible (for us by ourselves) to break. Paul's metaphor in Romans of being enslaved to sin is precisely accurate. All sin shares some of the dynamic qualities of the process of addiction: many forms of sin include patterns of self-seeking, childish impatience with delayed gratification and refusal to accept reasonable limits on behavior. Sin, like addiction, tends to split and bind the will, to work itself into a habit of the heart, and to hide itself under layers of self-deception. Moreover, people often commit sins in order to relieve distress caused by other sins—hence the familiar spiral shape of certain patterns of sin.[39]

Second, we note the relationship between addiction (or an ingrained

---

[38]Plantinga, *Not the Way*, p. 145.
[39]Ibid., p. 147.

sinful habit) and the process of practical reasoning. Each stage of intention, decision and execution becomes more and more distorted, more and more out of touch with reality. Any normal person can see that "I'll have just one more doughnut" (or one more glass of wine, or a few more minutes with the video game) is the wrong decision; it has no relation to the reality of needs and purposes, and it expresses a desire of a person who is avoiding something, compensating for some kind of pain or pursuing an underlying desire that is not focused and channeled properly. "Because they are human beings," writes Plantinga, "addicts long for wholeness, for fulfillment, and for the final good that believers call God. Like all idolatries, addiction taps this vital spiritual force and draws off its energies to objects and processes that drain the addict instead of filling him."[40] Augustine expressed this characteristic of sinful behavior to enslave:

> I . . . was bound not by an iron imposed by anyone else but by the iron of my own choice. The enemy had a grip on my will and so made a chain for me to hold me a prisoner. The consequence of a distorted will is passion. By servitude to passion, habit is formed, and habit to which there is no resistance becomes necessity. By these links . . . connected one to another . . . a harsh bondage held me under restraint. (*Confessions* 8.5.10-11)

It is the obvious helplessness of many addicts and the need for external intervention that provide us a model or analogy for the need for divine intervention in all of our lives to break free from the stranglehold that sin develops. Even if outwardly our lives have balance, order and purpose, without the presence of Christ there is a sinful orientation, patterns of attitudes and behavior that are misdirected, idolatrous and ultimately deadly to our souls. All of us are in need of conversion.

For Further Reading

Thomas Aquinas, *ST* I-II, qq. 71-89.

Karl Barth, *Church Dogmatics*, vol. IV.1, *The Doctrine of Reconciliation*, ed. G. W. Bromiley and T. F. Torrance (Edinburgh: T & T Clark, 1956), pp. 499-512.

Edmund Hill, *Being Human: A Biblical Perspective* (London: Geoffrey Chapman, 1984), chaps. 6-8.

---

[40]Ibid., p. 131.

Robert Jenson, *Systematic Theology*, vol. 2, *The Works of God* (Oxford: Oxford University Press, 1999), chap. 22, "Sin."

William Mattison III, *Introducing Moral Theology: True Happiness and the Virtues* (Grand Rapids: Brazos Press, 2008), chap. 12, "Sin: Corruption of Human Happiness."

Cornelius Plantinga Jr., *Not the Way It's Supposed to Be: A Breviary of Sin* (Grand Rapids: Eerdmans, 1995), especially chaps. 3-4.

7

CONVERSION TO CHRIST

IT IS PERHAPS NOT SURPRISING that the evangelical emphasis on conversion from sin to following Christ is difficult to find in the *Summa Theologiae* and has been largely lacking in the Roman Catholic tradition in general. More remarkable is the neglect of conversion in places where we would expect to find it. The works of Reinhold Niebuhr, for example, who drew the attention of a generation of liberal Protestants to the nature and reality of sin, offered "solutions" based on a realist use of coercion in society, and in the individual realm a rather dismissive view of the relevance of Jesus' call to discipleship. Neither personal conversion nor belonging to the transforming possibilities of the community of the body of Christ seems to have had much importance for him. Martin Luther King Jr. significantly wrote, "His pessimism concerning human nature was not balanced by an optimism concerning divine nature."[1]

Paul Ramsey, in his influential *Basic Christian Ethics*, offers a chapter on Christian vocation that begins with "The Problem of Christocentric Vocation."[2] Ramsey deals briefly with the tension between a general ethic and the particularism of the Christian vocation, but he gives no indication that the challenge of following Christ is something that we need to be persuaded and convinced of, or that this might be a different direction from what we are now engaged in or inclined toward, or that conversion might be required.

Even more surprising perhaps are recent evangelical works on ethics that

---

[1]Cited in Richard Hays, *The Moral Vision of the New Testament: Community, Cross, New Creation; A Contemporary Introduction to New Testament Ethics* (San Francisco: HarperSanFrancisco, 1996), pp. 222-23.
[2]Paul Ramsey, *Basic Christian Ethics* (New York: Scribner, 1950), chap. 5.

seek to broaden a general biblical approach by including the now more fashionable trend to virtue ethics and Christian character. One would think that for an evangelical theologian, writing under a title such as *Becoming Good*[3] or *Choosing the Good*[4] would provoke some reflections under the inspiration of Paul and Augustine that even well-intentioned human beings are not capable of becoming or choosing good without a fundamental re-orientation of life that we call conversion, involving the repudiation of sin and the affirmation of the priority of following the way of Christ. With a few exceptions, such as the work of Oliver O'Donovan and L. Gregory Jones (which I cite below), there is very little reflection on the need and relevance of conversion for Christian ethics.

Several explanations come to mind to account for this. First, conversion to Christ is simply assumed. An author writing on basic Christian ethics or building Christian character simply takes for granted that the reader is already a Christian, a committed church member, perhaps a seminary student; otherwise, the reader probably would not be interested in reading the book. Christian ethics as a discipline is assumed to be addressing those who are already committed to living the Christian life. The twentieth-century classic by C. S. Lewis, *Mere Christianity*, in which morality and Christian character and behavior are compellingly described, is exceptional in being directed to a general public (although with something of a Christian cultural background), and it offers the reader the reality of conversion and the challenge of accepting or rejecting Jesus Christ. The evangelical ethicist might reply that his or her own intention in writing was less evangelistic and addressed to the Christian believer. That may be an understandable strategy, but it not only makes assumptions about the reader's commitment, but also neglects the ongoing and continuous aspect of conversion and conformity to Christ.

Second, the more sacramental view of regeneration, part of the Catholic tradition that underpins much of the Roman Catholic, Anglican and Lutheran view of the Christian life, tends to downplay the importance of personal conversion relative to the sacrament of baptism. That is sound, theo-

---

[3]David Gill, *Becoming Good: Building Moral Character* (Downers Grove, IL: InterVarsity Press, 2000).

[4]Dennis Hollinger, *Choosing the Good: Christian Ethics in a Complex World* (Grand Rapids: Baker Academic, 2002).

logically, in preferring a confidence in the objective grace of God rather than
the quality of subjective experience; but psychologically and practically the
impression may be conveyed of complacency and acceptance of low-grade
standards and expectations for Christian discipleship. Thus the life of grace
begins with baptism, the new identity is conferred, and membership and
participation in the body of Christ are initiated. This new identity happens
once only: it is theologically and psychologically harmful to imply the necessity of reconversion. The seventeenth-century bishop Jeremy Taylor, in
his classic *Holy Living*, expressed this conviction well:

> For wee must know that there is but one repentance in a Mans whole life, if
> repentance be taken in the proper, and strict Evangelicall Covenant-sense,
> and not after the ordinary understanding of the word: That is, wee are but
> once to change our whole state of life, from the power of the Devil and his
> intire possession, from the state of sin and death, from the body of corruption,
> to the life of grace, to the possession of Jesus, to the kingdom of the Gospel;
> and this is done in the baptism of water, or in the baptism of the Spirit . . . and
> by our obedience to the heavenly calling, we working together with God.
> After this change, if ever we fall into the contrary state, and be wholly es-
> tranged from God and Religion, and professe our selves servants of unrigh-
> teousnesse, God hath made no more covenant of restitution to us.[5]

Even if we agree, as we should, that baptism is to be performed only once,
there is a need to reaffirm that signification, to reclaim that identity and to
continue the process of "living into" the calling of our baptism. L. Gregory
Jones reminds us of the meaning of the congregation's renewal of their bap-
tismal vows on the occasion of the baptism of a new member:

> The individual is baptized only once, for the induction is a singular event that
> provides a new story and tradition which defines her life and gives her a new
> identity; however, the task of responding in "newness of life," the life of
> friendship with God through discipleship, is an ongoing process of "un-
> learning" the old identity and "learning" the new identity characterized as
> "living into her baptism."[6]

---

[5]Jeremy Taylor, *Holy Living and Holy Dying*, ed. P. G. Stanwood, 2 vols. (Oxford: Clarendon, 1989),
1:246.
[6]L. Gregory Jones, *Transformed Judgment: Toward a Trinitarian Account of the Moral Life* (Notre
Dame, IN: University of Notre Dame Press, 1990), p. 139.

An even stronger description of the need to see ongoing conversion and renewal in connection to the sacraments of baptism and penance is found in the writing of the Orthodox theologian Alexander Schmemann:

> The *sacrament* of *penance* is not, therefore, a sacred and juridical "power" given by God to men. It is the power of baptism as it lives in the Church. From baptism it receives its sacramental character. In Christ all sins are forgiven once and for all, for He is Himself the forgiveness of sins, and there is no need for any "new" absolution. But there is indeed the need for us who constantly *leave* Christ and *excommunicate* ourselves from His life, to return to Him, to receive again and again the gift which in Him has been given once and for all. And the absolution is the sign that this return has taken place and has been fulfilled. Just as each Eucharist is not a "repetition" of Christ's supper but our ascension, our acceptance into the same and eternal banquet, so also the sacrament of penance is not a repetition of baptism, but our return to the "newness of life" which God gave to us once and for all.[7]

A third and more subtle explanation for the relative neglect of conversion in Christian ethics is related to the previous two considerations. It is assumed that once the orientation of the will is in place (either through an earlier Christian commitment or in the affirmation of Christian identity in baptism), the main problem of Christian ethics involves the details of biblical interpretation, the articulation of principles and the application of principles to current issues and problems. Oliver O'Donovan has pointed to the false dichotomy of instruction and obedience, of learning and repentance, of justification and sanctification, underlying which is the more fundamental problem: the divergence of reason and will.[8] When we divide or compartmentalize these things, we then conceive the Christian moral life as primarily a matter of the proper orientation of the will, and the intellectual discernment of complexities "is allowed no real moral significance."[9] In other words, if conversion and repentance are primarily a matter of the will and orientation of a person's intentions, we have a tendency to consider specific decisions and patterns of action as belonging to a separate category. If this is true, then we

---

[7]Alexander Schmemann, *For the Life of the World: Sacraments and Orthodoxy*, 2nd ed. (Crestwood, NY: St. Vladimir's Seminary Press, 1973), p. 79.
[8]Oliver O'Donovan, *Resurrection and Moral Order: An Outline for Evangelical Ethics*, 2nd ed. (Grand Rapids: Eerdmans, 1994), p. 104.
[9]Ibid., p. 262.

need to reintegrate justification and sanctification and intellect and will in instruction and repentance; and then the need for conversion is seen more clearly to be an ongoing feature of the Christian life and actually central to Christian ethics and the development of Christian character.

It is significant that conversion has been treated more thoroughly by systematic theologians than by moral theologians or ethicists. Emil Brunner, Dietrich Bonhoeffer and Karl Barth as major twentieth-century theologians highlighted either in separate chapters or entire books the centrality of discipleship and conversion.[10] In the exposition below I refer to insights from Barth and Bonhoeffer, but I will set the stage with a consideration of Brunner's articulation of conversion.

Not just in modern pietism, said Brunner, but in the whole of Scripture "conversion means the turning away of man from the previous way and life of his own choosing, and a turning to the will and way of God."[11] This is a theme not only in the Old Testament, of course, but also in the apostolic witness to Christ. *Shub* (Hebrew) and *metanoia* (Greek) refer not just to a change of mind (or heart) but rather to "the total act of the person which turns away from everything of its own in the past and turns to God."[12]

Repentance in the New Testament means that we "walk not according to the flesh but according to the Spirit" (Rom 8:4). Or as Colossians puts it, when we have repented, "You have stripped off the old self with its practices and have clothed yourselves with the new self, which is being renewed in knowledge according to the image of its creator" (Col 3:9-10). Faith as conversion is at the same time the end of the old—the end of the person whose center was the self—and the beginning of the new, God-created person; it is the end of my autonomy and the beginning of my acknowledgment of my Lord and Creator.[13] In faith, one understands oneself as a child of God, begotten by the Word, that being for which the Creator has designed us in love. But this happens in the act of turning away from self

---

[10]All of these theologians made important contributions to twentieth-century Christian ethics, but it is significant that they strove to integrate what they wrote on issues in ethics with their theological work.

[11]Emil Brunner, *The Christian Doctrine of the Church, Faith, and the Consummation*, trans. David Cairns and T. H. L. Parker (Philadelphia: Westminster, 1962), p. 277.

[12]Ibid., p. 278.

[13]Ibid., p. 283.

and turning to God, an act that is possible only in the act and word of God, in the cross and resurrection of Jesus Christ the Son of God, who is perfectly obedient to God and who bestows himself wholly and freely in love.[14]

Conversion depends upon responding to Truth: the truth or reality about ourselves and about God. As L. Gregory Jones has put it,

> In the recognition that God has befriended humanity which occasions conversion, people are convicted of their capacity for and the actuality of their evil, of the manifold ways in which their sin has prevented and continues to prevent them from growing morally because of their bondage to past distortions, deceptions, and rejections. It is only in seeing the truth about herself, brought about by God's grace, that a person can attain the true sorrow and forgiveness which constitutes her *metanoia*.[15]

Brunner pointed out that New Testament discipleship, following the way of the Lord, belongs to conversion, and involves a reorientation to reality:

> Man must really get out of himself, but this is precisely what he cannot himself do unless it happens in the reality outside of him, which is at the same time his reality and the reality of God. Only in this movement out of himself towards God does man find his true self, and with it his liberty, in unconditional dependence on the Power that created him.[16]

This coming out of oneself and being shaped by the reality of God is a continuous process. We do not find our true selves, or achieve our liberty or develop the unconditional dependence modeled for us by Jesus with one decisive reorientation. It requires the process of successive reorientations, the discovery of further blind spots and areas of resistance in our lives, of the combination of intellectual darkness and confusion as well as unwillingness and resistance that need to be brought before the wisdom and love of God in Christ.

DEATH TO THE OLD SELF

We will center our attention on Jesus' challenge to committed discipleship: "If any want to become my followers, let them deny themselves and take up their cross daily and follow me" (Lk 9:23). The process of conversion should

---

[14]Ibid., pp. 286-87.
[15]Jones, *Transformed Judgment*, p. 112.
[16]Brunner, *Christian Doctrine*, p. 289.

be seen as involving a fundamental decision about identity and direction, a daily reaffirmation of identity with Christ, and active following. But before being in a position to undertake such self-denial, let alone start on a path of discipleship, we must be roused from the slumber of sin, get our bearings and see our position accurately in order to reorient ourselves and follow Christ rather than the usual self-selected attractive paths.

Karl Barth describes powerfully the effect of sin that produces sloth and misery. The lazy stupor befuddles us and leaves us ineffective. Here the first aspect of conversion required is to wake up. We need above all to see the reality of our condition: befuddlement, heading in the wrong direction and preoccupation with the wrong priorities. In his section "Awakening to Conversion,"[17] Barth writes about Christians who have been awakened and are awake, but perhaps may fall asleep again. When they are awakened, sometimes with a jolt, they realize the way they were headed and that they now can and must take the opposite direction. Unlike actual physical sleep, people do not rouse themselves, but instead are in need of being roused; some intervention is required.

This is an excellent metaphor, capturing the moments in the parabolic depictions of conversion: the prodigal son in a far land, sharing food with the swine, finally "came to himself." In John Bunyan's *Pilgrim's Progress*, Pilgrim, after wandering from the right path (once again) spends considerable time in Vanity Fair before he realizes his error, folly and blindness.

Once the Holy Spirit has brought the reality of our plight to our attention and made clear that there is an alternative road that leads to life, we can take up the Lord's challenge of discipleship: self-denial, cross bearing and following Christ. Bonhoeffer puts it this way in the *Cost of Discipleship*:

> The cross is laid on every Christian. The first Christ-suffering which every man must experience is the call to abandon the attachments of this world. It is that dying of the old man which is the result of his encounter with Christ. As we embark upon discipleship we surrender ourselves to Christ in union with his death—we give over our lives to death. . . . When Christ calls a man, he bids him come and die.[18]

---

[17]Karl Barth, *Church Dogmatics*, vol. IV/2, *The Doctrine of Reconciliation*, ed. G. W. Bromiley and T. F. Torrance (Edinburgh: T & T Clark, 1956), pp. 553-55.

[18]Dietrich Bonhoeffer, *The Cost of Discipleship*, trans. R. H. Fuller (New York: Macmillan, 1963), p. 99.

The three components of the challenge of discipleship are explicated by Joel Green in his commentary on the Gospel of Luke. First, to deny oneself is to set aside the relationships by which one has constructed one's identity heretofore; radical self-denial means openness to constructing a whole new identity based not on ordinary human family associations or relationships of mutual obligation but in the new community centered on God and faithful to the message of Christ.[19] Second, taking up the cross is the identification with the suffering of Jesus, and a reemphasis on the death to the old self. Here the death involves being dead to the world that opposes God's purpose. Disciples are called to identify with Jesus in his suffering.

These first two actions of self-denial and bearing the cross are expressed in the aorist tense in Greek, implying that they are discrete actions, possible to finish, or actions that later reflection can situate in the past. This corresponds to Calvin's definition: "The true turning of our life to God, a turning that arises from a pure and earnest fear of him; and it consists in the mortification of our flesh and of the old man, and in the vivification of the Spirit" (*Institutes* III.3.5).[20]

Calvin, in his definition of repentance or conversion, implies that the turning away from self to God is in the past and sets the course of the rest of life. He also anticipates my emphasis on the resurrection in the next section by pointing to the vivification by the Spirit as part of the definition of conversion.[21] Thus there is the third emphasis in Luke on the ongoing nature of conversion indicated by the addition of "daily" to taking up the cross. The decision to take up the cross is a pattern for life that is established at one point, perhaps; but then it is reaffirmed on a daily basis. The following of Christ is expressed by a verb, *akoloutheō*, which is in the present imperative, indicating continuous action. Following Christ is active and ongoing. By adding "daily" to taking up the cross, Luke conveys the meaning that the disciple of Jesus is to live on a daily basis as though having been sentenced to death by crucifixion.[22]

---

[19]Joel Green, *The Gospel of Luke* (Grand Rapids: Eerdmans, 1997), pp. 372-73.

[20]Calvin, *Institutes of the Christian Religion*, ed. John McNeill, trans. Ford Lewis Battles, 2 vols. (Philadelphia: Westminster, 1960), 1:597.

[21]In his preface to the commentary on Psalms, Calvin used the word *conversion* to describe repentance that is thought of as lifelong. See ibid., p. 597 n. 14.

[22]Green, *Gospel of Luke*, p. 373.

In allegorical form, Bunyan portrays a fundamental and decisive orientation of the pilgrim to take the path that leads to God and the Celestial City. But in the wanderings off the path, Pilgrim portrays the possibility of temporarily forgetting or even deliberately ignoring the true destiny and identity of the pilgrim. Repentance and conversion is required to get back to the path; Christian does not have to reenter the "wicket gate" of conversion and begin the journey all over, but he must return to the path. As O'Donovan puts it,

> In examining the apparent meaning of our own past lives, we have to confess its ambiguity, its failure to give clear expression to the reality which must shape it. Therefore we continually turn back from these appearances of ourselves to the reality itself. In this sense it is true that conversion happens not once but many times. Yet it is always the one eschatological reality . . . each successive turning back claims and reclaims the one decisive encounter.[23]

THE RESURRECTION

This picture of conversion has considerable scope, but it is incomplete. Like the Gospel of Mark itself (in its presumed original version), with its emphasis on bearing the cross, and the identification of the disciple with the cross of Christ, it requires balancing with the good news of the resurrection. In the context of Mark 8 and Luke 9 and the focus of Jesus and the evangelists on the prediction of the passion, this can only be hinted at, just as the real identity of the Messiah is kept somewhat secret. But the resurrection is being indicated by both Mark and Luke in the promise immediately following: "For those who want to save their life will lose it, and those who lose their life for my sake will save it" (Mk 8:35; Lk 9:24). There will be ultimate vindication and the glory of the kingdom of God.

C. S. Lewis makes this process of "losing life" in order that real life may be "found" a fundamental biblical principle and points to the richly rewarding new life that will be ours:

> Give up yourself, and you will find your real self. Lose your life and you will save it. Submit to death, death of your ambitions and favourite wishes every day and death of your body in the end: submit with every fibre of your being,

---

[23]O'Donovan, *Resurrection and Moral Order*, p. 208.

and you find eternal life. Keep back nothing. Nothing that you have not given away will ever be really yours. Nothing in you that has not died will ever be raised from the dead. Look for yourself, and you will find in the long run only hatred, loneliness, despair, rage, ruin, and decay. But look for Christ and you will find Him, and with Him everything else thrown in.[24]

Paul, writing after Christ's resurrection, makes this principle of new life in discipleship even more vivid. The self-denial and death to self in following Christ is the same in Romans 6 as in Luke 9, but Paul links it to the resurrection life of Christ in a clear and compelling way:

> If we have been united with him in a death like his, we will certainly be united with him in a resurrection like his. We know that our old self was crucified with him so that the body of sin might be destroyed. . . . But if we have died with Christ, we believe that we will also live with him. . . . So you must also consider yourselves dead to sin but alive to God in Christ Jesus. (Rom 6:5-11)

There is a tendency to neglect this stark choice between death and life. An underestimation of the reality and power of sin is clearly a factor; so also is the minimizing of the eschatological significance of the kingdom of God. Converting to Christ means to put first the kingdom of God as the eternal reality in the light of which we judge all earthly life. The stark contrast between death and life that baptism symbolizes is not merely rhetorical; it points to the fundamental difference in identity and destiny that marks Christian discipleship. Oliver O'Donovan reminds us, "When the opposition of death and resurrection is collapsed, neither death nor resurrection remains. A moral authority which does not both judge and recreate is not the authority of Christ, but a purely natural authority, to follow which is to be conformed to the world."[25]

CONVERSION IS BOTH INDIVIDUAL AND CORPORATE

Conversion through Christ is through the Holy Spirit and the church. The Western emphasis, with the exaggerated individualism of the Enlightenment, has been on the solitary nature of Christian conversion. The existentialist focus by Søren Kierkegaard and in much twentieth-century theology highlighted the solitary Christian and his or her naked, isolated decision even

---

[24]C. S. Lewis, *Mere Christianity* (London: Collins, 1950), p. 188.
[25]O'Donovan, *Resurrection and Moral Order*, p. 105.

more. But consider this passage from Barth's *Church Dogmatics*, which points to the communal experience of conversion: "Thus the meaning of baptism is man's conversion—the conversion of all who have a part in it. It is the conversion which takes place in knowledge of the work and word of God. It is the common forsaking of an old way of life and the common following of a new way of life."[26]

The Catholic tradition and Eastern Orthodox are right to be critical of hyperindividualism and to recall the corporate nature of the church and life in Christ.[27] This has been expressed well by Rowan Williams:

> So to come to "be in Christ," to belong with Jesus, involves a far-reaching reconstruction of one's humanity: a liberation from servile, distorted, destructive patterns in the past, a liberation from anxious dread of God's judgement, a new identity in a community of reciprocal love and complementary service, whose potential horizons are universal.[28]

Likewise, N. T. Wright, in his recent book on ethics, takes pains to guard against an individualistic understanding of conversion and the life in Christ.[29]

With due acknowledgment of the dangers of overemphasizing individual conversion, we must, at the same time, avoid downplaying too much the importance of the individual decision.[30] The church and the congregation celebrate the Eucharist together as a community gathered by Christ, but each individual decides whether or not to participate. When Joshua issued his famous challenge, "Choose you this day whom you will serve," it was a challenge both corporate and individual. Strongly affected by the group, there is a certain pressure; but the decision to follow Joshua and the way of God's leading had to be made by individual households. Stephen Smalley makes the need for balance clear:

> The converted Christian is called to *be* converted, and the reborn person who is baptized needs perpetually to live out the implications of that status. Moreover, while conversion is initially an individual experience, those who

---

[26]Barth, *Church Dogmatics*, IV/4, p. 138.
[27]See Christos Yannaras, *The Freedom of Morality*, trans. Elizabeth Briere (Crestwood, NY: St. Vladimir's Seminary Press, 1996), chap. 3, "The Gospel's Rejection of Individual Ethics."
[28]Rowan Williams, *On Christian Theology* (Oxford: Blackwell, 2000), p. 138.
[29]N. T. Wright, *Virtue Reborn* (London: SPCK, 2010), p. 137.
[30]See Richard Mouw, *The God Who Commands* (Notre Dame, IN: University of Notre Dame Press, 1990), especially chap. 3, "On Being Fair to Individualism."

are converted belong to the community of the church, and are required to sustain their belief and exercise their service in a corporate context. In this sense, conversion and renewal by the Spirit are life-long features of the Christian life.[31]

THE RESULTS OF FOLLOWING JESUS

Conversion produces a change in attitude and outlook and inner harmony as well as behavior; as Barth inimitably put it, conversion is "the transition from the Before of self-will and anxiety to the After of obedience and hope."[32]

The Epistle to the Colossians links death to self and the new life in Christ: "So if you have been raised with Christ, seek the things that are above, where Christ is, seated at the right hand of God" (Col 3:1). The share in the resurrection of the Lord is meant to be the fundamental identity of the Christian disciple, but it presupposes the self-denial and cross-bearing implied by the challenge of Jesus: "For you have died. . . . Put to death, therefore, whatever in you is earthly. . . . You have stripped off the old self with its practices and have clothed yourselves with the new self, which is being renewed in knowledge according to the image of its creator" (Col 3:3-10).

It is obvious that the person who has gone from being asleep or stumbling in the wrong direction to self-denial, taking up the cross and following Jesus has undergone in that conversion a thorough change of attitude, priorities, ways of looking at things, of deciding what is good to do. In making decisions based on judgments about what seems good, the disciple no longer chooses actions that are characteristic of lust, greed, sexual immorality, anger and slander, for example, but is able to judge and decide on actions from the point of view of compassion, kindness, humility, gentleness and patience, forgiveness and peace (Col 3:5-15).

This is a conversion involving the entire mind and heart: reason, will and emotions. In Romans 12 Paul reminds the Christians in Rome that because of God's overwhelming love (Rom 8) and his will for both Jews and Gentiles (Rom 9–11), they should recognize how fitting it is to offer themselves as living sacrifices to the Lord: "Do not be conformed to this world, but be

---

[31]Stephen Smalley, "Conversion," in *New Dictionary of Theology*, ed. Sinclair Ferguson and David Wright (Downers Grove, IL: InterVarsity Press, 1988), p. 168.

[32]Barth, *Church Dogmatics*, IV/4, p. 138.

transformed by the renewing of your minds, so that you may discern what
is the will of God—what is good and acceptable and perfect" (Rom 12:2).

The renewing of the mind by breaking the conformity to worldly patterns
of thinking and having a new way of judging and a new way of wisdom is
the key to living out the new relationship of discipleship and fellowship with
Christ. In Romans 12:9-21 Paul draws out some of the practical implications
of this new pattern, echoing portions of the Sermon on the Mount in accepting persecution and not retaliating against those who hurt and insult.

It is the transformation of the mind (including principles of reason, the
orientation of the will and the emotions) that forms the basis for the new
life lived by the Holy Spirit. The Spirit does not (usually) lead by special
inspiration, but rather by reminding and making more vivid and attractive
those priorities and goals and values that belong to the kingdom of Christ,
enabling us both to see more clearly the right ordering of our lives and to
gladly and confidently choose those patterns (e.g., nonresistance) that
would have gone against our natural instincts or patterns of reaction.

Some readers may find the theme of conversion an especially Protestant
or evangelical emphasis, and that the Catholic focus on growth in grace by
the Holy Spirit through the sacraments and the development of the virtues
over time implies a kind of imperceptible change that is at odds with a break
with the past or sudden change in behavior that might be associated with a
doctrine of conversion. Yet we find both in the lives of the saints and in
Catholic theology the challenge of conversion, and the need to part company
with worldly points of view. A sophisticated theory of conversion was developed by the Jesuit Bernard Lonergan that corresponds rather well with
the treatment of Romans 12:1-2 just above. For Lonergan, there were three
types of conversion: intellectual, involving a judgment of the need to change
intellectual framework; a moral conversion, which involves the element of
choice or decision for one's life; and a religious conversion, involving a grasp
of what is ultimately important in life and a deep level of commitment or
self-surrender.[33]

These three types of conversion are not necessarily distinct in time or to
be thought of as different realities, but simply are aspects of a larger process.

---

[33]See Bartholomew Kiely, *Psychology and Moral Theology: Lines of Convergence* (Rome: Gregorian
University Press, 1987), pp. 212-17.

In Scholastic terminology, which typically is confusing for Protestants, this religious conversion involves a state of "habitual, operative grace," but there may be more overlap than is usually recognized between this Catholic view of "religious conversion" and the more evangelical terminology of self-surrender or being filled with the Spirit. In any case, biblical conversion involves the renewal of the whole person in a way that allows the intellect, will and emotions to be reoriented and strengthened in following Christ as his disciple. What it means to follow God's will and obey God's laws will be considered in the next chapter.

FOR FURTHER READING

Dietrich Bonhoeffer, *Ethics*, ed. Eberhard Bethge, trans. Neville Horton Smith (New York: Macmillan, 1955), part 3, "Ethics as Formation."

L. Gregory Jones, *Transformed Judgment: Toward a Trinitarian Account of the Moral Life* (Notre Dame, IN: University of Notre Dame Press, 1990), p. 139.

Livio Melina, *Sharing in Christ's Virtues: For a Renewal of Moral Theology in Light of "Veritatis Splendor,"* trans. William May (Washington, DC: Catholic University of America Press, 2001), chapters 1, 2, 6.

Gordon T. Smith, *Beginning Well: Christian Conversion and Authentic Transformation* (Downers Grove, IL: InterVarsity Press, 2001).

8

GOD'S WILL AND
GOD'S LAW

WITH CONVERSION, we have come to the turning point and cen-
terpiece of moral theology. When we have responded to God's grace
and experienced new life and new direction in our lives, the challenge for
us is to be confident in the correct direction we are taking, in the knowledge
of God's will, and the readiness to work out the framework of the priority of
God's kingdom and conformity to Christ into the decisions and actions of
daily life. The challenge involves the Holy Spirit, helping us not only with a
more accurate view of ourselves, and our relationships, but also with a better
knowledge of the way in which Scripture and theology in general provide
direction for us. The Bible supplies a mixture of direct guidelines, general
principles, an overall worldview and what may be called "focal images" for
consistent biblical guidance.[1]

In addition to knowledge, of course, we need hearts (wills and emotions)
that are in tune with our growth in understanding. Part of the struggle in
the Christian life (and the moral life for non-Christians as well) is that the
pattern of our emotional responses is not always in harmony with the
knowledge or principles that we have. This is especially true after any major
conversion: the new convert will have friends, familiar reactions to stimuli
and situations, and simple patterns of behavior that are difficult to bring in
line with new moral principles. The struggle with the inconsistency between

---

[1]For a detailed and careful guide to the application of the Scriptures to moral issues, see Richard
Hays, *The Moral Vision of the New Testament: Community, Cross, New Creation; A Contemporary
Introduction to New Testament Ethics* (San Francisco: HarperSanFrancisco, 1996).

our desires and our principles is something that all humans are familiar with. That is why the remainder of the book is devoted to analyzing the development of the virtues that shape the mind as a whole: our intellect in practical reasoning, the will and the emotions. But first we consider the need to be informed by God's will, not only in general terms, but also in the matter of specific guidance.

KNOWING GOD'S WILL

After conversion, Christian discipleship implies that the overriding goal is to turn away from the fulfillment of one's own will and toward the conscious seeking of God's will. The crucifixion of self and putting first the kingdom of God and his righteousness sets us in the right direction, but it does not make clear the small and intermediate steps that we need to take to keep moving in that direction. It may even seem impossibly difficult because the strong contrast implied by saying no to self and yes to God may imply that our ordinary human instincts, wisdom and cultural patterns are now suspect, and that we must look for some special guidance and direction that we do not expect or understand well. Old Testament wisdom literature reminds us, "Trust in the LORD with all your heart, and do not rely on your own insight. In all your ways acknowledge him, and he will make straight your paths" (Prov 3:5-6).

Paul reminds us in a famous passage in Romans, "Do not be conformed to this world, but be transformed by the renewing of your minds, so that you may discern what is the will of God—what is good and acceptable and perfect" (Rom 12:2). This verse follows the appeal to Christians to present themselves as a sacrifice to God, "a total setting of ourselves apart to serve and please God, as the entire business of our lives."[2]

There is a type of pietism that falsely exaggerates the difference between human knowledge of what is right and good, and what is actually God's will. By stressing the effects of original sin, the deceitfulness of the human heart, the contrast between the way to life and the way to destruction, confident Christian discipleship can be made more difficult by highlighting the incapacity of human beings to discern God's will.

---

[2]J. I. Packer and Carolyn Nystrom, *Guard Us, Guide Us: Divine Leading in Life's Decisions* (Grand Rapids: Baker Books, 2008), p. 117.

One key element, which may seem transparently obvious to many but is still worth putting into words, is that human beings, whether Christian or not, can agree on a great deal about what is good for ordinary human living. Matters of diet and health, physical exercise, music and the arts, family life, skills in social relationships and the world of daily working life, are part of the realm of creation that we can take part in and discern what is good and right (admittedly in a limited sense) by human understanding. A great deal of what civilization provides in opportunities for children's play and education, and for adults in commerce, education and the arts, is in harmony with (or at least not incompatible with) God's general will in creation. God has created a world in which human beings can work, play, enjoy friendship, marry, raise families and contribute their efforts to the welfare of their community. Without the benefit of revelation, most people recognize, correctly, that these are proper human activities. As Christians, with a doctrine of creation, and with scriptural affirmations to be fruitful, for example, and to work six days and observe a day of rest, we are even more confident that when we engage in meaningful work and raise families, we are living in God's will.

Of course, God may have a specific calling, an individual path for us to follow, which may involve remaining single, not raising a family, temporarily leaving friends to travel to some remote place on earth and so on; and in this case there is a need to be sensitive to the specific direction in God's will for *you*.

There is a danger in looking for direction from God and specific guidance of God's will when we are meant to use the abilities and gifts that we have. We can back this up with wise reflection from both Catholic and evangelical guides. First, we have the sensible advice of Francis de Sales, writing around four hundred years ago, who dealt with the question of how do we know when we should, for example, visit a sick friend or go to a church service.

> Ordinarily there is nothing of such obvious importance in one rather than the other that there is need to go into long deliberation over it. We must proceed in good faith and without making subtle distinctions in such affairs, as St. Basil says, do freely what seems good to us, so as not to weary our minds, waste our time, and put ourselves in danger of disquiet, scruples, and superstition.[3]

---

[3]Francis de Sales, "Finding God's Will for You," excerpted from *Treatise on the Love of God*, trans. John Ryan (Manchester, NH: Sophia Institute Press, 1998), p. 67.

And even in important matters, says de Sales, we must try not to force the issue by too much scrutiny and discussion. We ask for the light of the Spirit, take counsel with a director or others whom we trust and come to a resolution. To second-guess, to vacillate and doubt, is "a mark of great self-love, or of childishness, weakness, and folly of mind."[4]

This would mean that our ordinary method of practical reasoning, outlined in chapters two and three above, applies to Christians as well (given that intentions are ultimately ordered to God as chief good and final end, and the patterns of discernment, will and affection are not distorted). And here we can cite the helpful wisdom of theologian J. I. Packer, who affirms the validity of the ordinary pattern of reasoning and decision making. It carries extra weight for us not only because of Packer's long consideration of these matters, but also because at the conclusion of the section of the book on guidance he sums up a careful and wise treatment:

> Many Christians are still haunted by the fancy that real guidance from God for the making of each day's decisions is a direct ministry of the Holy Spirit in one's heart that entirely transcends the mental disciplines of analyzing alternatives, applying principles, calculating consequences, weighing priorities, balancing pros and cons, taking and weighing advice, estimating your own capacities and limitations, and engaging in whatever other forms of brainwork prudence in self-commitment is held to require. We emphatically agree that leading us to the best decision is a ministry of the Holy Spirit, first to last, but with equal emphasis we deny that under ordinary circumstances his ministry short-circuits or circumvents any of these sometimes laborious intellectual procedures. On the contrary, they are precisely the means by which the Holy Spirit of God leads us into seeing clearly what it is right and good to decide and do in each situation.[5]

In the following subsections we will turn to the role of objective laws and moral standards, both in the civil order and through the biblical revelation. How do we incorporate political laws and the moral laws of Scripture, such as the Decalogue, into our moral reasoning? Are civil laws binding? Are God's laws to be treated as absolute? These are matters that we consider when pursuing the question of fulfilling God's will.

---

[4]Ibid.
[5]Packer and Nystrom, *Guard Us, Guide Us*, pp. 136-37.

LAWS AND THE COMMON GOOD

Laws, by their nature, are general directives, prescribing and prohibiting behavior for everyone in a jurisdiction. The basic purpose behind all laws is the welfare of the community, the common good. This was recognized by Thomas Aquinas in his famous definition of law as "an ordinance of reason for the common good, made by the one who has the care of the community, and promulgated" (*ST* I-II, q. 90, a. 4). If a piece of legislation is manifestly for the advantage of a group of people and of little or no benefit to the common good (often the case in dictatorships, but also not unknown in democracies when interest groups and lobbyists can exert great pressure), then its fundamental justice may be brought into question.

Legislators are limited in their wisdom, even when they rely on experts and build on popular consensus. Laws often have to be modified in the light of how they actually work, and in view of changing circumstances. At any given point in a country (or other area of jurisdiction) there may be laws that are archaic and outmoded, poorly worded, unfair to a sizable group of citizens and so on.

Yet a citizen is under obligation to obey laws. The Christian citizen, moreover, is expected to respect and obey governmental authority (which, according to Rom 13, has divine sanction) as part of Christian discipleship. Can laws, then, be disobeyed?

Thankfully, we have had the contours of our situation clarified by experience and by extensive reflection on political theory, both philosophical and theological. Many Christian countries went through a period of the "divine right of kings" when the sovereign was assumed to have absolute authority on the grounds that God simply transferred authority within a realm to its rulers. We can also see a connection between the development of absolute monarchy and the late medieval and early modern view of law as based on the imposition of will rather than on principles of reason. In many areas of Europe influenced by Luther's view of the "two kingdoms," God was seen as sovereign in the spiritual sphere, while in the social and political sphere the earthly sovereign had complete control. But with the vivid examples of the horrors of untrammeled political power, most Christians are well aware that there are lines that mark out a territory where they ought to obey God rather than human authority.

In the more ordinary world of taxes, traffic laws, building codes, commerce, contracts and the workplace, laws impinge on us and require our obedience on the grounds that they serve the common good. They may seem at times contrary to our personal wishes (and depending on our philosophical views, perhaps even misguided aspects of government interference), but obedience is required.

Exceptions may occur at times, when the "letter of the law" is not followed, but the real intention of the law is honored. Aquinas uses the example of a medieval walled city where a law would require the city gates to be barred at a certain time in the evening. The gatekeeper might notice a few soldiers of the city on the other side of the wall after the gates were locked, and he would be right to open the gates to let them in, since their presence inside is helpful not only to them personally but also to the welfare of the city (ST I-II q. 96, a. 6).

In a more modern situation, you may be in a car, facing a medical emergency and the need to get to the hospital as quickly as possible. The speed limits, which are meant to promote public safety, envision normal circumstances. In your case, strict adherence to the speed limit might well endanger someone's health, and going above the speed limit (while still driving with due care) is still in keeping with the law's intent for the common good.

What happens in such cases is not simple disobedience of the law, but a recognition of the higher intention of the law. If law is seen as the intelligent ordering of means to an end, then a person may sometimes be able to recognize that the purpose of a given law is, in unusual circumstances, sometimes better served by taking exceptional action.

The potential is present here, of course, for self-deception and abuse. That is why cases in secular law courts often concern the correct interpretation of the relevant laws and are resolved by judges who have the experience, knowledge of the law and wisdom to discern its application. But not every situation can be (or needs to be) taken through tedious and expensive trials. The Scholastic tradition spoke of the need for *epikeia* as the intellectual discernment used for the proper application of law.[6] This is the term that moralists generally have used, while in jurisprudence lawyers use the term

---

[6]See Thomas Aquinas, *ST* II-II, q. 120, aa. 1-2.

equity to denote basically the same thing. *Epikeia* is the virtue by which Christian persons discern the inner meaning of a human law so as to obey it intelligently in the majority of cases and, if need be, go beyond it in a reasonable way in the exceptional case.[7]

What about more obviously unjust laws? What should be the Christian attitude toward laws such as those that maintain discrimination, including the segregation laws in parts of the United States before the civil rights movement of the 1960s? In a very real way, such laws are essentially defective because they fail to promote the common good, properly understood (that is, they promoted what seemed to be the good of a section of the populace). From this perspective, drawing on principles of Augustine and Thomas Aquinas, Martin Luther King Jr., in his famous "Letter from Birmingham Jail," argued that discriminatory laws can be seen as lacking the essential characteristic of law: justice. Even though such laws have been validly legislated and command the support of the majority, they do not deserve true obedience.

Civil disobedience requires wisdom as to targeting and timing and tactics. Even bad laws are still valid in the sense that the government may enforce them, and those who disobey must be willing to suffer the consequences (which the nonviolent section of the civil rights movement explicitly accepted).

Ordinarily, it should be clear, the Christian citizen obeys all laws, even those that he or she disagrees with—those that are unwise, and even those that are unjust. The rationale for this is again the common good: the harmonious operation of society is such an important good, and the habit of living as a community under "the rule of law" so important, that it is in the interests of all of us to obey even the bad laws, and then take the steps that are available to challenge and change legislation, when it seems necessary, through the channels of the legislatures and courts.

GOD'S LAW AND MORAL ABSOLUTES

For the Christian, God's moral law is binding in a way that other types of law are not. Human law is subject to the imperfections of human intelligence—limited understanding, unforeseen circumstances, faulty legislation. It is necessary sometimes, as we have seen, to seek the proper intention of

---

[7]Timothy O'Connell, *Principles for a Catholic Morality*, rev. ed. (San Francisco: Harper & Row, 1990), p. 232.

the law in a situation not adequately covered by a particular law. But God's law is the product of wisdom and love that are by nature perfect, and it is received by God's people as binding on their conscience.

Some will point out that Jesus himself provides precedent for the use of *epikeia* in understanding God's law. In his controversies with the Pharisees about Sabbath observance, and whether it was legitimate to heal or pluck grain on the Sabbath (considered to be a form of work), Jesus enunciated the underlying intention of the law: "The sabbath was made for humankind, and not humankind for the sabbath" (Mk 2:27). Overly burdensome regulations about how far one may walk on the Sabbath or use the kitchen in the preparation of food undermine the real purpose of the Sabbath, which is to share in the rest of God. But Jesus' use of *epikeia* was directed at the human interpretations and specifications of the command not to work, and these regulations, of course, shared in the limitations of all human legislation. We cannot take the principle "The sabbath was made for humankind" as a relativizing of the command itself to keep holy the Sabbath day.

Along with much of the rest of the Mosaic law, the fourth commandment was often treated by the Christian theological tradition as a part of the ceremonial law no longer binding on Christians. Christians observe Sunday not as a transferred Sabbath, but as a feast of new life in Christ. The Calvinist tradition, and much of Western Christendom until the last generation or two, took seriously the prohibition of work; but much of the church has reverted to treating this as part of the old law that no longer has binding force.

It is different, however, with the "moral" law. The Roman Catholic and Reformed branches of the church have understood that there is a core moral content enunciated in the Decalogue (and not confined to it) that has permanent and binding validity. The features of universality and permanence are strengthened by the notion of "natural law"—the idea that these moral regulations can be known by reflection on the nature and requirements of human society. The force of the prohibitions against murder, stealing and adultery, for example, or the requirement to be fair and honest in business dealings, are not only injunctions in God's revealed law, but are also to be found in nearly all human societies. Thus the convergence of moral norms reached by human reflection and experience with the moral laws in revelation has a powerful claim on the Christian conscience: they cannot be set aside as the old law of Moses or as having only limited and temporary relevance.

The binding character of moral laws varies with their form as positive or negative norms—that is, as positive injunctions, such as "Be honest," or prohibitions, such as "Do not defraud anyone." Negative commands, or prohibitions, can have a precise legal or moral definition that makes it fairly clear when they are being violated, whereas positive injunctions are, by nature, often imprecise and difficult to fulfill perfectly. This is true of all laws, whether we speak of the Decalogue or of mundane traffic laws. There is a fundamental difference between "Don't speed through school zones," "Don't blast your horn," and so on, and "Always be a safe and courteous driver." We can learn to be accurate about school zones and proper use of the horn. Courtesy and safety are much more imprecise and vary with the driving habits in different areas. Moreover, we all also have moments of inattention or frustration that usually cause no problems, thankfully, but do detract from our claim for the "best driver of the year" award.

Before we consider the Ten Commandments in some detail, consider this further example of the moral injunction "Pay your debts." From the view of deontological ethics, this is nearly a direct implication of a norm of justice or fairness. It would be a primary specification of treating others as one would want to be treated. From a utilitarian perspective also, this would be basic, since social relations and functions depend on people keeping their word. The biblical or theological foundation is similarly strong: "Owe no one anything, except to love one another" (Rom 13:8). The importance of paying wages on time and of keeping short accounts is a theme of the parables and of the Epistle of James. For the Christian, the conclusion must be that there is an obligation to repay debts faithfully, keeping to arrangements for long-term loans and making sure that paying what is owed to others has a higher priority than personal convenience or self-indulgence.

As obvious as this may be, the injunction sometimes cannot be fulfilled. Even where there is no question of negligence, there can be unforeseen financial burdens and catastrophic circumstances where employers cannot meet their payroll and must close down, or individuals are forced into declaring bankruptcy. As fundamental as this moral norm is, we cannot treat it as binding in an absolute sense—not from any disagreement about its truth, but because sometimes it simply cannot be fulfilled. That brings out the logical form of positive commands: they can function as hard-and-fast goals, but not as absolute or unqualified imperatives to be fulfilled.

Thus it is only prohibitions such as "Never touch a high-voltage wire" or "Do not commit adultery" that can function as absolute norms. A very high percentage of society easily goes through life without ever touching a high-voltage wire; a considerably smaller group, though still surprisingly large given a society where the pleasures of illicit sex are described and celebrated, manage to stay faithful to their spouses. These are norms meant to be fulfilled.

Turning to the norms of the gospel, it is not only the demands in the Sermon on the Mount that are difficult, but also, especially, the foundational ones. "Seek first the kingdom of God and his righteousness"; "Love God with all your heart, soul, and strength, and love your neighbor as yourself." There are so many ways in which we are preoccupied, weak and lacking in focus or enthusiasm that we can never come to a point (short of the new kingdom itself) when we can say that we have fulfilled what our Lord demands of us. When we confess that we have sinned, and that "by what we have done and by what we have left undone" we have not loved God or our neighbor properly, this is always strictly accurate.

What we can make a point of strictly adhering to, however, are the commands that point to some of the ways in which it is possible to offend God or harm our neighbor. That is the function of the prohibitions in the Decalogue, specifying some of the kinds of unloving behavior that we must avoid, and it is these that we must treat as absolute norms to be kept.

THE DECALOGUE: TEN GOOD SUGGESTIONS?

In the not-so-distant past when the 1662 *Book of Common Prayer* was the norm in the Anglican communion, the eucharistic liturgy included the recital of the Decalogue (omitted more often than not, we should note). After each commandment the people were to respond, "Lord, have mercy upon us, and incline our hearts to keep this law." This was an opportunity to acknowledge transgressions of the commandments in the past and pray for "grace to keep the same for the time to come," as the prayer book rubric advised.

In the 1979 *Book of Common Prayer* of the Episcopal Church the recital of the Decalogue is removed from the eucharistic liturgy and included as an optional part of an extra "penitential order." The traditional (rite I) version follows 1662, while the more common "contemporary" version (p. 350) predictably truncates and modifies the commandments. What is noteworthy is the congregational response: "Amen. Lord, have mercy." This implies agreement with the Lord's commands and an admission of the need for forgiveness, but there is no expression of the need to follow or keep the commands.

There is a very revealing question about the Decalogue in the Episcopal Catechism:[8]

Q: Since we do not fully obey them, are they truly useful at all?

A: Since we do not fully obey them, we see more clearly our sin and our need for redemption.

Here is a clear instance of the Lutheran view of the law (in an otherwise not very Lutheran denomination). The *primus usus* (first use) of the law is to convict one of sin, and that forms the main theological view of the law, because for Lutheran tradition there is no *tertius usus* (third use) as directive norms for the Christian to live by, which the Reformed or Calvinist tradition emphasized. (There was basically no disagreement about the second use of law, which is to maintain order in civil society.)

This neo-Lutheran view in the catechism is the opposite of Pelagianism, the view that humans are able to keep the moral law if they strive properly to do so. The contemporary Episcopalian is given the assumption that we are not going to be able to "fully obey" the commandments, thus encouraging the notion that we should not let our consciences be overly sensitive about trying to "keep" them. This assumption that we are not going to be able to fulfill the commandments does make some sense in the context of the 1979 Catechism because all of the commandments are rewritten as positive duties to perform and attitudes to have (which I will analyze further below), eliminating the prohibitive "Thou shalt not . . ." form.

This is a fundamental flaw in the Episcopal Catechism. By associating the prohibitions that are meant to be strictly kept with the positive general com-

---

[8]*Book of Common Prayer*, p. 848.

mands that cannot be fully realized, the Christian is given the impression that it is not realistic to expect to obey *any* of the Decalogue or of God's moral law. The flaw lies in not appreciating the logical difference between positive commands and negative prohibitions.

Let us take a moral norm common to Christians and to the wider culture: "Parents must love their children." Then let us treat as a specification of showing love this norm: "Never strike your child in anger." This prohibition will also receive very wide acceptance, as it does not prohibit moderate and properly applied corporal discipline. All parents will admit to falling very short of the ideal of showing consistently wise love; but many parents, Christian or not, have managed to discipline without angry physical blows. It is simply not right (and quite possibly highly dangerous when it comes to norms dealing with crossing sexual boundaries in families) to give the impression that many moral norms—the prohibitions—are not meant to be treated as absolutely directive of our behavior.

When we look at all Ten Commandments, we see that most of them are in the form of prohibitions:

1. You shall have no other gods before me.

2. You shall not make for yourself an idol.

3. You shall not make wrongful use of the name of the Lord your God.

4. Remember the Sabbath day to keep it holy; you shall not do any work.

5. Honor your father and mother.

6. You shall not murder.

7. You shall not commit adultery.

8. You shall not steal.

9. You shall not bear false witness against your neighbor.

10. You shall not covet . . . anything that belongs to your neighbor.

Only the fourth and fifth commands—keep the Sabbath holy (we dealt with the special status of this commandment above) and honor one's parents—are in the positive format, which prevents them from complete fulfillment due to our imperfections in "keeping holy," and our defective honoring. The rest, being prohibitions, are meant to be kept.

There are further difficulties with the first three commands because they deal with attitudes toward God in the face of our inveterate tendency to exalt ourselves and of our own self-deception. But once a false god or idol is recognized, it must be absolutely rejected as incompatible with loving God. As William Cowper put it in his hymn "O, For a Closer Walk with God": "The dearest idol I have known, whate'er that idol be, help me to tear it from thy throne, and worship only thee."

The last commandment is also exceptional in that it deals with attitudes rather than observable behavior, and thus it is subject to vagueness and frequent self-deception in facing the true nature of coveting things.

Thus for our purposes we focus on the four commandments that deal with external actions, that part of the moral law linked most closely with the norms provided by natural law. These laws, which deal with murder, stealing, adultery and lying, should be treated as absolute and binding, not as guidelines subject to setting aside in difficult situations.

We consider here two wrong approaches to understanding these moral commandments. The first is to transpose and expand them into positive requirements as the 1979 Prayer Book Catechism does:

- To show respect for the life God has given to us; to work and pray for peace; to bear no malice, prejudice or hatred in our hearts; and to be kind to all the creatures of God

- To use all our bodily desires as God intended

- To be honest and fair in our dealings; to seek justice, freedom and the necessities of life for all people; and to use our talents and possessions as ones who must answer for them to God

- To speak the truth, and not to mislead others by our silence[9]

There certainly is a value in reflecting and expanding on the moral values behind the commands and their implications for us; but in this form they become positive standards that we never fully live up to. This is most evident in the ninth commandment: to turn the prohibition against bearing false witness into a general obligation to speak the truth makes us reflect on all the situations where telling the plain truth must be qualified, and how none

---

[9]Ibid.

of us can (or should) always be open and transparent. The transmutation into positive guidelines can easily leave us with the impression that the important thing is to have right attitudes and intentions, and that we need not worry about complete obedience.

The second error starts with the real need to be more precise in definition. Not all killing is prohibited, such as self-defense, war and capital punishment. Therefore, to treat this as an absolute prohibition, we need to describe the action of killing as "unwarranted" or "disproportionate": "Do not kill anyone unless it is warranted." Similarly with the other commands: "Do not commit illegal theft"; "Do not have wrongful sex"; and "Do not intentionally deceive unless you work for the National Security Agency or have some other good reason."[10] The trouble with this approach is that absoluteness is purchased at the price of vacuity; they become tautologies, commands that all will agree with, but then we differ widely on, for example, what constitutes wrongful sex or what circumstances permit lying and deceit.

A full interpretation of the commandments will need to deal more precisely with the meaning of murder, bearing false witness and so on (adultery is the least susceptible to qualification); but once that is made more clear, Christians need to realize two things about these commandments: (1) they refer to a set of objective actions (independent of subjective intention); (2) they are absolute (i.e., norms without exceptions). There are some more complex cases, often dealing with life-and-death situations, where an action may have more than one set of effects and more than one "object" for the action. We will consider these in the treatment of prudence (chapter ten).

There is another recent Anglican Catechism that provides a sharp and valuable contrast to the approach of the 1979 Episcopal Catechism: the Anglican Church in North America has produced a catechism entitled *To Be a Christian*.[11] In section four, on Christian behavior, the new catechism presents a picture of Christian living based entirely on interpreting the Decalogue, and our understanding of the commandments should be guided by these

---

[10]See the discussion in John Finnis, *Moral Absolutes: Tradition, Revision, and Truth* (Washington, DC: Catholic University of America Press, 1991), p. 36. See also the response and further reflection by Oliver O'Donovan, "John Finnis on Moral Absolutes," *Studies in Christian Ethics* 6 (1993): 50-66.

[11]*To Be a Christian: An Anglican Catechism* (Ambridge, PA: Anglican House Publishers, 2013).

four principles: "Each commandment calls for positive action, forbids whatever hinders its keeping, calls for loving, God-glorifying obedience, and requires that I urge others to be governed by it."[12]

While this is a welcome counterpart to the Episcopal Catechism that reflected the era of situation ethics, there is an element of overreaction in that the primary moral category is simply assumed to be obedience to law. However, Christian discipleship is often presented in the New Testament in the framework of virtue, such as the imitation of Christ, growing in grace and living by the Spirit. The relationship between law and virtue, and what is to be our fundamental motivation in living the Christian life, are left unclear.

There is an understandable concern for the loss of Christian standards in modern Western societies, but this should not lead us to overemphasize the role of law in the Christian life by stressing absolute moral norms, and to assume that obedience is the chief virtue.

LAW AND THE CHRISTIAN LIFE

Not only Protestants or Anglicans were influenced by the popularity of situation ethics and were drawn to modify traditional moral norms. In Roman Catholic circles, in spite of (or perhaps partly because of) the well-worked out catechetical teachings in theology and ethics, many moral theologians developed ways of relativizing moral norms, through techniques such as the "fundamental option" (see chapter six), "proportionalism" (a means of disguising a consequentialist morality) and so on.

The 1993 encyclical *Veritatis Splendor* (*The Splendor of Truth*) by John Paul II[13] was in large part addressed to this problem, in the Roman Catholic context, of new moral theologies that tended toward situation ethics, or types of consequentialism or undue individualism in matters of conscience. The encyclical made a number of valid lines of critique of some of the new styles of Roman Catholic ethics. And it should be noted that the criticism came after a fine introduction with a strong treatment of Christian discipleship as attraction to the truth and goodness that God offers us in Jesus Christ. But one cannot help sensing that the trap of nomism—the under-

---

[12]Ibid., pp. 107-8.
[13]John Paul II, *The Splendor of Truth, Veritatis Splendor: Regarding Certain Fundamental Questions of the Church's Moral Teaching* (Washington, DC: US Catholic Conference, 1993).

standing of morality as obedience to law—has not been entirely avoided. In this line of thought I follow the comments of the late Herbert McCabe, OP, who responded to these issues with insight and wisdom from the 1960s on, and provided penetrating analysis of some weak points in *Veritatis Splendor*.

As McCabe put it, if you want to play football (soccer, for Americans), there is both a rule book and a training manual. The rule book will inform you about shots that are free kicks, what actions are fouls, when a player is offside, and so on. But there is another kind of book, a training manual (probably including, in our time, a series of video clips), produced by an experienced coach, which summarizes ways in which to acquire the skills of the game: how to practice evasive moves and attacking techniques, how to develop the ability to disguise your intentions and so on. The first kind of manual determines whether you are playing the game correctly or not, but it will not help you become a good player. Even the spectators in the stands can know and recognize when shots and plays are legal or not. To be a good player, one might begin with the material in the training manual, but skill is a matter of being able to translate these tips into actual moves on the field or pitch, and practicing and making these things second nature until one hardly needs to refer to the manual anymore.[14]

Veritatis Splendor, in McCabe's view, seemed to be an attack on those who want to read the rule book as though it were a training manual by those who want to read the training manual as though it were a rule book. "Neither seems to have averted to the act that they are logically quite different kinds of discourse. The rule book, for example, is about individual acts, whereas the manual is about how to acquire dispositions."[15] McCabe concluded,

> I think it [the encyclical] fails, because, despite its frequent references to
> St. Thomas, it is still trapped in a post-Renaissance morality, in terms of law
> and conscience and free will. Amongst Christians this commonly shows itself
> in attempts to *base* an account of Christian morality on the ten command-
> ments, and this can only lead to a sterile polarization of "legalism" or "liber-
> alism." You cannot fit the virtues into a legal structure without reducing them
> to dispositions to follow the rules. You can, however, fit law and obedience to

---

[14]Herbert McCabe, "Manuals and Rule Books," in *Considering "Veritatis Splendor,"* ed. John Wilkins (Cleveland: Pilgrim Press, 1994), pp. 61-68.
[15]Ibid., p. 63.

law into a comfortable, though minor, niche in the project of growing up in the rich and variegated life of virtue.[16]

If this analysis by McCabe has validity, and we apply it to our Anglican context, then the two catechetical treatments of the Decalogue considered above are also representative of the fruitless standoff between liberalism and legalism, each heading in contrary directions, but both sharing the mistake of trying to describe Christian behavior entirely on the basis of the Ten Commandments.

What this implies about the Christian moral life is that the larger constellation of goals and interests that shapes our actions and characters and course of life is determined by our personality, temperament and attractions toward certain friends, hobbies, careers, marriage partners, social commitments and so on, and how all of these are related to our vision of what is supremely good. There is no "rule book" for these major directions in our life, because they reflect our individual interests and sense of calling. The rules of morality come into relevance as operative principles for affirming or filtering out certain means for accomplishing goals. Lying and deception may tempt us by offering an easy way out of a potential problem; a sexual liaison may entice us; a shady business deal may generate quick profit; but we judge these actions as things to avoid. The system of law and moral rules and duties, as important as these are, has an occasional and secondary role to play within an overall motivational scheme of desire for God and an accurate view of discerning the goods that attract us to a fulfilled life.

What should we use as a training manual then? What should be the positive moral teaching or presentation to supplement the Decalogue? As a basic answer we could say, correctly, that Christ himself, the pattern of his relationships to God and other people, his attitudes and concerns, the qualities of his character are the revelation of God's will for us, provide the perfect and reliable exemplar. But more specifically, the teaching of Jesus in the Sermon on the Mount and especially in the Beatitudes, the list of spiritual qualities presented by Jesus as defining features of the Christian disciple, provide a compact summary. Many commentators have noted that the Beatitudes correspond closely to a description of Christ himself, as does the

---

[16]Ibid., pp. 67-68.

list of character qualities enumerated by Paul in Galatians 5 as the fruit of the Spirit.

In part two we consider the presentation by Thomas Aquinas of the seven virtues, the three theological virtues (faith, hope, love) coming from Scripture, of course, and the four moral or "cardinal" virtues coming from the Greek philosophical tradition. Did Aquinas make a strategic mistake in not using the Beatitudes or the fruit of the Spirit as the model?

The preliminary answer here is that the structure of the virtues used by Aquinas actually does incorporate the character qualities in the Beatitudes and Galatians 5. In the case of the Beatitudes, he links a specific beatitude with each virtue as a way of capping his explication, considering each beatitude as a sort of perfection of each virtue, made possible by the Holy Spirit.[17] It can also be demonstrated, as we see in the next chapter, that there is a close correspondence and overlap between the traditional virtues and Paul's list of the fruit of the Spirit.

For Further Reading

Thomas Aquinas, *ST* I-II, qq. 90-108.

Pamela Hall, "The Old Law and the New Law," in *The Ethics of Aquinas*, ed. Stephen Pope (Washington, DC: Georgetown University Press, 2002), pp. 194-206.

Herbert McCabe, *Law, Love and Language* (New York: Continuum, 2003 [1968]).

Oliver O'Donovan, "Christian Moral Reasoning," in *New Dictionary of Christian Ethics and Pastoral Theology*, ed. David Atkinson and David Field (Downers Grove, IL: InterVarsity Press, 1995), pp. 122-27.

---

[17]See Yiu Sing Lúcás Chan, *The Ten Commandments and the Beatitudes: Biblical Ethics for Real Life* (Lanham, MD: Rowman & Littlefield, 2012), p. 144.

PART TWO

9

VIRTUES

Moral Dispositions for Acting Well

A CHARACTER TRAIT OR moral disposition (or *habitus*) develops as a person chooses the actions that help to form and are characteristic of that disposition (see chapter five). Generosity, patience, fairness, perseverance, the ability to work under pressure and so on are virtues, or good dispositions and qualities of character that reveal themselves in patterns of observable behavior but are generated by a complex set of causes: basic temperament plays a role, but so do training, relationships, attitudes and examples that one holds as role models. It is easier to work on the virtues that come more naturally to us, or maybe to focus on one challenge at a time; in the moral life, however, that is not an option, and Christian discipleship needs to involve growth in all the virtues as an ensemble.

In view of the discussion in chapter eight, on the proper role of law in the Christian life, and at the beginning of my presentation of a virtue ethic based on Thomas Aquinas, we can benefit from the wisdom of the systematic theologian Stanley Grenz:

> The Christian vision, therefore, is neither a life of slavish devotion to duty nor the attempt to cultivate the proper set of virtues. Instead the ethical life emerges as we desire to be transformed according to the image of Christ. For the Christian the Lord Jesus Christ—and neither a list of virtues nor a delineation of duties—is the focus of the ethical life.[1]

---

[1]Stanley Grenz, *The Moral Quest: Foundations of Christian Ethics* (Downers Grove, IL: InterVarsity Press, 1997), p. 220.

This is not merely a useful reminder; it is an absolutely necessary starting point for a clear doctrine of the virtues: the Christian life is centered on conformity to Christ, and both fulfillment of the law and the supreme expression of human virtues were demonstrated for us in Christ.

What follows in the description of virtues has a "list" aspect, but only for the purposes of analysis and description. Atomizing the moral life into individual actions and norms, and into discrete character qualities or virtues, is a necessary but unfortunate aspect of any systematic moral analysis. But in contrast to Plato or Aristotle, or Confucianism, or any other system of virtues, the Christian life has an exemplar who is not merely a model, but is actually drawing us to be conformed to his image. The reader should keep in mind that in what follows in part two, which is organized around the virtues, duty and law are not set aside by this framework, but rather are subsumed and integrated, and that the "system" or network of virtues is both exemplified and transcended in the person of Christ.

The Interconnection of the Virtues

Following the function of practical reasoning (chapters two and three) and the development of patterns of intellectual and emotional dispositions (chapter five), we need to be able to choose correctly those actions that are best for our goals and purposes, and to establish by sound judgments (the virtue of prudence) a pattern of considering other people's needs and interests (which is the virtue of justice), of dealing with obstacles, discouragement and threats (the virtue of fortitude), and of managing well the enjoyment of life's pleasures (governed by the virtue of temperance or self-control).

But we can also see that good choices and actions depend on having the moral virtues already in place. Without a sense of justice, for example, we cannot have the virtue of prudence and be able to make wise choices, because our practical reasoning will be skewed toward a selfish perspective, fulfilling our own needs and desires at the expense of recognizing the claims of others. Similarly, without proper courage, we will not be able to carry through with our decisions, even when knowing clearly what ought to be done, in the face of hostility or adversity. And lacking temperance, and being inclined toward self-indulgence, we will tend to make choices in favor of experiencing pleasure or avoiding pain, and this, as we can easily imagine, may sabotage the wisdom and good choices that we may be capable of making.

This means that a person cannot have any of the moral virtues without having them all, at least in partial measure. We cannot be prudent and selfish, or courageous and self-indulgent. We cannot focus on one or two of the easier or more attractive virtues and develop moral character in a lopsided way.

Of course, the acquisition of specific virtues is easier for some than for others. Personality and temperament play a role, as do cultural, familial and educational background. We also find that certain character traits are easier for us to develop than other traits that are more of a challenge. Humility and self-control, for example, seem much more natural to some people than to others. It is worth noting, as Aristotle did, that it is possible to have the wrong kind of humility (poor self-esteem), or too much patience (never being provoked by injustice) and so on, so that some people have to work in the other direction to bring their affective responses up to the proper level for good moral character.[2]

Some may question whether we are now in a kind of circular logic: if practical reasoning depends on having the moral virtues, and if the moral virtues depend on the virtue of prudence (or practical wisdom), where is the starting point, and how can progress be made? If I am lacking prudence, I may never develop courage either, because that depends on making wise choices in the face of adversity, and that will be impossible for me if I lack prudence.

This difficulty is indeed part of the reason why the attainment of good moral character is far from easy, takes time and requires all the help we can get. Part of the answer is in education and training. The training of moral character is not just a matter of communicating moral principles, but of showing and living out the examples of the virtues, of enabling them to be patterns for others. One of the goals of bringing up young people is to provide an appropriate structure of disciplined living, so that the patterns of good actions are followed, become part of the lifestyle and later, we hope, become their own character traits. The process of habituation will occur, although in a somewhat external way until the actions are freely chosen, and for the right

---

[2]See the section "Emotion, Will and Moral Weakness" in chap. 5.

reasons, without the need for a pattern of behavior to be imposed. That this frequently breaks down, and that many young people go through a period of rejecting these patterns and then redeveloping their own patterns of behavior, shows the challenge and difficulty of cultivating virtue.

Another important part of the answer for the Christian is the church community, including friendships with other Christians. This is a consistent theme in the moral theology of Stanley Hauerwas, who points out to us the vital importance of having our minds shaped by the values and attitudes of the biblical narratives, and by sharing life in communities where we see and experience how lives and behavior are actually to be lived in accordance with the gospel.[3] Not only does the worship and life of a Christian community shape our minds and hearts, but also relationships with other Christians become occasions to see what is lacking in our own characters, to learn from the examples of others and to be accountable to each other in the mutual desire to grow in Christian discipleship.

THE FUNCTION OF THE VIRTUES

In the description of practical reasoning (chapter two) I established that our decisions are made by the joint operation of intellect and will: a judgment that an action is good with the concurrence of the will. This basic pattern of practical reasoning covers a great deal of our daily decisions, especially those that are ordinary or routine, that do not involve perplexity or a sense of conflict. Nevertheless, it represents an idealized pattern for practical reasoning unless the role of our affections and emotional life is properly included.

The decisions that we are most conscious of are precisely those where we experience doubt and conflict, the ones that do not go smoothly. There are the cases in which we are simply not clear about what is the right path to choose, when deliberation, analysis, advice and prayer are required. This is a matter of practical reasoning in its deliberative mode—a matter of discernment, analysis perhaps, and deliberation. What we are concerned with here, however, are the cases where there is a lack of harmony between the

---

[3]See Stanley Hauerwas, *A Community of Character: Toward a Constructive Christian Social Ethic* (Notre Dame, IN: University of Notre Dame Press, 1981); see also the essays in William Brown, ed., *Character and Scripture: Moral Formation, Community, and Biblical Interpretation* (Grand Rapids: Eerdmans, 2002).

judgments of our practical reasoning and the actual things that we do. We make decisions at the beginning of a day (perhaps writing out an agenda list) and then reflect at night that our intentions were imperfectly carried out. This could be the result of poor or overly ambitious planning, in which case these experiences may help us with more realistic practical reasoning.

In many other cases we may simply not "feel like" doing something. The laundry is postponed in favor of reading a magazine; we omit the exercise that we had decided to do; we eat more at dinner than we had originally planned; we curtail or omit our prayer time. We do not get around to writing the letter that we had planned, and we find that we had spent unplanned time on video games, or internet surfing or a number of other things not wrong in themselves but that in reference to our plans and prior decisions amount to a deflection from our aims. This is part of the human condition, of course, and part of the material for our reflection that "we have left undone those things which we ought to have done, and we have done those things which we ought not to have done."

More serious are the omissions and commissions that we recognize as sinful: actions contrary to the love of God and neighbor and corrosive of our character. We may know that we ought to be patient and kind, but in certain circumstances we feel provoked and incensed—perhaps by a totally unfair insult—and might respond with verbal attack or even physical aggression. When we cool down, we talk about the heat of the moment, the surge of passion that overtook our better judgment. We call this a lack of emotional control or a lack of patience, but a deeper analysis might reveal a wide range of possible factors.

Further, if we take the model of practical reasoning seriously, that actions are the product of intellect and will, and we say that an angry retaliation was purely an emotional response, then we remove it from a decision of practical reason altogether, and such actions become irrational. In other words, in some way an angry person, when provoked by another, sees the provoker as having deserved the attack and thus judges it as a good thing to do in that situation. There are actions triggered by psychological disturbances, such as Tourette syndrome, where a person utters shocking verbal abuse with no control. But in the case of a person who needs help with an "anger management" problem, the counselor does not solve the problem by prescribing a strong sedative. There is a moral dimension to ordinary human anger that needs addressing on all levels: intellect and will as well as emotion.

The angry person may have a warped perception both of himself and of others. He may feel that others are putting him down or "out to get him" (paranoid in a nonclinical sense); she may feel that she is not respected properly (and there may be a complex set of personal and experiential factors that have affected her self-image, and where psychiatric counseling can provide insight). But such persons may also have an unarticulated principle to teach others a lesson that they need to get what is coming to them; and we need to admit that this is a reasonable principle in certain situations where rebuke and punishment are sometimes the correct action to take. The person's will is too set on a perception of what is good in terms of his or her own self-interest. There is a failure to hold the good of others and of society in general sufficiently important. From a Christian point of view, this selfishness is an aspect of the fallenness of human nature and of original sin.

On the level of emotions, there are varieties of dispositions and temperaments. We talk about choleric or hot-blooded people, on the one hand, and calm or mild-mannered people, on the other hand. But the strength of angry emotions does not cause the aggressive response without being validated by the decision of intellect and will. All of us feel provoked at times, but we are expected to moderate and channel our aggressive impulses. What is required in the management of anger (and other emotional reactions) is the education of the emotions, the training over time of improving the way one sees situations, to improve the patterns of intellect and will so as to guide the emotional reactions in a better way.

Note how this explanation differs from a psychological model where the function of the will is to control or suppress the emotion. In widespread popular thinking, often found in Christian circles, the easy explanation for wrong actions involving emotion is that the conscience knows the right thing to do, but the person lacks enough "will power" to keep the emotions in check to follow the right course. The assumption is that the intellect through conscience has the right perspective, and that it is largely the irrationality of the emotions that threatens correct action. It is then the role of the will as arbiter to choose between obedience to conscience or to give in to the pressure of emotion. If one's will is weak, then irrationality triumphs.

This simple and common model has explanatory force in describing the experience of conflict and temptation, but it fragments the agent into separate agencies: a rational and objective conscience; unintegrated and dangerous emotions; and a will that becomes the moral center because it alone is responsible for the choice to obey or disobey. The Christian who wants to improve his or her moral character seems to be faced simply with the need to develop more will power to combat emotional force. It is too crude a model because it is unrealistic, a setup for discouragement, and far too limited in its ability to describe comprehensively the unity of the moral agent and the many ways in which grace is meant to assist in the growth of Christian character.

CLASSIFYING AND NAMING THE VIRTUES

Once we break away from the traditional four moral and three theological virtues, then the lists and different combinations proposed seem to become an arbitrary selection of character qualities that seem attractive or seem to be neglected and could benefit from attention and highlighting. Admittedly, there is a fair bit of variety in the lists of character qualities found in Scripture from the Old Testament, the Sermon on the Mount, the gifts of the Spirit in Galatians 5, and other lists of virtues, such as Colossians 3:12-16.[4]

Robert Roberts, for example, writes about a set of Christian emotion virtues: contrition, joy, gratitude, hope, peace and compassion.[5] What is the relationship of these to wisdom and justice? What about fear and courage? How do joy and peace relate to love? And what is the principle of selection and organization?

In his inspirational book *Becoming Good*, David Gill has organized fifteen character qualities under five different functional headings: (1) the "disciple" as faithful, holy and wise; (2) the "servant" as open, responsible and gentle; (3) the "leader" as righteous, just and merciful; (4) the "peacemaker" as loving, sacrificial and genuine; (5) the "ambassador" as hopeful, courageous

---

[4]See, for example, the treatment of Galatians 5:19-23 and Romans 5:3-5 in Daniel Harrington and James Keenan, *Paul and Virtue Ethics: Building Bridges Between New Testament Studies and Moral Theology* (Lanham, MD: Rowman & Littlefield, 2010), chap. 13, and pp. 109-13.

[5]Robert Roberts, *Spiritual Emotions: A Psychology of Christian Virtues* (Grand Rapids: Eerdmans, 2007), pp. 97-198.

and joyful.[6] With fifteen different virtues here, most of the classical Christian virtues (moral and theological) are included, but with the notable exception of temperance or self-control. Control of appetite for pleasure is perhaps not so attractive to modern consumer society; but then again, it is perhaps one of the most neglected and needed. Another problem here is that the true importance of some of these virtues is obscured when the basket of virtues is so generously expanded. Wisdom, for example, is dealt with in two pages tacked onto a chapter primarily about faithfulness. The reader is misled into thinking that wisdom is a desirable, experience-based, richer perspective on life rather than the absolutely essential sine qua non for any kind of moral life or the development of any other virtue.

There is a certain vagueness and lack of precision in N. T. Wright's recent book *Virtue Reborn*,[7] which sets aside the framework of the classical moral virtues, preferring the Christian character description given us by Paul in Galatians 5 under the heading "the fruit of the Spirit."[8] Even though Wright wants to emphasize the importance of Christians living in the real world with their feet on the ground, so to speak, he seems uninterested in the kinds of virtues that we may share in common with other people (the moral virtues) and draws our attention to four distinctly Christian virtues: humility, patience, chastity and charity. The question of the harmony of the theological virtues and the classical moral values is important, and it underlies my discussion below and in the following chapters organized around the virtues.

Even with the virtues indicated by N. T. Wright, however, distinctions need to be made between entirely new virtues (which Augustine and the Christian theologians following Paul did with faith, hope and charity) and those that overlap with the virtues of classical thought. Christians have a

---

[6]David W. Gill, *Becoming Good: Building Moral Character* (Downers Grove, IL: InterVarsity Press, 2000).

[7]N. T. Wright, *Virtue Reborn* (London: SPCK, 2010). The American edition is *After You Believe: Why Christian Character Matters* (New York: HarperOne, 2010).

[8]Note, however, the high degree of convergence, perhaps surprisingly, between the fruit of the Spirit and the traditional moral and theological virtues: if gentleness and patience are seen as central aspects of fortitude (as Aquinas did), and kindness and generosity as features of justice, then Galatians 5:22-23 forms a more detailed and spiritual picture of the traditional moral virtues, with the discernment and judgment of the Spirit understood to be the Christian's underlying source of wisdom (prudence).

distinctive emphasis on sexual self-control, certainly, but the virtue of chastity clearly is an aspect of temperance and self-control rather than a separate virtue. Likewise, patience seems to be best treated as a subvirtue of fortitude, not a separate virtue: the ability to resist pain, suffering, boredom and discouragement are related to the same character trait required to face other obstacles and dangers that cause fear; all of these tempt us toward escape and turning away from difficulty. Humility too, as Wright and others point out, is contrary to the Greek ideal of the self-confident "great-souled" individual, and it would seem to have more of a claim to be a distinctive Christian virtue.

In the Middle Ages there was flexibility in the number and treatment of the virtues, especially in sculpture and artistic depictions, sometimes because the artist needed a specific number of virtues to fill up the spaces needing to be decorated. For instance, on the door panels of the baptistery in Florence, Andreas Pisano depicted eight virtues and included humility (which with patience was often included) along with the three theological and four traditional moral virtues.

The problem with the contemporary listings of "free-floating" virtues is that they become the character traits most significant to the author and may reflect our culture's strengths and weaknesses. Our current liberal culture certainly would include tolerance as a prime moral virtue.

In contrast with a procedure of selecting virtues that to us seem relevant to the Christian life, Oliver O'Donovan reminds us that Plato linked the four cardinal virtues with a tripartite analysis of the human soul: temperance of the virtue of the appetite, fortitude of the spirited part (*thymos*) and prudence of the intellect, with justice as the virtue of the whole where each part finds its proper position subordinate to the part above in the hierarchy of the soul. Augustine took the emphasis on charity and Christian love and tended to subsume the moral virtues under the dominant virtue of love, signaling the shift to an emphasis on intention and state of the heart as the dominant moral factor.[9]

Thomas Aquinas, though a Christian theologian whose theology is based on Augustine's teaching and often offered as commentary and refinement

---

[9]See Augustine, *De Doctrina Christiana* I.39; see also Oliver O'Donovan, *Resurrection and Moral Order: An Outline for Evangelical Ethics*, 2nd ed. (Grand Rapids: Eerdmans, 1994), pp. 222-23.

on Augustinian principles, clearly retains the basis of the moral virtues as linked to the division of the soul. While it is true that love (*caritas*) is the form of the virtues, this is developed in a much more complete and subtle fashion than Augustine's sketchy account.

Following the treatment of practical reason, the *Summa Theologiae* contains a lengthy and masterful treatment of the passions and emotions, the will and intellect having been treated earlier.[10] This then sets up a thorough description of the development of dispositions, attitudes and patterns of reaction that apply to the intellect, will and emotions. These dispositions, when put into a moral context of choosing actions, become what we understand as virtues and vices, good and bad dispositions for action. The proper "subject" for each virtue (i.e., the appropriate aspect of the soul for the "location" of each virtue) is explained primarily in *ST* I-II, q. 56. Thus prudence, or wisdom for action, is the virtue of the intellect, and justice of the will. Prudence is the ability to reason well about actions: to deliberate, decide and execute actions well. Justice is the attitude of the will that considers the good or well-being of others, and it can be identified with a spirit of fairness.

So far, this is clear. But rather than a generalized virtue dealing with emotion, and rather than multiplying virtues for separate emotions, Aquinas divided the sensitive appetite, that part of the human psyche that experiences emotion, into two general groupings: those directly related to desire, and those related to an obstacle to our desire. Love (not the virtue *caritas*, but the basic emotion of desire, *amor*) and hate are basic emotional frameworks that we have toward many objects, while joy and sorrow are affective reactions to the presence or absence of the desired object.

Emotions such as fear and anger arise in us when we see something threatening our well-being; there is some kind of threat to us, or an obstacle to accomplishing our purpose, that must be dealt with. Hope and despair describe our possible attitudes toward attaining our purpose in the light of our assessment of the obstacle.

With this sketch of a summary of emotion to which Aquinas devoted a very detailed analysis, we can see the basis for the separate virtues of temperance and fortitude. Temperance governs those affections that may be

---

[10]The general nature and function of psychological powers was described by Aquinas in the general section on creation, at *ST* I. qq. 78-89.

called "desiring emotions" and are directly related to sense desire, including food and drink, sex, and other activities that we take delight in. Fortitude governs the contending emotions that arise when we feel attacked or thwarted in our purposes.

The moral virtues, in distinction from the theological virtues, may be acquired rather than "infused" (which is the technical term the tradition has used to designate the influence of grace). These moral virtues are developed by a pattern of good actions that gradually become part of one's character. A person who has good intentions, deliberates and decides well, and executes good actions, and is not deflected by contrary emotions, and has a developed consistent pattern of so acting, is developing the moral virtues.

We saw above that the moral virtues are a kind of package: they are interdependent and cannot be developed individually or in isolation. One cannot have the virtue of justice, for example, without having the prudence or wisdom to make good decisions at the right time and without the courage and persistence to act justly when tempted or pressured otherwise. A person cannot have one or two strong virtues and lack the others, because a virtuous person not only performs good actions, but also does so for the right reasons. For example, a person's sexual behavior may on the surface appear to be chaste and virtuous, without promiscuity or illicit affairs. But this abstinence from sexual activity could primarily result from fear and insecurity rather than reflect a properly developed virtue of temperance.

Let us take a real-life example. Shortly after the terrorist attacks on the World Trade Center in New York City in 2001, television commentator Bill Maher got into a controversy and lost his job for remarking on the bravery of the terrorist pilots, whereas most of the public was inclined to describe the attacks as acts of cowardice. The commentator was right in a technical sense, because carrying out the attack exhibited a certain highly developed form of steely nerve. Without the virtue of justice, however, and prudence, which the jihadists clearly lacked, their "courage" could not be considered a moral virtue, since their aims and intentions were immoral. One can give credit to the clever and efficient operations of the Nazis and be consistent in denying them any moral virtue. Actions directed to immoral ends become all the worse when carried out with ruthless determination and zeal.

THE CENTRAL ROLE OF PRUDENCE

Prudence, or practical wisdom, or wisdom in action is the acquired ability to reason well about actions, and it involves good deliberation, sound judgment and excellence in execution. Clearly, prudence is the key to good behavior and to the other moral virtues. The patterns of one's behavior, as well as the moral virtues, are built up by the many different decisions that are made, and they need to be made by a person with prudence.

We can go further and say that in a very real sense prudence forms the other cardinal virtues by setting their standards of rationality. In Thomistic terminology, prudence is the *regula*, the rule of the other virtues. This makes sense, because a virtue such as justice, which in itself is a sense of fairness, and a sensitivity to the needs of others, is rudderless without the discernment and judgment of prudence. In each situation where a decision needs to be made—for example, whether debts should be paid—it is obviously the practical reason that must discern and help execute the appropriate action.

This role of prudence as the measure for the other virtues is even more evident with fortitude and temperance. The emotions that have to do with fear and courage, for example, need to be regulated and channeled by reason, not ignored or suppressed, on the one hand, nor simply followed, on the other hand. The virtue of courage exhibits that quality of the "mean" that Aristotle analyzed (and perhaps pushed a bit too far in implying that all virtues have this character): the standard of right reason avoids the extremes of excess and lack in emotional appraisal and reaction. One can be too fearful (with phobias and the like) or react with fright in situations that ought to be faced. But one can also have too little fear, where risks are ignored or belittled, and life is endangered. Such a person we call reckless rather than courageous. Thus courage finds a kind of intermediate point between timidity and bravado.[11]

The very fact that we cannot beforehand say what is the "right amount" of courage or justice for someone to have shows that practical reason must be aware of the person's needs and goals and the circumstances, and make fitting decisions and actions in the light of each situation.

But the relationship of prudence to the other moral virtues is not only

---

[11]See Thomas Aquinas, *ST* I-II, q. 64; see also chap. 5 above.

directive and regulative. Prudence in turn depends on the soundness of the will and emotional management. In order for good decisions to be made, the overall orientation must be sound, with an attitude of justice toward the implications of social and personal relationships; otherwise, there may be pretty good deliberation and effective decisions made, but they may well tend in a selfish direction.

Similarly, we need to manage our anger and fear if we are to get the right benefit of our practical reasoning. Anger often will interfere with calm deliberation, and fear can be a factor any time, especially at the point of execution. Since execution, the production of an action, is really the point of practical reasoning, there is no prudence if a person comes to a sound decision about what to do and then through fear (perhaps of the consequences, or of others' opinion, etc.) omits or delays the action. Thus the acquisition of prudence requires the simultaneous acquisition of the other virtues. The moral virtues are manifestly interdependent. One cannot have one moral virtue without the others, just as one cannot develop one theological virtue (faith or hope or love) without the other two.

One question remains in this general account of the virtues: What is the relationship between the theological and moral virtues? This may be divided into two further questions: Can the moral virtues really exist without the theological? Are the moral virtues changed in quality by the theological virtues that are "infused" in us by the grace of the Holy Spirit?

The Augustinian reading (see *The City of God*) was inclined to write off pagan virtues as "splendid vices." In other words, the generosity, patience and self-control of the non-Christian, because they developed outside of a relationship of love for God, are so fundamentally flawed that they only appear to be virtues. When the apparent charm, kindness and fairness of distinguished citizens are merely surface qualities that mask an overriding selfishness (and all of us have met such people), then we can agree that true virtue is lacking. But there is something deeply problematic in denying to all individuals and cultures outside of a commitment to Christian faith the possibility of developing any of the moral virtues—prudence, justice, self-control and courage.

This issue is far from being just an academic theological point; it is of great importance in the attitude of the church to non-Christian religions, how missionary work and ministry are conducted, and, in this context of moral theology, how we view the possibility of shared moral values and cooperation with non-Christians in a multicultural society. In a helpful historical study (from Aristotle to the Enlightenment), Jennifer Herdt has described the problems that arise from restricting virtue to the influence of grace in a Christian context, arguing that we should not drive a wedge between love for God and love for self, or between the work of divine grace in our lives and the role of human agency.[12]

If we take a certain analysis of the Thomistic criteria of good action from chapter five above, we could easily draw a negative conclusion about the moral value of the actions of a non-Christian. If the overall end or ultimate telos for action is the wrong one, then there is a fundamental defect, and we could consider a person's character or actions as bad. This would be consistent with the moral analysis of actions that I described, where the aim, object and circumstances all must be correct for action to be considered good.

Thomas Aquinas, however, did not draw so rigid a conclusion. In his discussion of the question "Can moral virtues exist without charity?" (ST I-II, q. 65, a. 2) Aquinas provided a kind of twofold or qualified answer. In the framework of the natural ends of this life (such as friendship, fulfillment through work, raising a family and so on) the moral virtues can be cultivated and be said to exist in a limited sense, with qualification. If we take the larger view, including the spiritual dimension of life—truth and the ultimate end— then the virtues lack their correct orientation and are defective. This enables Aquinas to be faithful to the essential need for charity in the moral life, while still being able to affirm that from a human point of view the person who "lives a good life" with honesty and generosity, takes good care of a family, works at a job conscientiously, is involved in community, and so on, can be said to have moral virtues (in a qualified but real sense).

In response to the second question, on the change in the moral virtues in the life of grace, we may first of all say that the moral virtues become true virtues when God becomes the true object of faith, hope and love. All the aims and attitudes of the person become properly ordered to their final end. But beyond this there is an aspect of each moral virtue in the Christian that

---

[12]Jennifer Herdt, *Putting on Virtue: The Legacy of the Splendid Vices* (Chicago: University of Chicago Press, 2008).

receives an "infused" quality as a result of operative grace. Thus prudence, justice, fortitude and temperance are strengthened and receive an additional dimension by the work of the Holy Spirit.

At the conclusion of the treatment of each virtue Aquinas works out an appropriate gift of the Holy Spirit and a beatitude that corresponds to the moral virtue. The gifts of the Spirit are drawn from Isaiah 11:2-3 (and had become part of the tradition before Aquinas), while the beatitudes, of course, come from Matthew 5. Aquinas is somewhat aware of the artificiality of this medieval penchant for matching up these lists of qualities, yet the correspondences are not strained. For example, prudence has the gift of counsel, the leading of the Holy Spirit in matters that exceed our natural vision. Justice has the gift of piety, by which we are able to see what is implied in our worship of and service to God. There is a gift of spiritual fortitude that enables a person to accomplish the performance of actions in spite of adversities and perils. The deeper point being made here (beyond the terms or labels for these gifts) is that the incomplete and limited nature of the acquired moral virtues is given an added development and richness by the work of the Holy Spirit in our lives.

THE THEOLOGICAL VIRTUES

What we need are the virtues—all of them, for all aspects of our personality involved in behavior. We need to have our intellect, will and emotions strengthened, corrected and perfected if we are to be the human beings God means us to be.

Thomas Aquinas accepted this definition of virtue that had been pieced together from Augustine and become standard in the textbooks: "Virtue is a good quality of mind [*qualitas mentis*] by which one lives righteously, of which no one can make bad use, which God works in us without us." At first glance, this would seem to be unduly restrictive because it implies, first, that virtues belong only to our rational nature (and not our sense appetites or emotions), and, second, that there are only God-given virtues, no natural ones. For the first, virtues do operate primarily in intellect and will, but they become part of our affective or emotional natures as well, to the extent that they are guided by reason and so participate in the correctness of reason and will. For the second, Aquinas clearly affirms the possibility of natural virtues in a real (but limited) way; he could hardly be a follower of Aristotle without doing so.

But the Augustinian definition does point more directly to the theological virtues. The theological virtues are faith, hope and love, based on 1 Corinthians 13, but based also on certain logic of the relationship between intellect and will and our need for their proper orientation and perfecting. The "greatest" of these is love (1 Cor 13:13), not because the moral life can be reduced to some sort of essence or supreme principle of love, but because love is the principle of union within the Trinity, and is the principle of our own union with God. Love for God is at the very heart of morality because it fixes on God as our final end, that the truly supreme good is in fact the object of our desire, the overarching purpose for which all our actions are conducted. In this life faith and hope are necessary virtues, but once we leave this life for the presence of God, faith and hope are no longer necessary: the intellect enjoys the beatific vision directly, while the will comes to its full and lasting completion and enjoyment in continued love.

The theological virtues are supernatural in that their origin and goal is God himself. The natural powers of the soul that we have—intellect and will—are oriented to truth and goodness, but only as they are encountered in the observable world. Grace through the Holy Spirit is required for us to have God himself as the object of our hearts and minds, and thus these virtues are known as infused virtues. They are acquired not by our actions, but by our sharing in the divine life through the Spirit.

Love is a virtue of the will (which is directed to the good), while faith is a virtue of the intellect (directed to truth), and hope is the virtue directed to God as our final end and supreme happiness. The integration and interrelationships of the three theological virtues is a task that has been neglected somewhat, due to a number of factors, including the separation of theology into systematic, ascetical and moral compartments; and the confusion in the period following Aquinas about the relationship between intellect and will. We note the contribution that Oliver O'Donovan has made in his critique of Karl Barth's use of the structure of faith, hope and love in the *Church Dogmatics*, and his own provocative reflection linking faith, hope and love to self, world and time.[13] It will be a great benefit to the church if this is a

---

[13]Oliver O'Donovan, *Self, World and Time*, vol. 1, *Ethics as Theology: An Induction* (Grand Rapids: Eerdmans, 2013).

sign of future theological efforts toward a more fruitful grasp of the heart of the Christian life, helping us both intellectually and practically.

Note that there would be no virtue of love without faith. This follows from the description of the relation of intellect and will. The will, oriented to the good, is dependent on the intellect for the presentation or interpretation of the object that it can desire. A principle important for both Augustine and Aquinas is that an object not apprehended cannot be loved.[14] Of course, God is beyond our ordinary understanding, which is why the virtue of faith as a gift of the Spirit for our understanding is essential for us to be able to love God and our neighbor truly.

This is an important safeguard against the kind of vagueness that plagues many types of Christian ethics that reduce morality to love. There is often an indifference (if not hostility) to the relevance of dogmatic theology, and a desire to fashion an ethics that centers on an emphasis on love to generate an attractive system of morality. This is a legacy of the Enlightenment, which valued the moral teachings of the Bible and the Christian heritage that could be adapted to our common social life over the supernatural features of the death and resurrection of Jesus Christ, and the depreciated need for conversion, redemption and sanctification. A kind of culmination was reached in the situation ethics of Joseph Fletcher, in which the one guiding principle, "Always do the loving thing," apparently was completely severed from any sense of the need for love to be rooted in the worship of God in spirit and in truth.

Thus the theological virtues are united, and one cannot have one virtue without the others. There is no love without faith and hope, no faith without love and hope. The devils who are said to believe and tremble (Jas 2:19) have a kind of "belief" in that they recognize the existence of God and know certain things about him, but are actually devoid of faith because they absolutely lack any dimension of love and hope.

The theological virtues must be actualized in the concrete thoughts and actions of our lives in order to grow and flourish. This is where we have some control and responsibility. Regular worship and prayer and participation in the sacraments are the means not only through which our minds

---

[14]See Thomas Aquinas, *ST* II-II, q. 4, a. 7, on the primacy of faith among the virtues.

and hearts are reminded of the reality of God as creator, redeemer and sanctifier, but also through which we have the opportunity to realign and affirm with our whole beings this fundamental relationship. We then bring this vision and conviction ("Go in peace to love and serve the Lord") to the framework by which we make all our decisions. Our intentions, deliberations and decisions are conducted in the light of the truth that we have about God, our acknowledgment of him as the overarching object of our love and the hope we have in God as our final happiness.

In the treatment of the individual virtues that forms the last section of the book I treat the moral virtues first, followed by the theological. This was not the pattern of Thomas Aquinas, who began the long section in the *Summa Theologiae* on individual virtues with faith; but we note that there is good precedent for beginning with the moral virtues that we share with human beings in general. This allows us to highlight a certain basic shared moral development (e.g., fairness, regard for others, basic kindness, control of anger), followed by the difference made when the theological virtues of faith, hope and love are added. They are, of course, not simply layered on top of the moral virtues; rather, they deepen and transform the other virtues within the context of a relationship with God and his kingdom.

FOR FURTHER READING

Thomas Aquinas, *ST* I-II, qq. 55-70.

Romanus Cessario, *The Moral Virtues and Theological Ethics*, 2nd ed. (Notre Dame, IN: University of Notre Dame Press, 2009), pp. 45-71.

Joseph Kotva, *The Christian Case for Virtue Ethics* (Washington, DC: Georgetown University Press, 1996), pp. 69-142, on the theological links and biblical connections.

Livio Melina, *Sharing in Christ's Virtues: For a Renewal of Moral Theology in Light of "Veritatis Splendor,"* trans. William May (Washington, DC: Catholic University of America Press, 2001), chap. 5, "A Christocentric View of Ethics."

Jean Porter, *The Recovery of Virtue: The Relevance of Aquinas for Christian Ethics* (Louisville: Westminster John Knox, 1990), chaps. 4, 6.

10

WISDOM IN ACTION

S OME VERY FINE treatments of virtue continue to use *prudence* for the virtue of good practical reasoning, while others use *practical wisdom* (the Latin word is *prudentia*, the Greek term is *phronēsis*). In modern English *prudence* conveys a cautious approach to planning for the future, often referring to the management of investment portfolios and more specifically to self-protective strategies that seek to reduce potential risks.

Though an improvement, *practical wisdom* can be somewhat misleading by giving the impression that it is basically a matter of good reflection and analysis before a decision is carried out, and the problem with that will be dealt with below. No term is completely apt, so the reader will find that for reasons of variation and because the correct description is more important than the label we use, the terms *practical wisdom, prudence* and *wisdom in action* are used interchangeably in this chapter.

What kind of virtue is the intellectual virtue required for acting well? In his recent book on Christian character N. T. Wright devotes a chapter to being "transformed by the renewal of the mind," referring to Romans 12:2.[1] Wright helpfully expounds Romans 12 and relevant portions of Ephesians and Colossians to develop the importance of seeing situations and actions from a new point of view, to let the Spirit and the Christian community shape our vision and reactions along the lines leading us toward Christ's kingdom. Decisions and actions must be guided not by feelings but by a renewed intellect, a mind that has good reasons for seeing things in certain

---

[1]N. T. Wright, *After You Believe: Why Christian Character Matters* (New York: HarperOne, 2010), pp. 135-79.

ways. In commenting on Philippians 1:9-11, where Paul prays that love may abound, Wright points out that love needs to increase with knowledge and discernment, so that love is informed by "a thought-out habit of the heart."[2]

There is also much insight and helpful spiritual advice in the recent practical book by J. I. Packer and Carolyn Nystrom on divine guidance.[3] But there is some lack of consistency in explaining the nature of wisdom and prudence (similar, of course, to the Bible itself in its unsystematic language of heart, mind and wisdom). Packer and Nystrom treat Christian prudence with reference to C. S. Lewis's definition of "practical common sense," but then they define wisdom in a rather narrow sense as "the hard thinking that . . . the assessing of advice requires."[4] Components of this kind of wisdom are a clear grasp of the gospel of Christ, with the liberation of forgiveness; a conscience that responds to biblical truths and values; and a "resolute realism in facing the true and full facts of every situation."[5]

In an earlier section on wisdom, however, wisdom becomes a very broad and inclusive virtue indeed:

> First, wisdom is about understanding; second, it is about worship; third, it is about goals and the ends that should be in view in the life we live; fourth, wisdom is about strategies, or means to these ends; fifth, wisdom is about relationships; sixth, wisdom is about self-control; and seventh, wisdom is about humility.[6]

This description accomplishes something similar to Augustine's recasting of the moral virtues in terms of love, because Packer and Nystrom's list pretty much covers the entire gamut of moral virtue except for fortitude. Self-control ought to be considered a separate virtue, and "wisdom in relationships" is really the domain of justice and love. That wisdom easily becomes a catch-all for moral character in general (just as love has) points to the fact that wisdom and the other virtues are mutually interdependent, a point already made and expanded below. Removing these aspects that belong to other moral virtues from their definition, we can focus on the three ele-

---

[2]Ibid., p. 157.
[3]J. I. Packer and Carolyn Nystrom, *Guard Us, Guide Us: Divine Leading in Life's Decisions* (Grand Rapids: Baker Books, 2008).
[4]Ibid., pp. 160-61.
[5]Ibid., p. 162.
[6]Ibid., p. 122.

ments identified by Packer and Nystrom as features of practical wisdom: understanding, recognizing goals and overall purposes, and perceiving the means or strategies for achieving these goals.

In this chapter I will concentrate on the basic human virtue, the traditional cardinal virtue of prudence, which is shared, in its basic characteristics, by Christian and non-Christian alike. This implies that the classical thinkers could speak of *phronēsis* or *prudentia* and describe a moral virtue that, in some limited sense, is a good character quality able to produce actions that show some measure of wisdom and goodness.

WISDOM (AND WILL) FOR ACTION

At the outset I draw attention to the real standard or "bottom line" measurement of prudence or practical wisdom: right actions. The person who is good at thinking through moral issues, the ethicist who can analyze case studies with helpful insight, the counselor who gives wonderful advice to clients are not examples of the virtue of practical wisdom unless their own lives are following the right pattern. There is often a gap between knowledge and performance, and well-informed and clever people can have blind spots in relationships, be poor at making decisions or at carrying them out at the right time and in the right way. This stage of practical reason, which we call execution, is the most critical and important part of the virtue of prudence or practical wisdom. This is stressed by Thomas Aquinas in the introductory question on what the virtue of prudence actually is:

> The activity of reason goes through three stages. The first is taking counsel, which as we have seen, is inquiry in order to discover. The second is forming a judgment on what has been discovered. So far we have not left theory. Practice, however, is another matter. For the practical reason, which is meant for the doing of something, pushes on to a third act, namely of commanding; this consists in bringing into execution what has been thought out and decided on. And because this approaches more closely to what the practical reason is for, it is the chief act of the practical reason, and so of prudence as well. (*ST* II-II, q. 47, a. 8)

Some very fine Christian philosophers, theologians and communicators have written clearly and persuasively about the true nature of prudence but have neglected to emphasize this point. C. S. Lewis and Herbert McCabe drew attention to the feet-on-the-ground nature of this wisdom, that it is more like "good sense" (McCabe) or "practical common sense" (Lewis), and brought out the feature of good judgment.[7] This is a good antidote to the emphasis on knowledge of cases (casuistry) and the intellectual application of principles in moral reasoning. But what Aquinas wants to emphasize even further is that the ability to deliberate well and make discerning judgments about what should be done is only preparatory to action. If you do not carry out in action your brilliant insights and decisions, you lack the virtue of prudence. The coach may have spent hours on analysis and developed a clever game plan, but if in the hustle of the game the coach is distracted and fails to execute it in actual competition, there is a definite lack. Your good intentions, your "to-do lists" and plans for the future, are all very good (and may exhibit a certain insight, practicality and wisdom), but if they are not translated into actions, there is no true virtue of practical wisdom in action/actuality.

Of course, the reason for the gap between good thinking and action, between plan and performance, is often due largely to emotional factors (assuming for now that the preceding thought and judgment is thorough, clear and well-founded). For example, a book is recommended to us, and we decide that it would be useful for the essay we need to write, but then we postpone reading it because of some interesting television programs. Fear and anxiety keep us from marching ahead with very fine plans that we make; psychologists can multiply and amplify the various emotional obstacles that distort our lives and prevent us from achieving what we are called to do (and perhaps have many times definitely decided to do).

This underscores the importance of the point of the interdependence of the virtues. It may indeed be sloth, fear, attraction to certain pleasures that keep us from doing certain things and the lack of the virtues of courage and self-control are directly related to those emotional patterns; yet the lack of those virtues means that we also lack prudence, the true wisdom for acting well. Self-control and fortitude require reason and prudence for their correct development; but so does practical wisdom require the ac-

---

[7]See Herbert McCabe, "Aquinas on Good Sense," in *God Still Matters*, ed. Brian Davies (New York: Continuum, 2002), pp. 152-65. C. S. Lewis dealt briefly but helpfully with prudence in the chapter on cardinal virtues in *Mere Christianity* (first published in 1952).

quisition of the other moral virtues for a person to truly have the wisdom for acting well.

There are a couple of important reasons why practical reason and the virtue of prudence have not been understood so well. The first involves the bias that we put on reason itself, and on wisdom being a fascinating mental process rather than the vital connection between reason and action. From Plato we have understood vision and contemplation as the highest form of human activity, and then we have subtly restricted intellectual activity to be equivalent to logical reasoning and analysis. In so doing, we forget that what Aristotle had in mind as a model for *phronēsis*, practical wisdom, was not the clever critic or even skillful adviser, but rather a person fully engaged in civic and political affairs and leadership responsibilities, such as Pericles. It is a mistake, I am quick to admit, most likely to be made by those in a position to be writing treatises on ethics— philosophers and academics.

The second reason why the performance of the concrete action is not associated with the virtue of prudence is our faulty model of practical reasoning, which splits intellect and will. I have alerted the reader to this earlier (chapters two and three), but the emphasis on will as the "deciding" factor in action is extremely hard to root out. Our inherited explanation (or default model, if you like) is basically that the practical reason (and so the virtue of prudence) is responsible for deliberation, analysis of choices and a kind of identification or selection of the suitable action in the circumstances; but then the will is the force that puts the choice into action: it is "really" the will that decides. This is indicated by the persistent translation of *liberum arbitrium* ("free choice") as "free will," as if the will is the responsible factor in choice of action, and the intellect is not a principle of freedom.[8] In this faulty will-centered view of human action, if emotions or other factors interfere with carrying out good actions, then the fault lies with the will (perhaps for not keeping emotions "in check"). We must consciously set aside this faulty reductionist model (of the will determining action) if we are to understand that practical wisdom, a virtue of the intellect, is responsible for the execution of good actions.

---

[8]See the evidence and more technical discussion in Daniel Westberg, *Right Practical Reason: Aristotle, Action, and Prudence in Aquinas* (Oxford: Clarendon, 1994), especially chaps. 6 and 7.

WISDOM FOR THE STAGES OF PRACTICAL REASON

At the heart of practical wisdom is the ability to make good judgments. In the process of practical reasoning (chapter three) I highlighted the judgment at the stage of decision as the conclusion of the practical syllogism "This is the good thing to do." It is that judgment, the *krisis* aspect of *prohairesis*, which translates our desires and intentions and freedom to act into a specific concrete action. It is a judgment of the intellect because it involves seeing a situation, awareness of desire and making the rational connection between purpose and specific action leading to it.

Good judgment is also required at the stages of deliberation and execution. When we deliberate by considering possible options, or by asking the advice of others, or perhaps even consulting books or technical manuals, we use judgment in sorting through the variables and narrowing down the options to one course of action.

Good intentions, good ability to deliberate by analyzing and comparing options, and even the ability to make good decisions are no substitute for actually carrying out good actions in the right way and the right time. That is why Aquinas makes the stage of execution the characteristic and key aspect of practical wisdom: the person who has good practical reasoning is, above all, the one who acts well.

The judgment required at the stage of execution is awareness of the appropriateness of the decision to act. In most cases the decision to act leads to action because there is no doubt or conflict. In cases where there is an element of doubt, or the need to act in a way contrary to feelings that we might have, the judgment in the stage of execution is one that affirms the correctness of the choice of action for the circumstances. Execution is not simply the will carrying out what the mind has already decided. A slight change in circumstances, or the realization that the nagging doubt that one tried to silence in deliberation and decision, requires a reassessment and reconsideration of the decision itself, and instead of performing the action the agent reconsiders. But even in the majority of cases where the action follows upon decision, the person makes the continuing judgment that the decision previously made is indeed correct and appropriate. This certainly requires good judgment and the virtue of wisdom.

Many of us have decided to send a sharply worded email in reply to a criticism or insult or to a view so erroneous that it requires clear and forceful rebuttal. Sometimes we are saved from making a bad situation worse because although we had already decided in favor of this action (by setting aside other tasks and sitting down at the computer to write a paragraph or two with the strong intention of letting a person know our thoughts and reactions), having good judgment at the moment of execution reminds us to reconsider that the indignant reply that we were about to send does not fit the situation; this may be because in a calmer frame of mind we recognize that it would be counterproductive, or that it would unfairly hurt the other person.

How to discipline a child is an illustration of the many facets of practical wisdom. On the level of knowledge there are competing theories forming a rather wide spectrum between lax indulgence and rigorous demands. Much of this variation is cultural, and is subject to shifts in custom and outlook. The generation of baby-boomers supposedly raised on the laissez-faire methods of Benjamin Spock contrasts sharply with the contemporary "tiger mom" approach of severely high demands and harsh discipline.

From a Western point of view, Japanese parents are very indulgent to young children, letting them engage in tantrums, yell at their parents and so forth, with a minimal amount of correction. From a North American point of view, this ought to result in undisciplined and ill-mannered citizens when these children are older; however, the cultural pattern develops otherwise. Through a combination of society and school (where teachers and society as a whole provide a strong structure of discipline and expectations), and supported by family relationships, the child makes the transition from indulgence to discipline and conformity that perhaps work all too well in shaping adult Japanese attitudes and behavior (there are indications that this traditional pattern has lost some of its hold on the current generation).

Part of the reason why parental wisdom resists being systematized into neat techniques is that there is no one-to-one correlation between parental discipline and how children turn out. Other factors, such as peer pressure, general culture and individual temperament, play a major role. All of us probably know children who have come from horrific family situations of abuse and neglect but who developed into mature, attractive and fulfilled adults, while other children from much more benign and affirming environments develop patterns of negative reaction or rebellion.

Good judgment is required in assessing situations. Parents need to develop skills of sensitivity to the child's temperament and make judgments about the severity of guilt, when the child is likely to be avoiding the truth.

There is a level of theoretical knowledge, and a level of awareness of the particular child. But an important part of parental wisdom is self-awareness and the management of patterns of reaction modeled by parents and led by emotional reactions. One reason behind the contemporary disapproval of corporal punishment is the difficulty of punishing without anger.

Take, as another example of the need for practical wisdom, telling the truth to a patient afflicted with an incurable and fatal condition. You might be part of the medical team, a chaplain or a close relative. You might well have a high regard for the importance of being truthful and having integrity as well as a conviction that patients have a right to know about their condition. Yet wisdom in such a situation involves having not only good truth-telling principles, but also skills in assessing the condition and needs of the patient, the circumstances. The psychology of the patient (perhaps feeling angry) will be a factor in the decision to share and communicate the truth in a gradual disclosure.

Also, the decision of the caregiver is certainly affected by his or her own psychology and attitude toward death. Fear of death sometimes can lead to an inability to share openly and constructively, or instead it can distort the communication of information in a clinical and distant fashion so that the "truth" is communicated in a poor or clumsy fashion.

This kind of wisdom is built up by instruction, experience and reflection. There will be a value in texts, seminars and workshops, following the advice and examples of mentors. Medical and psychological experts offer a theoretical basis of conditions and patterns. There is no substitute for personal knowledge of the patient's attitudes, desires and reactions. But wisdom will also require self-awareness and the ability to keep personal feelings and attitudes from interfering with what is the best care for the patient.

ASPECTS OF PRACTICAL WISDOM

Along with memory, insight and the ability and willingness to learn from others, practical wisdom involves skill in reaching decisions quickly. The ability to consider options and deliberate well is an important aspect of practical wisdom, but one can envision situations where the disposition to go through detailed comparisons of alternatives can sometime militate against effective decision and action.

An ability to recognize the features of a situation with shrewdness and insight is an important asset. There are occasions, of course, when time for diligent deliberation is required, but there are other situations that call for wisdom and good judgment but also require accuracy and quickness.

Being good at deliberation is not the same as having the ability to make sound judgments.[9] As Thomas Aquinas puts it, "Many are good at counsel yet lack the good sense to form a sound judgment" (*ST* II-II, q. 51, a. 3). Excessive caution and lack of courage can keep a person from reaching a firm decision in a timely fashion. Those with special training and affinity to see and understand different angles and aspects of a question or course of action (such as academics and lawyers) may be able to give good advice but lack the ability to make effective decisions themselves.

Practical wisdom may sometimes recognize that an unusual situation occurs where the ordinary rules are no longer a good guide. Aquinas cites the common example (going back to Plato) of returning a weapon to one who planned to do harm. Ordinarily the owner of the gun or knife has a legitimate claim to have it returned; but when the owner has malicious intent, the ordinary rules of property no longer apply. In such situations, wrote Aquinas, "we ought to judge matters of this kind by certain principles higher than the ordinary rules." The specific name, *gnōmē*, used by Aquinas (and borrowed from Aristotle) for this subvirtue,[10] is not so important as the recognition that in some situations the ordinary line of reasoning is subject to a higher principle; here the common good or the safety and well-being of the community is of more relevance than the provisions for private property.

Failures in wisdom can occur predictably from various causes. Simple lack of information and training, along with the inability to recognize the complexity of a situation, often are factors. If this is a result of mere lack of experience, there may be little responsibility or culpability, and the mistake may be a fruitful part of the development of the virtue of practical wisdom. But there can also be inordinate haste, a lack of patience to examine and deliberate (or to take counsel from other sources). In some of these cases

---

[9]See Thomas Aquinas, *ST* II-II, q. 51, a. 3.
[10]For Aquinas's treatment of *gnōmē*, see *ST* II-II, q. 51, a. 4.

the ignorance can be willful, in the sense that a person is unwilling to take the care or attention that most people would recognize as necessary.

There are instances of psychological barriers to good deliberation, decision and execution because of desire to avoid the full consideration of an issue. An obvious example is the difficulty of facing one's own death, which results in lack of planning. But patterns of avoidance develop in most people having to do with resolving conflicts.

Accurate vision of the situations that we face and deal with is essential. As William Mattison puts it, "How we see the way things are, whether our vision is accurate or not, drives how we act."[11] Extreme examples of this are anorexic individuals who see themselves as "fat" even when the evidence on the scale, and in objective appearance, is clearly otherwise.

Less extreme and more common examples are the ways in which we read into other people's actions and statements malicious or insidious motives. Relationships often are injured as a result of drawing the wrong conclusions, misunderstanding motivations. The injunction from Jesus, "Do not judge, so that you may not be judged" (Mt 7:1), applies primarily, it seems, to the attempt to discern and judge the motivations of others. Here the comparison between the log in our own eye and the speck in the eye of our brother or sister is apt: we often deceive ourselves, assume that our own attitudes are above criticism and have the temerity to be unduly harsh in the judgments that we make about the attitudes and motives of others.

The many ways in which practical reason and good judgment can go astray or be distorted and the need we have for real wisdom here are well expressed by Packer and Nystrom:

> We fallen humans excel at self-deception when it comes to decision making. We shut our eyes to inconvenient facts, we naively rely on our own imperfectly trained consciences, we make exceptions to rules to favor ourselves, we listen only to people who say what we want to hear, we decide on policies and courses of action in unawareness of our own deep-down motives, ambitions, and rivalries; and so it goes on. In decision making we must ever seek honesty, humility, and prudence, and without the gift of wisdom we shall always miss all three.[12]

---

[11]William Mattison III, *Introducing Moral Theology: True Happiness and the Virtues* (Grand Rapids: Brazos Press, 2008), p. 96.

[12]Packer and Nystrom, *Guard Us, Guide Us*, p. 137.

SPECIALIZED PRUDENCE IN DILEMMA SITUATIONS:
THE PRINCIPLE OF DOUBLE EFFECT

There are some situations where taking action may have bad immediate effects that are intrinsic to the action itself. In order to rescue a child who has been left too long in an overheated, locked automobile, you might have to smash one of the windows for access. Any hesitation about damaging someone's property or the cost of repair is completely outweighed by the good of rescuing the child.

But there are other situations in which the action taken appears to contravene an absolute moral principle, such as the taking of an innocent life. An operation to remove a cancerous uterus from a pregnant woman will unfortunately result in the removal and death of her fetus. Or a police officer attempting to disarm a terrorist may have no recourse but to use violent force that will result in the death of a hostage, say, or of innocent bystanders.

It would be different, of course, if the physician did not know that the woman was pregnant (if the fetus was at a very early stage), or if the police officer was not aware that hostages had been taken. But we want to focus on situations where the action taken involves knowingly taking innocent life.

The principle of double effect hinges on the question of intention: What is the primary intention of the action? In the one case, it is to save the life of the mother by a surgical procedure to which there is no alternative; in the other case, it is to disarm a threatening terrorist by the most effective use of force that the police officer can determine. The surgeon does not intend to perform an abortion, and the police officer does not intend to kill innocent civilians.[13]

A common objection is that if one knows these evil outcomes ahead of time, how can one choose the actions that produce them without really intending them? Could you buy a lottery ticket and say, "I want to purchase a chance to the win the big jackpot coming up, but I don't believe in supporting the gaming industry"? One cannot split intentions in this way. If you have moral scruples about supporting gambling, then you should not indulge your desire to cash in on a chance to win big.

---

[13]For much more detailed description of consideration of further difficulties in understanding or applying double-effect analysis, see Steven Jensen, *Good and Evil Actions: A Journey Through Saint Thomas Aquinas* (Washington, DC: Catholic University of America Press, 2010), especially chap. 2, on intention.

In what way is "double effect" different? It involves two effects only accidentally and not inherently related. Surgical removal of the uterus (hysterectomy) is normally a therapeutic procedure, and it is an unfortunate and undesired circumstance that a fetus is also involved. Police action is a lot less predictable, and some groups of terrorists may routinely use hostages as "human shields"; even so, the lethal actions needed to disarm them are essentially directed at the terrorists, with every possible precaution used to minimize harm to civilians caught up in the situation.

One way to come at this is to ask whether there would have been an abortion if there had been no surgery indicated. If both mother and physician had been planning on gestation and delivery, then the fact of the abortion is, strictly speaking, *praeter intentionem*, beyond intention. The surgery that unfortunately resulted in an abortion was aimed (in the morally relevant way) strictly to the indicated surgical procedure, even when they know that the surgery will destroy the fetus.

Wars are messy, confusing, sometimes unbelievably horrific and notoriously corrosive of moral ideals and standards. For Christian ethics, the application of moral principles to waging war is made all the more difficult by a significant and respectable body of Christian thought that considers warfare inherently immoral from the beginning, and the admission that one is intending to kill enemies automatically disqualifies the action from moral justification. Despite this, and despite the ambiguities in some actual situations, we can see how the principle of double effect may be applied. In the bombing of a German munitions factory in World War II, let us say, we can separate, morally, the intention to damage the war-making capabilities of the Nazis from the death of civilians, even if the crude guidance systems provided little accuracy, and it was known that many ordinary people would die. Yet such bombing was fundamentally different (again morally) from bombing whole swaths of the cities of Dresden and Leipzig with the specific aim of damaging morale, causing panic, or just general destruction.[14]

It is important to note that the double effect analysis does not at all become equivalent to justifying an evil action by the good results that it produces. First, there must be a primary action with its own intended object

---

[14]For much more extensive and refined assessment of double-effect reasoning in warfare, see Nigel Biggar, *In Defence of War* (Oxford: Oxford University Press, 2013).

that is good (or at least indifferent). The evil effects are accompaniments ("collateral damage," if you like) that occur at the same time and are inseparable from performing the intended act. Second, the ends-justifies-the-means type of reasoning applies to results that occur some time after the action. In traditional double-effect analysis, the kind of situation where the fetus is aborted by direct action for the sake of the mother's health, for example, would not be considered licit.[15]

Finally, we must note that just because a police or military action is justified (e.g., to disarm a terrorist), the action taken must bear in mind the type and imminence of threat, the likelihood and scope of incidental damage that could well occur. Bombing entire residential city blocks where a suspected shooter might be hiding certainly would be effective in removing the threat, but it would be grossly contraindicated by the loss of life.

With these points in mind, we can summarize the criteria required for an action to come under bona fide double-effect analysis:

1. The act itself is good or at least indifferent.

2. The good effect of the act is what the agent intends directly, and only permits the evil effect.

3. The good effect must not come about by means of the evil effect.

4. There must be some proportionately serious reason for permitting the evil effect to occur.[16]

Another area in which double effect analysis is applied is in end-of-life situations, where the distinction between euthanasia and proper care for the dying person may appear to be murky. A physician may prescribe a morphine drip to ease the pain of the patient, perhaps in increasing dosages. One effect of the morphine may be on heart and lung function, so that along with relief from pain, the patient's life may be shortened. In such a case the caring physician is intending to provide relief from suffering, not to cause death to occur more quickly, even though that may well be the effect of the medication. Here there will be little observable difference between proper

---

[15]For the traditional Catholic analysis, see "Abortion," in *Dictionary of Moral Theology*, ed. Pietro Palazzini (London: Burns & Oates, 1962), pp. 6-11.

[16]William E. May, "Double Effect," in vol. 2 of *Encyclopedia of Bioethics*, ed. Warren Reich, rev. ed. (New York: Macmillan, 1996), p. 316.

care and euthanasia (hence the murkiness), but there is a very real difference possible in the attitudes and intentions of those providing care.

In these difficult situations it is still necessary for the intention to be directed to a good action. And one value of considering these cases of double effect is to make even clearer the moral impossibility of choosing an evil act in order to produce good results.

Can Non-Christians Develop a Virtue of Practical Wisdom?

Can one be wise and have the virtue of practical wisdom without being a believer in Christ or following God's will and the Holy Spirit? In the important and comprehensive sense, true practical wisdom is possible only for those rightly related to God: "The fear of the Lord is the beginning of wisdom" (Ps 111:10).

The wisdom for action that Plato and Aristotle described as *phronēsis* was not completely illusory, however. We know that non-Christians can have wisdom within certain spheres and can develop admirable characters (from certain points of view). Thomas Aquinas distinguished two different kinds of practical wisdom or prudence found in non-Christians. The first type is the kind of ability to succeed well at a line of activity, but where the purpose is defective morally. A safecracker could be highly trained and skilled and plan a bank break-in and safecracking operation meticulously, but as with the World Trade Center terrorists, this is to use skills in deliberation and decisiveness for immoral purposes. The defect in wisdom is obvious here.

There are, however, many people whose lives are directed to proper goals and purposes: a respectable and productive career, raising a family and contributing to the community. People need not be believers to be able to have good goals and the wisdom to plan and choose actions to lead to these goals. According to Aquinas, we can see this as a genuine but incomplete kind of wisdom (*ST* II-II, q. 47, a. 13)—incomplete because it lacks a fully comprehensive view of the nature of reality and the meaning of life. Thus complete prudence, or wisdom for action, is connected with understanding God and his kingdom, and actually directing one's life toward the kingdom of God and his righteousness.

This is partly related to natural law or, more loosely, to the natural grace available to human beings in understanding some of the correct elements of a successful, productive and happy human life. Herbert McCabe has expressed this aspect of the ordinary acquisition of wisdom and the moral virtues by people who lack faith in God or even any knowledge of him:

> You don't need God to reveal it to you that there are ways of eating and drinking and generally conducting your life that will keep you healthy. And you don't need God to reveal it to you that there are other ways that will be bad for you. You learn these things from traditions of human knowledge and from your own experience. In the same way, you don't need God's revelation to tell you that there are ways of living with others, ways of behaving, that will encourage friendship, a peaceful harmonious society, and a reasonably flourishing human life: ways of living that will enable you to grow out of being infantile, greedy, selfish and aggressive into a mature person that people enjoy having about the place. And you don't need God's revelation to tell you that there are ways of living that have just the opposite effect. You don't need the Bible to tell you that.[17]

Of course, all human beings, Christian or not, experience a tension between knowledge and inclination, and the tendency toward selfishness. This is partly addressed by the cultivation of other virtues that train emotional patterns and inclinations in line with the good principles that we hold; but as Christians, we also know that knowledge of God and the Spirit that directs and strengthens us in that ultimate direction is critically necessary for true wisdom, and is available only through grace.

PRACTICAL WISDOM DEPENDS ON THE OTHER VIRTUES

We know that the development of character and virtue depends on the development of a pattern of performance: by performing repeated acts representing good and wise choices, we develop a positive trait of practical wisdom. In a simplistic and mundane way, the ability to drive a car well is developed by a pattern of making good driving decisions in various situations, such as assessing road conditions and anticipating the maneuvers of other vehicles. Skills in cooking, deer hunting or trombone playing are developed by good memory and judgment, and improvisation when necessary.

---

[17]Herbert McCabe, *God, Christ and Us*, ed. Brian Davies (London: Continuum, 2003), pp. 63-64.

The skills and patterns and the judgment to use them appropriately become second nature.

As we ought to expect, the development of practical wisdom as a guiding virtue of our entire pattern of action is much more complex and difficult to acquire than learning to drive a car. That is partly because the ability to act well depends much more on having not only correct principles and good judgment, but also good emotional dispositions and attitudes toward others. Being able to control feelings of fear and anger through the virtue of fortitude, to control desires relating to pleasure through the virtue of self-control and to be well disposed to the claims and needs of other people through the virtue of justice are essential if practical wisdom is to be effectively developed. Otherwise, good decisions will be compromised by reluctance to carry them out through fear, laziness, self-indulgence and neglect of others.

There is actually still some force in the analogy with good automobile driving that allows us to see the importance of attitudes and emotional disposition. All of us have observed drivers who have technical skills but lack courtesy. There are drivers who, when a slowdown occurs in a construction zone, give themselves the permission (contrary to justice and not just to courtesy) to pass by on the shoulder and jockey for a superior position at the front of the line of traffic. On the other hand, there are drivers who may be intimidated by the speed and volume of traffic and lack the confidence necessary to take their turn at a four-way stop or to accelerate in a timely fashion when entering an expressway at rush hour. We can see that the driver with the finest driving habits is the one who not only knows and observes the rules of the road, and has technical competence and experience to correctly judge tricky driving situations, but also has respect for other drivers, and a kind of Aristotelian mean with respect to confidence behind the wheel, being neither hesitant nor aggressive.

Thus, being able to develop a virtue of practical wisdom depends not only on the ability to have good judgment, but also directly on the development of the virtues of justice, fortitude and self-control. Without the other moral virtues, a person may have good intentions, a knowledge of correct actions and even good decisions, but lack an ability to carry out the corresponding good actions. Since, as I stressed at the beginning of this chapter, actually performing good actions is the crucial and revealing characteristic of wisdom, no one can have the virtue of practical wisdom without the other moral virtues. People cannot perform a pattern of good actions and cultivate the virtue of wisdom in actions without also developing the qualities of character that deal with the importance of relating well with others, and with the complex assortment of attitudes and emotions in their personalities.

By the same token, justice, fortitude and self-control cannot be developed without practical wisdom, because it is good judgment that recognizes the ways in which to relate well to others, the correct occasions and degrees of the enjoyment of pleasure, the appropriate blend of caution and boldness, perseverance and stubbornness. The moral virtues depend on practical wisdom, but practical wisdom cannot be developed without the simultaneous development of the other moral virtues.

For Further Reading

Thomas Aquinas, *ST* II-II, qq. 47-56.

James Keenan, "The Virtue of Prudence," in *The Ethics of Aquinas*, ed. Stephen Pope (Washington, DC: Georgetown University Press, 2002), pp. 259-71.

Herbert McCabe, "Aquinas on Good Sense," in *God Still Matters*, ed. Brian Davies (New York: Continuum, 2002), pp. 152-65.

Josef Pieper, *The Four Cardinal Virtues: Prudence, Justice, Fortitude, Temperance*, trans. Richard Winston et al. (Notre Dame, IN: University of Notre Dame Press, 1966).

Charles Pinches, "Pagan Virtue and Christian Prudence," *Journal of Religious Ethics* 23 (1995): 93-115.

Daniel Westberg, *Right Practical Reason: Aristotle, Action, and Prudence in Aquinas* (New York: Oxford University Press, 1994), chaps. 13-17.

11

JUSTICE

W HEN WE COME TO the moral virtue of justice, we encounter considerable difficulty in part because the meaning of the term *justice* (*iustitia* in Latin, *dikaiosyne* in Greek) in English has shifted away from the moral virtue toward describing a political or social condition, and because the category of justice has been broadened in the last few centuries to include important areas of political theory such as human rights and equality.

In the rather lengthy account of justice by Thomas Aquinas (*ST* II-II, qq. 57-122) we recognize the sections dealing with stealing, lying, and personal injury and self-defense as aspects of justice, where a criminal justice system is something required by society. But there are other topics, such as gossip, slander, cursing and hypocrisy, and more positively gratitude and generosity, and areas of religious practice, such as tithing, prayer, true worship and the avoidance of idolatry, that seem completely out of place in a discussion of justice.

Oliver O'Donovan has pointed out that the Western Christian tradition has inherited three different senses of justice.[1] First, there is a state of affairs, "a kind of moral equilibrium" between the members of a group or society. In the Roman legal tradition the term *ius* ("right") described this moral equilibrium, providing one stream of justice, and this sense is closest to the modern sense of justice. We can think of many examples of the call for justice meaning rectifying injustice in society for marginal groups, such as the battle against slavery and various civil rights move-

---

[1] Oliver O'Donovan, *The Ways of Judgment: The Bampton Lectures, 2003* (Grand Rapids: Eerdmans, 2005), pp. 6-7.

ments. Second, there is justice as a moral virtue, the disposition to render to others what is their due, described by Plato and Aristotle, and the background, of course, to the treatment by Aquinas. Third, there is justice as effective performance, the act of "judgment" that sets wrong right. The source for this sense is mainly from the Old Testament with the concern of God for righteousness, and the hopes, expressed often in the Psalms, that God would step in, vindicate his people and bring about justice. There are different words for justice and righteousness, but they clearly overlap, as in Jeremiah 9:24: "Let those who boast boast in this, that they understand and know me, that I am the LORD; I act with steadfast love [*ḥesed*], justice [*mišpāṭ*], and righteousness [*ṣĕdāqâ*] in the earth, for in these things I delight." When people "demand justice," they are expressing a desire for vindication and rectification, reflective of the biblical desire for the application of judgment; they want somebody to do something about an existing wrong.

Thus Roman law, Greek philosophy and the Bible have played major roles in the formation of our rather complicated conception of justice. While I bring out the main features of the focus on justice as a moral virtue in the Thomistic account, we should note that justice as right and justice as judgment were included and briefly dealt with by Aquinas in *ST* II-II, q. 57 (*ius*) and q. 60 (*iudicium*), although judgment is treated in its philosophical rather than biblical sense.

JUSTICE AS A MORAL VIRTUE

If you were called on by a lawyer or a court of law to be a favorable character witness for a colleague, neighbor or friend, you probably would comment on aspects of the person's civic character—being law-abiding, volunteering for things, showing a sense of responsibility, courtesy and friendliness to neighbors, having general interest in community affairs, and so on. You probably would want to use such words and phrases as *decent, honest, reliable, polite* and *a good citizen* (assuming that there is truth to these descriptions of your friend).

These qualities that make up the virtue of justice or uprightness have to do with our relationships with other persons. Wisdom, courage and self-control, the other moral virtues, deal with our behavior and actions, which

of course affect other people around us, but the area of concern for each of
these virtues is within the mind or soul: having the correct outlook, principles and judgment (practical wisdom), and having the right kind of emotional response, control and expression (courage and self-control). With the
uprightness form of justice, the focus is relational, treating people as they
deserve or need to be treated. In brief, the heart of this moral virtue is the
attitude of mind and the developed disposition to give people what is due
to them, expressed in the traditional definition of justice in the Roman legal
tradition by the third-century jurist Ulpian: "The perpetual and constant
will to render to each one his right."[2]

A good place to start is the Old Testament picture of the just or righteous
person. In Psalm 15 the question is posed about who may dwell in and share
the presence of God. The answer is a fine list of character traits: those who
do right, who speak the truth from the heart, who do not slander or take
revenge, who keep their word (even when it is costly), who do not take
bribes. The reader may note a couple of omissions from the ideal pictured
in this psalm. One is that the upright person "does not lend money at interest" (Ps 15:5), and this was part of the biblical case against the practice of
usury, which was banned throughout the Middle Ages. In the *Summa Theologiae* account of justice we find a question of several articles (*ST* II-II, q. 78)
devoted to a defense of the prohibition of charging interest. Without going
into the details of the refinements in biblical interpretation and philosophical and theological analysis, we can affirm, even though the position
on usury has changed, that there is still continuity in emphasizing fairness
in finances, and a moral line drawn between reasonable interest and the
shadier practices of predatory lending.[3]

More importantly, we note in Psalm 15:4 that the righteous are those "in
whose eyes the wicked are despised, but who honor those who fear the
LORD." Even removing the malicious overtones of despising, and also
making the distinction between sin and the sinner (so that people are not
despised as people but rather for behavior that is wicked in the sight of God),

---

[2]See *Digest* I.1; *De Justitia et Jure* 10 (cited in Thomas Aquinas, *ST* II-II, q. 58, a. 1).
[3]The standard treatment on the medieval prohibition of usury has been John Noonan, *The Scholastic Analysis of Usury* (Cambridge, MA: Harvard University Press, 1957). More recently, see
several important studies on Aristotle and the medieval theologians by Odd Langholm.

this points to an apparent attitude of smugness and self-righteousness that emerges now and then in the Psalms.

A central part of the gospel of Jesus Christ has to do with clarifying the relationship of being right with God (*dikaiosyne*). Only Jesus himself was fully righteous, with a clear conscience before God. All other human beings are unrighteous and cannot make themselves right in the sight of God. By accepting the offer of forgiveness made possible through the punishment suffered by Jesus, we can enjoy the position of standing guiltless before God.

It is has become difficult to convey to the modern mentality the dynamics of sin and punishment, the wrath and judgment of God, and the necessity for the atonement. I can do very little here to help convey these things more clearly (without straying off topic), but I can point to an important aspect of the traditional treatment of justice or uprightness: God is among those who are due something from us. If there is a God, then he is due our worship and devotion and obedience. God is meant to be the object of our love, and his grace makes possible a divine and transcendent friendship. But underneath this—or before this, if you like—there is what we owe God, what he has a right to expect from us: allegiance and obedience. It is because God actually has a right to our complete obedience that sin is a fatal problem; we can do nothing ourselves to make amends for failing to give God his due.

Now we can understand the Decalogue as the precepts of uprightness, because they deal with the different types of persons we owe something to. The first set of four commandments speaks of what we owe to God, while the rest deal with authorities (such as parents) and then how other people deserve to be treated by us.

Is the Decalogue relevant outside of the Jewish-Christian-Muslim heritage? One can reply with Paul's teaching in Romans 1 that there is some knowledge of God available to all, even without the knowledge of the Mosaic law. It is noteworthy too that in the discussion of religion as a part of justice, Thomas Aquinas quotes from Cicero, that religion is a part of justice because "it consists in rendering service and ceremonial rites to some superior being that men call divine."[4]

The commandments direct us to having a proper view of God and not

---

[4]Cicero, *De Inventione Rhetorica* II.53 (cited in Thomas Aquinas, *ST* II-II, q. 80, a. 1).

fashion a false or idolatrous view of God. Prayer, tithing and keeping the Sabbath constitute part of the set of attitudes and behaviors that we offer to God. There is no limit to what we owe to God, of course, and there is a certain open-endedness in that we can never tell ourselves, "I have offered God enough now"; but the whole framework or conception of repaying God from a sense of duty or justice is swallowed up in the offering of our whole selves to God in love.

Somewhat like our obligation to God is our relationship to our parents, wider family, community and nation. The English term *piety* does not really express the Latin *pietas*, which refers to that virtue combining respect, affection, devotion and sense of duty. It springs from a proper reflection that we literally would not exist without our parents, nor would we be who we are without our community, culture and country. The sense of civic responsibility may be shown in donations to charitable organizations, offering volunteer time and efforts, and supporting educational institutions where we received training. Like our worship of God, there can be no question of putting an amount or value to what we owe; what we are able to offer in return is an expression of thanks and recognition for benefits and blessings that are inestimable.

RESTITUTION

One requirement of justice is to restore what rightly belongs to another. A person may borrow an item with the consent of an owner, with or without a written contract, and simple justice requires the return of the item.

In the case of theft or obtaining property unlawfully, it may be that in addition to restoring the property a penalty will be imposed. Restoring the item (e.g., paying back the money) restores the equilibrium; but there is also the sinful nature of the action that may be dealt with by a fine or some other form of punishment.

In the ordinary course of life we discover that we incur debts that we are not aware of at the time, or we neglect to return favors (such as an invitation to dinner); people forget to return books that they have borrowed from us; and we neglect or forget to make amends. Since we are both on the giving and receiving ends of injustice, there is often a kind of rough equalization that works things out. But the cultivation of the virtue of justice is to develop a greater sensitivity to what we owe to others. In the words of Josef Pieper, "The just man recognizes when wrong has been done, admits his own injustice, and endeavors to eradicate it. Who would deny that we touch here the sore spot in all reciprocal relationships, and that the basic way to realize commutative justice does in fact have the character of restitution?"[5]

Oliver O'Donovan might be one to deny this. He has been critical of the way the metaphor of exchange and equality has been embedded in the modern Western notion of justice. While the analysis of Aristotle had a certain broader scope and flexibility, it has been overly simplified, and the principle of exchange, or "reciprocity in giving and receiving," has been taken to be, for example by Wolfart Pannenberg, as a fundamental natural law principle underlying all societies. The consequences of this focus in Western political thought have not been helpful:

> Treating reciprocity as the sole matrix of justice has its practical result in that totalizing of market-theory which was such a feature of late twentieth-century political and social thought. In order to find exchange equivalencies within complex political and social relations, we are sometimes forced to treat as loss what any sound philosophy regards as gain.[6]

Thomas Aquinas's theory of justice does not share the same problems as that of many modern political philosophers; yet his emphasis on justice as reciprocity and rendering what is due must be noted as a limitation in scope that might have been corrected by more attention to Scripture and more independence from the inherited categories.

JUSTICE AND SOCIAL VIRTUES

The limitations of the term *uprightness* become more apparent when we consider the outgoing moral qualities that should characterize relationships with each other.

Thankfulness and gratitude are attitudes that we ought to have, and ought to express, when we consider the benefits that we receive; in a very real sense thankfulness is something that we owe. To God we owe thanks for, as *The Book of Common Prayer* says, our "creation, preservation, and all the

---

[5]Josef Pieper, *The Four Cardinal Virtues: Prudence, Justice, Fortitude, Temperance*, trans. Richard Winston et al. (Notre Dame, IN: University of Notre Dame Press, 1966), p. 80.
[6]O'Donovan, *Ways of Judgment*, p. 36.

blessings of this life" and for salvation through Christ above all else. God as the cause of all else is our supreme benefactor, and being reminded of this and returning thanks is our joyful duty.

We also owe thanks to our parents and other caregivers, and to many other people who give something of their time, resources, thought and care. There are social conventions that govern the appropriate expression of gratitude, such as written thank-you notes for wedding gifts and dinner invitations; but much of the benefits that we receive from other people is subject to judgment about the nature of the gift and whether we should return the favor with a similar gift, or if an expression of thanks only is what is required in the situation.

The ungrateful person can be defective at several different levels. Let us take as an example someone who goes out with close friends for lunch but rarely picks up the bill and so usually is on the receiving end. This could be a failure of practical reasoning in carrying out the act of paying: someone else grabs the check first, or the person in question is disorganized, forgetting to bring cash and having no credit card handy. But the moral fault could be deeper, such that the person is failing to notice how many times others are actually paying, and thus how he or she is receiving a benefit from someone else; or it may even be that the person has such an inflated, self-important view of things as to think it only natural that others would pay for his or her meals.[7]

To say that our judgment of the situation is always involved is to say that our assumptions and attitudes about who we are, what we deserve from others and our valuation of the concern and efforts of others can easily be distorted and affect the way we regard circumstances where we benefit, and thus our sense of gratitude or entitlement.

To keep social relationships working smoothly, there is a virtue of amiability or friendliness that is also part of what we owe to each other. To be pleasant and courteous is not an optional extra; it is part of what other people deserve from us and what we ought to contribute to the people we come in contact with, because the fruitful ordering of relations in society in a very real sense requires this expression of good will on the part of everyone.[8]

---

[7]See the treatment by Thomas Aquinas, ST II-II, q. 107, especially a. 2.
[8]See Thomas Aquinas, ST II-II, q. 114.

TRUTH AND DECEPTION

Honesty, truth-telling and integrity constitute a basic virtue in virtually every culture, as it is apparent what damage and breakdown in society can result from dishonesty and deception.

If we start an account of truth-telling from a natural law point of view, analyzing the purpose and nature of speech, then consistency requires a prohibition of saying anything false (any statement not in accordance with reality), because this would contravene what human nature is meant to be. This extreme approach has the attraction of a kind of heroic zeal for moral purity, which we can see in the treatment by Immanuel Kant: "To be *truthful* (honest) in all declarations is therefore a sacred unconditional command of reason, and not to be limited by any expediency."[9] Kant is famous for his conclusion, consistent with his principles, that one must tell the truth even if it means disclosing the hiding place of someone fleeing a murderer.

Withholding or disguising the truth in response to certain questions from young children or dying patients takes into account primarily what they need and what we owe them, the primary concern of justice. Here being people of truth cannot mean the telling of direct lies; however, the question of timing and how much of the truth to share, and in what way, becomes part of the judgment that we bring to the situation. As Gilbert Meilaender has put it, "As long as we think of ourselves as having taken the first step on a road that leads ultimately toward 'the whole truth,' we do not necessarily lie or deceive when we disclose less than we know."[10]

If we place truth-telling in the context of uprightness, the dynamic of personal relationships and what is owed to other persons, then certain difficult situations can be handled without sacrificing honesty or commitment to truth. An obvious area is a warlike situation of conflict with enemy nations or other hostile groups (such as drug dealers, organized crime rings and so on); assuming that taking forceful action against them is the right thing to do, then deception and disguise and withholding the truth are part

---

[9] Thomas Kingsmill Abbott, trans., *Kant's Critique of Practical Reason and Other Works on the Theory of Ethics*, 6th ed. (London: Longmans, Green, 1923), p. 363.

[10] Gilbert Meilaender, *Bioethics: A Primer for Christians*, 3rd ed. (Grand Rapids: Eerdmans, 2013), pp. 76-77.

and parcel of the modus operandi: the enemy has forfeited the right to truth and honesty (and of course will not be expecting it).

Oliver O'Donovan has taken such occasions (extreme though they may be) when we need to make a judgment to hide or disguise the truth, even to practice "outright deception," as the chief example of the need for discerning wisdom in Christian moral reasoning.

> If we decide that a demand to know the truth [e.g., by the secret police searching for a dissident] is weakened when it is asserted with a hostile and illegal purpose, then we have discerned something important about what truth itself demands of us and the conditions for the exercise of truthfulness. We have not merely decided that mercy should prevail in this case; we have gained an understanding of the law of truth itself.[11]

LIFE, DEATH AND SELF-DEFENSE

Suicide represents an assault on one's own life by one's own hand. As such, there is a deep contradiction, as we read in the treatment by Thomas Aquinas, to both natural law and *agapē* love. A basic inclination of the nature of all beings (not just animals) is to keep themselves in existence, and so suicide is a violation of a basic law of being. It also violates the love that we should have for ourselves and our bodies as objects of God's love and as a person for whom we have primary responsibility.

Further, suicide is contrary to justice and what we owe to others. We are members of a community and belong to society as a whole. When we eliminate ourselves, we harm and do an injustice not just to society at large, but also the various overlapping communities that we belong to: family, the set of relatives and friends, the neighborhood, and the local church community. And, of course, suicide is an injustice to God. As Aquinas puts it, life is God's gift to us, and he retains the right to decide matters of life and death. If we make this judgment, we usurp the role and privilege of God (*ST* II-II, q. 64, a. 5).

In considering self-defense against attack (*ST* II-II, q. 64, a. 7, following the discussion of suicide in a. 5), Aquinas uses the same starting point of the

---

[11]Oliver O'Donovan, "Christian Moral Reasoning," in *New Dictionary of Christian Ethics and Pastoral Theology*, ed. David Atkinson and David Field (Downers Grove, IL: InterVarsity Press, 1995), p. 127.

natural inclination to keep oneself in being. The kind of forceful action required to defend oneself is morally legitimate, as long as it is proportionate to what is required, and as long as harming the assailant was not directly intended. This provides the basis for the famous and controversial doctrine of double effect (for further explanation, see chapter ten above, on prudence).

What we are interested in noting here, however, are two points. First, judgment is required to assess the situation, and to make sure that the response matches the need. Presumably, Aquinas would have agreed that in some cases a call for help, or running away, would be the wiser course. Second, Aquinas's appeal to a natural inclination to self-preservation is not a requirement of justice or the determining principle, as though self-defense, by lethal force if necessary, is a kind of automatic principle based on natural law. If so, there would be a conflict with Jesus' teaching in the Sermon on the Mount about turning the other cheek, and not returning evil for evil.

In some questions later on in the section on justice Aquinas raises the question of whether one ought to endure verbal attacks or insults (*contumelia*). He quotes Augustine's commentary on the passage in Matthew about turning the other cheek (Mt 5:39) and concludes this way: the Christian always needs to be prepared to take the course of patience and turn the other cheek, but is not always bound to do this actually. His reasoning is that our Lord was not always consistent: sometimes he was silently patient, while at other times he answered back, as in the instance when he was before the high priest and was struck on the face, and then challenged those who had hit him (Jn 18:23).[12]

What this indicates is that Aquinas did not forget about the Sermon on the Mount or let a principle of natural law take precedence over the gospel and example of Christ; rather, discernment and good judgment are required about the time and mode of fulfillment of all moral directives, whether from natural reasoning or from revelation and the teaching of Jesus.

PUNISHMENT AND JUSTICE

There is an uncomfortable but undeniable aspect about uprightness and justice: sometimes in recognizing what someone deserves, we conclude that

---

[12]Cited in Thomas Aquinas, *ST* II-II, q. 72, a. 3.

on the basis of that person's faulty behavior, he or she should get some sort of rebuke, reprimand or penalty. Thus the willingness to give people what is due to them also includes willingness to "teach them a lesson," perhaps. The virtue of being willing to give to each person what is due thus includes punishment, which can be defined as the infliction of pain on those who have voluntarily violated codes of conduct.[13]

Here we are not speaking of a personal virtue of justice or uprightness, directing our choices and actions in our ordinary human relationships, because the right or obligation to punish belongs to a person in authority. In civil society there are judges trained and appointed for this; and in more informal situations, such as the work place or educational institution, the need for punishment falls on those designated with authority.

Parents are expected to punish children, and institutions may punish members of the community for violating certain rules. These less serious cases enable us to understand the essential dynamics of justice as punishment. If a teenager breaks a curfew rule (and it is established that there was negligence or intentional fault involved), then the parent may impose a punishment of, say, grounding for some days. In the case of this kind of punishment, the purpose of punishment is primarily for training. It is educative in nature, so that the teenager will be able to understand the rules of behavior and live in accordance with them. Justice comes into the picture in relation to the fairness of the rules, the assessment of circumstances and the imposition of punishment.

The object is not mere external obedience, either; rather, it is to bring about an appreciation that structures of behavior are not simply imposed to limit freedom, but are framed for the common good of the family, for secure and healthy life, and lessons of authority. There may also be a deterrent aspect, also a social function, especially if there are younger siblings who are watching to see how seriously to take the household rules. The principles and patterns apply, obviously, also to society at large.

The purpose of punishment is not primarily retributive—that is, to "pay back" the teenager, to impose some pain or cost—simply because he or she has done something wrong. Normal parents have no interest in causing pain

---

[13]This definition of punishment is drawn from the article on punishment by D. W. Van Ness in Atkinson and Field, *New Dictionary of Christian Ethics*, p. 710.

or difficulty per se (although at times they are indeed tempted!); rather, they have an interest in the character development of their children. Thus punishment in a family setting (or in other social organizations) is rehabilitative and disciplinary, with an eye on the deterrence of others. Thus punishment is not retributive in the sense that the person has done something that needs to be paid back, which some theories, including some conservative Christian views, attach to the commission of crime.

This is one of the problems generated by understanding punishment as primarily a matter of retributive justice (the influence of justice as reciprocity?): there is supposedly a moral imbalance that occurs with crime and wrongdoing, and the wrongdoer must suffer a penalty that matches the offense. This is the theory of punishment as pure retribution, the moral necessity of inflicting punishment commensurate with the crime. This theory imagines that there is a kind of moral equilibrium that is thrown out of balance with a crime, and that equivalent punishment in the form of pain or cost to the offender must be suffered. It lies behind phrases such as "paying one's debt to society" in reference to a prison sentence having been served out.

To be sure, there is a retributive element to punishment, in that the offender must deserve to be punished. This is important in order to keep a proper check on the other purposes of punishment. If deterrence is the only or primary goal of punishment, then there is a certain logic in the proposal to take a few criminals and punish them very hard to "put the fear of God" in the rest of the population. That might be effective, in the short term, perhaps, but it would be unjust in punishing people out of proportion to their offense.

Or if we take correction, training or rehabilitation as the primary purpose, then what is to stop authorities from continuing the punishment until the desired reform occurs? If the "lesson has not been learned" or the prisoner seems incorrigible, then the theory might well tell us to extend the punishment until the correct level of reform has been reached. This was a favorite technique of the Soviet treatment of dissidents, and of the Chinese Cultural Revolution under Mao Zedong, and virtually permanent imprisonment could be meted out under the guise of psychological or ideological rehabilitation. Thus keeping the retributive aspect, and closely connected with the notion of what the offender deserves, a reasonable limit may be set to the extent and severity of punishment.

Let us consider a plausible basis for the biblical authorization of retaliation or retribution, the so-called *lex talionis*, and its context from Leviticus.

> One who blasphemes the name of the LORD shall be put to death; the whole congregation shall stone the blasphemer. Aliens as well as citizens, when they blaspheme the Name, shall be put to death. Anyone who kills a human being shall be put to death. Anyone who kills an animal shall make restitution for it, life for life. Anyone who maims another shall suffer the same injury in return: fracture for fracture, eye for eye, tooth for tooth; the injury inflicted is the injury to be suffered. (Lev 24:16-20)

Setting aside the matter-of-fact brutality (distasteful to modern sensibilities) characteristic of ancient Near Eastern judicial punishment (and in some respects surviving in Islamic justice), we must realize that some of these provisions are judicial rhetoric, or the statement of a principle of retribution that would not actually be applied as such. The passage about "eye for eye, tooth for tooth," well-known because of its citation by Jesus, if taken literally, meant that if someone knocked your tooth out, then the attacker must suffer the loss of an equivalent tooth. Or if someone hacked off your foot or gouged out one of your eyes, then the same thing would be done to the assailant in return; and Leviticus 24:20 does seem to put this into a general principle by saying, "The injury inflicted is the injury to be suffered."

The impracticality and waste involved in this mode of punishment would quickly become apparent: the loss of your own eye would not be much easier to take just because you knew that your attacker was also missing an eye; and now two families have disfigured and handicapped members. Hebrew criminal law developed a system of compensatory fines, so that for the loss of an animal or injury to the body, compensation appropriate to the loss incurred had to be paid out.[14]

A principle of strict retribution thus was not applied in less severe criminal cases, but only in the case of premeditated murder, in which case compensation was not allowed: the principle of "life for life" must be literally enforced

---

[14]Gordon Wenham, *The Book of Leviticus* (Grand Rapids: Eerdmans, 1979), p. 312.

because human beings are made in the image of God.[15] We will briefly consider the relation of Jesus and the New Testament to this; but this much at least can be said about crimes other than murder: they were not to be punished by strict retribution—that is, with imposition of the same amount and kind of harm—but rather by a fixed scheme of compensatory fines.

When Jesus, in the Sermon on the Mount, says, "You have heard that it was said, 'An eye for an eye and a tooth for a tooth.' But I say to you . . . " (Mt 5:38-39), it could be thought that he was overruling the retributive features of the Mosaic law in favor of forgiveness. But it is more likely that Jesus was attacking those who turn the retributive principle into a maxim for personal conduct. The followers of Jesus were not meant to live their lives in relation to others on a tit-for-tat basis, and Jesus was not making a comment about how official judges should hand out punishments.[16]

There is a section in Romans 12 on a Christian attitude toward punishment presented just before the famous passage on government responsibilities and obedience to authorities (Rom 13:1-7). Paul writes, "Do not repay anyone evil for evil, but take thought for what is noble in the sight of all. If it is possible, so far as it depends on you, live peaceably with all. Beloved, never avenge yourselves, but leave room for the wrath of God; for it is written, 'Vengeance is mine, I will repay, says the Lord'" (Rom 12:17-19). In the light of what follows in Romans 13, Paul is not at all removing the need for forceful punishment; but he is reminding us that faith in the sovereignty of God and responsibility for justice should take from us the need for complete retaliatory justice.

The function of punishment often combines purposes of preventing the repetition of the crime, the deterrence of others, the communication of societal standards and attitudes, as well as hopes (at least in the instance of lesser crimes) for the possibility of amendment of life and reintegration with society. For this to be an expression of real justice, all such purposes must be connected to a retributive intent—that is, inflicting punishment because the offender deserves it.[17] However, we need to separate the punishment

---

[15]Bernard Jackson, *Essays in Jewish and Comparative Legal History* (Leiden: Brill, 1975), pp. 75-107.
[16]Wenham, *Leviticus*, p. 313.
[17]See Adrian Speller's principles for Christian thinking about penal policy in *The Future of Criminal Justice: Resettlement, Chaplaincy and Community*, ed. Christopher Jones and Peter Sedgwick (London: SPCK, 2002), pp. 10-11.

even of a serious crime such as murder (which ought to have a serious punishment) from some inherent need to express the full measure of justice. To punish a person as fully and completely as he or she deserves must be left to the only wise and righteous judge, God himself.

JUSTICE AND RIGHTS

In contemporary moral and political discourse, issues are often framed exclusively in terms of rights, and the points of disagreement are reduced to competing rights. The abortion debate in America is a good example, where large sections of the population, with a variety of perspectives and concerns, are segmented into supporting either the right of the fetus to live or the right of the mother to choose. One reason why the argument for the right of gay and lesbian partners to enter into marriage has been so successful recently is that the issue is seen as the mere extension of the right to marry (on grounds of justice) without taking away any of the rights of the heterosexual members of the society. We may predict that euthanasia, presented as the right to die with dignity, will also be presented as an expansion of rights (for those so inclined) without taking away the rights of the rest of the population to die in the way they so choose. Needless to say, this view of human rights would be baffling to classical philosophers, medieval theologians and thinkers of the Reformation and early modern era.

Some of the problems and ambiguities in the modern view of human rights are notable when we consider this somewhat condensed (but still lengthy) list of human rights included in the United Nations Charter:[18]

- Everyone has the right to life, liberty and security of person.

- No one shall be held in slavery or servitude; slavery and the slave trade shall be prohibited.

- No one shall be subjected to torture or to cruel, inhuman or degrading treatment or punishment.

- All are equal before the law and are entitled without any discrimination to equal protection of the law.

- No one shall be subjected to arbitrary arrest, detention or exile.

---

[18]The full document of thirty articles is available at www.un.org/en/documents/udhr/.

- Everyone charged with a penal offence has the right to be presumed innocent until proved guilty according to law in a public trial at which he has had all the guarantees necessary for his defense.

- Men and women of full age, without any limitation due to race, nationality or religion, have the right to marry and to found a family.

- The family is the natural and fundamental group unit of society and is entitled to protection by society and the State.

- Everyone has the right to own property alone as well as in association with others.

- No one shall be arbitrarily deprived of his property.

- Everyone has the right to freedom of thought, conscience and religion; this right includes freedom to change his religion or belief, and freedom . . . to manifest his religion or belief in teaching, practice, worship and observance.

- Everyone has the right to freedom of opinion and expression.

- Everyone has the right to take part in the government of his country, directly or through freely chosen representatives.

- The will of the people shall be the basis of the authority of government; this will shall be expressed in periodic and genuine elections which shall be by universal and equal suffrage and shall be held by secret vote or by equivalent free voting procedures.

- Everyone has the right to work, to free choice of employment, to just and favorable conditions of work and to protection against unemployment.

- Everyone has the right to equal pay for equal work.

- Everyone who works has the right to just and favorable remuneration ensuring for himself and his family an existence worthy of human dignity, and supplemented, if necessary, by other means of social protection.

- Everyone has the right to form and to join trade unions for the protection of his interests.

- Everyone has the right to rest and leisure, including reasonable limitation of working hours and periodic holidays with pay.

- Everyone has the right to a standard of living adequate for the health and well-being of himself and of his family, including food, clothing, housing and medical care and necessary social services, and the right to security in the event of unemployment, sickness, disability, widowhood, old age.

- Everyone has the right to education. Education shall be free, at least in the elementary and fundamental stages. Elementary education shall be compulsory. Technical and professional education shall be made generally available and higher education shall be equally accessible to all on the basis of merit.

- Parents have a prior right to choose the kind of education that shall be given to their children.

Much of this enumeration of human rights is unexceptionable and is basic to most people's view of the implications of the intrinsic importance of human life and dignity, and the minimum requirements of a just society. Such would be the provision of fair trials, protection of property, prohibition of slavery, the rights of conscience and freedom of speech.

The more controversial sections of the charter of rights have to do with the assumption of rights to goods and services, including education, medical care, paid employment, unemployment benefits and paid holidays. Many have commented that these so-called rights reflect a point of view belonging to Western, developed nations, not taking into account sharp economic and cultural differences. And even in Europe, when the United Nations Charter was adopted in 1948, not all countries allowed women to vote (Switzerland granted this right in 1971). Is the right to vote as fundamental a right as freedom of conscience or freedom from arbitrary arrest? To include perhaps laudable goals such as every worker having paid holidays and access to higher education, along with fundamental rights of life and property, seems to confuse what is at stake: the moral basis of human rights. Rather than strengthening the argument for fundamental human rights, the inclusion of some marginal or questionable provisions, or rights that even some highly developed countries fail to provide, makes it easier for brutal dictatorial regimes to refuse the applicability or relevance of the most basic principles of justice.

One common line of criticism of the modern expansion of rights is that rights must be correlative to duties. Rights are not some abstract concept attaching to all human beings, as the United Nations Charter implies, but correspond to the specific duties of others to provide them. Employment, for example, while certainly necessary and desirable for any economy, is not a fundamental political right, because no employer has the obligation or duty to employ anyone. Americans have yet to agree that medical care is a fundamental right, related to a lack of consensus about it being society's duty to provide it. Even education, though it has been mandatory for a hundred years or so and is universally provided by state or local government (at primary level, at any rate), is also questionable in regard to being a fundamental human right. Education in the basic general sense of providing training and knowledge to children of the next generation has always been the duty of parents and the society; but perhaps formal education in the modern sense of school classrooms and curricula is not really a fundamental human right.

Thus, if there are fundamental rights to life and belief, and expression, and ownership of property, there are those with duties to provide for these rights: parents must provide for the needs of their children; governments must provide safety and protection for citizens by means of police forces and national defense; and law courts must be provided to uphold contracts, resolve disputes and maintain the rule of law.

Although this is a strategy used by political conservatives to resist the intellectual underpinnings of the welfare state, there are good arguments to question the restriction of human rights to areas where there exists a manifest duty. While there is a great deal of overlap between rights and duties, they are not coterminous: there are some rights that people have by virtue of being human, that need to be respected, even if no one has a specific duty to ensure that right.[19]

While much of the contemporary political arguments from rights seem to have little to do with Thomas Aquinas, and other medieval theologians, or the magisterial Protestant reformers, and seem to become more and more secular or humanist in tone and orientation in the twenty-first century, it is important to see the roots of concern for human rights as stemming from not only the classical legal and philosophical traditions, but also from

---

[19]See Nicholas Wolterstorff, *Justice: Rights and Wrongs* (Princeton, NJ: Princeton University Press, 2008), chap. 12.

Christian teaching about the creation of human beings in the image of God and the dignity and respect that human beings are meant to have on that ground. This consideration enables Christians to recognize some theological truth in the modern concern for justice, and to be able to participate in discussion and proposals for change.

FOR FURTHER READING

Thomas Aquinas, *ST* II-II, qq. 57-122.

Oliver O'Donovan, *The Ways of Judgment* (Grand Rapids: Eerdmans, 2005), chap. 3.

Jean Porter, "The Virtue of Justice," in *The Ethics of Aquinas*, ed. Stephen Pope (Washington, DC: Georgetown University Press, 2002), pp. 272-86.

Martin Rhonheimer, "Sins Against Justice," in *The Ethics of Aquinas*, ed. Stephen Pope (Washington, DC: Georgetown University Press, 2002), pp. 287-303.

Nicholas Wolterstorff, *Justice in Love* (Grand Rapids: Eerdmans, 2011).

12

Fortitude

A T THE BEGINNING OF the treatment of fortitude, Thomas Aquinas offers one of his occasional but very helpful summaries:

> Virtue is that which makes its possessor good, and renders his work good. Actions are good when in accordance with reason, and this happens in three ways: first by rectifying reason itself, which is done by the intellectual virtues; secondly by establishing the rectitude of reason in human relationships, and this belongs to justice; thirdly by removing the obstacles to this establishment of this rectitude in human affairs.
>
> Now the human will is hindered in two ways from following the rectitude of reason. First by being drawn by some object of pleasure to something other than what the rectitude of reason requires; and this obstacle is removed by the virtue of temperance. Secondly through the will being disinclined to follow that which is in accordance with reason, on account of some difficulty that presents itself. In order to remove this obstacle fortitude of the mind is required, with which to resist the difficulty. (*ST* II-II, q. 123, a. 1)

It is in this aspect of the will being hindered either by being drawn to a different object of attraction, or by seeing and being hindered by a difficulty, that the type of ethical system that emphasizes virtue makes an obvious and notable contribution.

Other ethical systems, such as utilitarianism and Kantianism, have versions of practical reasoning and a focus on justice that parallel Aristotelian and Thomistic ethics. But they have very little helpful to say about improving defective decisions and actions other than to encourage greater clarity of reasoning and will power.

This observation is true for systems of Christian ethics that follow from a model of divine command theory or of natural law and conscience: improvement and growth in character are based on better understanding, better reasoning and sensitivity to circumstances in application, and above all a will that is not disobedient and does not deviate from the judgment of conscience.

The Thomistic incorporation of emotions in the moral virtues, and the need for their direction by reason, are not an appendix or supplementary explanation, but a central concern for the development of moral character, especially when we consider Christian character being shaped by the Holy Spirit in the image of Christ. Only a bit of honesty in reflecting on the shape of our moral lives makes clear to us that the difficulty we share with Paul in knowing the good that we should be doing but are failing to do results not from a lack of moral knowledge, but rather from the psychological weakness or inability to carry it out: we are drawn from our purpose by something that seems more attractive, or we are discouraged and hindered by fears and difficulties.

Our own experiences, and those of whom we know well and tragic figures in works of both history and fiction illustrate this aspect of the human condition: dreams abandoned, ideals compromised, talents undeveloped, enormous amounts of time wasted, misunderstandings between relatives and friends left unresolved, grudges perpetuated, depression, anxiety, abuse of drugs and medication, various types of addictive behavior, and so on. In many cases the individuals affected have been instructed with moral principles, and perhaps they have been faithful church members, but they find themselves drawn into a pattern of thinking and behaving contrary to their better ways of thought.

Although I will treat, as Thomas Aquinas did, the virtues of fortitude and temperance as separate and distinct cardinal virtues, there is a real sense in which they overlap. All the emotions are reflections and patterns of reaction to the objects of love, and so in a fundamental sense the development of virtue with respect to our emotional life is a matter of perfecting the way in which we love.

If we take a concrete example of someone succumbing to alcoholism, there is a clear combination of the two categories of emotion. A person sees in the relief and euphoria induced by alcohol a kind of pleasure that is both easy and attractive. At the same time, what drives a person to dependence on this particular kind of pleasure is the sense of weakness in the face of life's obstacles. Often there is a lack of self-confidence, which, when compounded with difficult problems, job loss and other challenges, can develop a dangerous pattern of retreat, denial and avoidance. What is lacking in the person with a drinking problem (or other kinds of addiction) is both temperance and fortitude.

COURAGE: THE ARISTOTELIAN BASIS AND SUBSEQUENT TRADITION

If we take a quick look at the Aristotelian source behind the Thomistic account, we find it a little thin or restricted and somewhat confusing as well.[1] First, there is not the expanded view of courage that we find in Thomas Aquinas covering many different kinds of threats, but rather a concentration on the courage or bravery of the soldier on the battlefield, and perhaps *valor* would best capture this range and quality. Thus Aristotle does not discuss courage in everyday life, such as would be seen in pressing on in spite of handicaps or difficulties, or making a difficult moral choice and showing the courage of one's convictions.

It is likely, also, that Aristotle folds into his analysis two different aspects of courage. When he applies his doctrine of the mean to compare the cowardly person and the brave person, he asserts that the brave person has the right amount of courage, whereas the coward is deficient in courage, and the person who has too much courage is rash. Aristotle probably should have distinguished between fear and confidence, because each has its own distinct object, pattern of response and spectrum of balance between deficit and excess. It is too much fear that makes a person a coward, whereas the brave person has the right amount. The spectrum of confidence looks different: an excess of confidence is rashness (overconfidence), while the deficiency of it is overcautiousness. The mean is to be "cautious," acting wisely under potentially threatening circumstances.

Someone might have a fear that the economy is heading for recession, thus making it difficult to keep up with mortgage payments and retain

---

[1]In the account offered here I am basically following J. O. Urmson, *Aristotle's Ethics* (Oxford: Blackwell, 1988), pp. 63-67.

home ownership. This is not the same kind of fear that one would have on the battlefield.[2] The neighbor who is not so worried about a recession would be seen not as brave but as confident, as this is a different set of external threats and internal responses (perhaps the presence or absence of adrenalin is an indicator here). It is interesting to see that in the later tradition of moral theology very little interest or space was devoted to courage or *fortitudo*. John Capreolus (ca. 1380–1444) gave much more attention to the theological virtues, and all the cardinal virtues were downgraded somewhat.[3] In the Anglican tradition we find in Jeremy Taylor's work several of the virtues highlighted and developed—faith, hope and love, of course, plus justice and "sobriety" or soberness, under which he includes temperance, chastity, modesty and humility. Prudence is virtually replaced by conscience,[4] and courage has no special treatment. Taylor (who also wrote *Holy Living* and *Holy Dying*) was naturally concerned with the Christian facing death, which ought to fall under the category of patience and courage, but it is as a type of "contentment" that Taylor gives the Christian advice about spiritual character in the face of the threat of death.

The treatment in the Roman Catholic handbooks is also lopsided, and a section on courage by Henry Davis,[5] for example, is extremely sketchy, with the main topic of interest being martyrdom; in our own era, which produced more Christian martyrs than previous centuries, this obviously has more relevance in some places around the globe than others.

Kenneth Kirk, with his interest in using contemporary psychology to enhance his description of moral theology and spirituality, might have been expected to show more interest in fear, anxiety and courage in the Christian life, but there is disappointingly little.[6] This lack of attention to courage is

---

[2]Ibid., p. 66.

[3]See John Capreolus, *On the Virtues*, trans. Kevin White and Romanus Cessario (Washington, DC: Catholic University of America Press, 2001).

[4]See Oliver O'Donovan's remarks on the tendency in Taylor and other moralists of the seventeenth century to exalt the authority of conscience, emphasizing its "rational character as well as divine institution" (*Resurrection and Moral Order: An Outline for Evangelical Ethics*, 2nd ed. [Grand Rapids: Eerdmans, 1994], p. 118).

[5]Henry Davis, *Moral and Pastoral Theology*, vol. 1, *Human Acts, Law, Sin, Virtue*, 2nd ed. (London: Sheed & Ward, 1941).

[6]Kenneth Kirk, *Some Principles of Moral Theology and Their Application* (London: Longmans, Green, 1934).

also true in more recent treatments of virtue and the Christian life, such as that by Robert Roberts.[7]

In his treatment of Anglican moral theology Herbert Waddams allows the cardinal virtues almost to disappear, compressed into a four-page account paired with the seven vices.[8] This offers some insight into the perception that courage was not so useful, since it was not opposed to any one of the vices directly, and since fear was seen as an emotion rather than a vice.

The relevance of courage and the Thomistic account comes much more clearly into view when we consider the importance of fear and anxiety in twentieth-century theology and spirituality, and the problems of depression and neurosis that afflict many. It is here that a contemporary account of the Thomistic virtue of *fortitudo* can begin to demonstrate the richness of outlook provided by Thomas Aquinas and also make connections to the best contemporary psychological and sociological research.

THOMISTIC FORTITUDE

Fortitude can be defined in general as firmness of mind, and more specifically firmness in the face of threat or danger.[9] It is the quality of character that enables a person not to be diverted by difficulty or danger from carrying out an action or plan for achieving some good purpose.

Thomas Aquinas clearly is using Aristotle as a basis, and he retains the ability to face death as a central paradigm of fortitude, but there is a great expansion in the coverage of the virtue. In his helpful study comparing the virtue of courage in Aquinas with that of the Chinese philosopher Mencius, Lee Yearley points out that Aquinas was juggling and combining disparate elements from Greek, Roman, Stoic and biblical sources, as well as the thinking of the early church fathers.[10] Aquinas is faced with the task of describing courage as a combination of three different notions:

1. Courage refers to qualities needed in hand-to-hand combat.

---

[7]See Robert Roberts, *Spiritual Emotions: A Psychology of Christian Virtues* (Grand Rapids: Eerdmans, 2007), where he treats contrition, joy, gratitude, hope, peace and compassion.

[8]Herbert Waddams, *A New Introduction to Moral Theology*, rev. ed. (London: SCM Press, 1972), pp. 124-28, 207-13.

[9]See Thomas Aquinas, *ST* II-II, q. 123, a. 2.

[10]Lee Yearley, *Mencius and Aquinas: Theories of Virtue and Conceptions of Courage* (Albany: State University of New York Press, 1990), p. 33.

2. Courage is a general enabling virtue in situations involving fear and confidence.

3. Courage underlies the psychological attitude of detachment crucial to survival in bad times.[11]

In order to solve the problem of unifying this larger ensemble of virtue, Aquinas makes four different virtues parts of courage: two of them, perseverance and patience, are central to the Christian tradition, while the other two are central to classical Greek schemes and come to Aquinas from Aristotle: magnanimity and magnificence. At first sight, we might agree with Lee Yearlee (and others) that Aquinas shows lack of historical and cultural awareness, and that there is a fundamental incompatibility between a New Testament emphasis on the virtue of humility in a Christian and the Aristotelian conception of the virtue of "great-mindedness" and the daring involved in undertaking great projects. First, however, we can demonstrate the similarities in treatment of Christian fortitude between the Bible and the virtue theory of Thomas Aquinas.

PATIENCE AND PERSEVERANCE IN THE NEW TESTAMENT

Greek words in the *hypomenō* family describe patient endurance: "The one who endures [*hypomenō*] to the end will be saved" (Mk 13:13); "If we hope for what we do not see, we wait for it with patience [*hypomonē*]" (Rom 8:25); "If you endure [*hypomenō*] when you do right and suffer for it, you have God's approval" (1 Pet 2:20). As Friedrich Hauck indicates, there is a major difference from Greek ethics, which considered *hypomonē* the steel-willed resistance of the virile spirit against attacks, whereas the Christian attitude extends to patient suffering and endurance even when injustice is being done.[12] And certainly this is what Jesus demonstrated for his disciples.

The term *proskartereō* overlaps with "patience," but instead of endurance in a passive way, it has the active element of perseverance, to persist or keep on doing some vital activity.[13] The disciples after Pentecost persisted, "de-

---

[11]Ibid.

[12]Friedrich Hauck, "μένω, κτλ.," in *Theological Dictionary of the New Testament*, ed. Gerhard Kittel and Gerhard Friedrich, trans. Geoffrey Bromiley, 10 vols. (Grand Rapids: Eerdmans, 1964–1976), 4:582.

[13]Walter Grundmann, "καρτερέω, κτλ.," in Kittel and Friedrich, *Theological Dictionary of the New Testament*, 3:618-19.

voting [*proskartereō*] themselves" to teaching, fellowship, breaking bread, and prayers (Acts 1:14). Paul instructs disciples, "Devote yourselves [*proskartereō*] to prayer" (Col 4:2 [cf. Lk 18:1]), and he uses both words when he writes, "Rejoice in hope, be patient [*hypomenō*] in suffering, persevere [*proskartereō*] in prayer" (Rom 12:12).

PATIENCE AND PERSEVERANCE IN THE TEACHING OF AQUINAS

The virtue of fortitude or courage often is associated with bravery in the face of death. This is because death is the ultimate danger for us (our physical existence in this life) and thus threatens all that we love in this life. Soldiers, police officers, and firefighters, who risk their own lives to protect the lives of those in their country and community, are obvious examples of fortitude.

The martyrs who gave their lives as witnesses to the cause of truth and justice exhibit fortitude in a special degree. Giving up one's life for the cause of truth in the face of oppression and persecution and in conformity to the example of Christ is the proof of the perfection of charity, because such a person is willing to give up what is most dear in this life for the sake of love for God and for others.[14]

If we take the ability to face death as the prime instance of fortitude, we see right away that fortitude sometimes takes the form of decisive action in spite of, or to repel, a dangerous threat (such as entering a burning house or resisting an attack). At other times, as in the case of martyrs, fortitude consists in an unflinching acceptance of pain and death. This points to the necessity for the ability to judge the character of a situation and respond with clarity and confidence; fortitude needs the guidance of prudence.

For most of us, the relationship to death will not likely be physical persecution, war or imminent danger to life and limb. But there is for all of us either the potential threat of death in serious illness or its eventual and certain arrival with advancing age. Fortitude, guided by wisdom, is able to face death appropriately: not giving up too soon, and not trying to resist death "heroically" when we ought to recognize and prepare well for the inevitable and natural course of events.

The relationship between grace and fortitude, the quality of character and

---

[14]See Thomas Aquinas, *ST* II-II, q. 124, a. 3.

attitude that one will have in the face of death, ought to be significantly different for a Christian than for a person who has no kind of faith in an afterlife, for whom life in this world contains all the good that is worth striving for. Of course, there are pagan philosophers such as Socrates and other non-Christians who accepted death with staunch fortitude, just as there are Christians whose faith and hope are insufficiently developed to counter a fear of death; yet the Christian confidence in the work and salvation of Christ ought to be determinative in the formation of Christian fortitude:

> The first thing that must be said, and which can never be said powerfully and triumphantly enough, is that human fear has been completely and definitively conquered by the Cross. Anxiety is one of the authorities, power, and dominions over which the Lord triumphed on the Cross and which he carried off captive and placed in chains, to make use of as he wills.[15]

There is a need for wisdom to face the challenge of death appropriately (depending on circumstances)—whether resistance or acceptance is appropriate. This is also a feature of fortitude in general: there are times when patience and endurance are called for and are the qualities characteristic of fortitude, and there are times when an aggressive or attacking mode is the path of wisdom and courage.

In the Christian tradition the aspect of patient endurance has been central to our view of the virtue of fortitude, partly from the example of Jesus' acceptance of the way of the cross, and the martyrs of the early church, and the high profile of Jesus' teaching in the Sermon on the Mount about nonresistance and turning the other cheek, and the highlighting in the Beatitudes of blessings in store for the meek, the persecuted and the insulted.

Josef Pieper, however, has pointed out that there is a distortion in the received picture of what the virtue of fortitude involves. We certainly can say that the person who has fortitude will have patience; but it does not follow that the patient person is necessarily brave. That is because patience and endurance are not the only qualities characteristic of fortitude: "The brave man not only knows how to bear inevitable evil with equanimity; he will also not hesitate to 'pounce upon' evil and to bar its way, if this can

---

[15]Hans Urs von Balthasar, *The Christian and Anxiety*, trans. Dennis Martin and Michael Miller (San Francisco: Ignatius Press, 2000), p. 81.

reasonably be done. This attitude requires readiness to attack, courage, self-confidence, and hope of success."[16]

Here the example of Jesus is instructive. His mental anguish in the garden of Gethsemane shows that his acceptance of suffering and death was not merely passive. And Thomas Aquinas points out in his commentary on the Gospel of John that Jesus did not always literally turn the other cheek in response to attack. There were times in the presence of Pilate or the chief priest when Jesus was silent and apparently passive; but there were also times when Jesus challenged his questioners:

> "I have always taught in synagogues and in the temple, where all the Jews come together. I have said nothing in secret. Why do you ask me? Ask those who heard what I said to them; they know what I said." When he had said this, one of the police standing nearby struck Jesus on the face, saying, "Is that how you answer the high priest?" Jesus answered, "If I have spoken wrongly, testify to the wrong. But if I have spoken rightly, why do you strike me?" (Jn 18:20-23)

Thomas Aquinas argues that a brave person will sometimes make use of anger in his action.[17] Fortitude has two types of action: endurance and aggression, and it employs anger in actions that are aggressive, because it is characteristic of anger to "strike at the cause of sorrow." Of course, the anger must be moderated and properly guided by reason, and be judged appropriate in the circumstances.

We can note here that this is part of the reply to the misunderstandings of Friedrich Nietzsche, Sigmund Freud and others of the passivity implied in the Christian tradition of patient suffering. Nietzsche belittled the "slave mentality" of Christians in comparison with heroic courage, and Freud was critical of the Christian attitude toward aggression. Freud took aim at the spirit of self-sacrifice in the doctrine of love for neighbors, strangers and enemies, thinking that with a naive underestimation of human aggressiveness, Christians leave themselves vulnerable to hostility and aggression.[18]

The reply to this charge involves two points. First, the Christian some-

---

[16]Josef Pieper, *The Four Cardinal Virtues: Prudence, Justice, Fortitude, Temperance*, trans. Richard Winston et al. (Notre Dame, IN: University of Notre Dame Press, 1966), pp. 129-30.

[17]See Thomas Aquinas, *ST* II-II, q. 123, a. 10.

[18]Sigmund Freud, *Civilization and Its Discontents*, cited in Craig Steven Titus, *Resilience and the Virtue of Fortitude: Aquinas in Dialogue with the Psychosocial Sciences* (Washington, DC: Catholic University of America Press, 2006), p. 303.

times is called to lay down his or her life for someone as friend or neighbor, but this comes from strength not weakness; it is a confident following of the example of Christ, a desire and calling to defend the weak, and sometimes in order to promote the cause of justice. Second, there is a limit to the counsel of turning the other cheek (as Jesus himself showed), and there are also situations that call for resistance, righteous wrath and forceful defense or intervention.[19]

The active nature of fortitude is also underscored by the subvirtue of perseverance, which is what enables a person to persist in pursuing a good in spite of the difficulty and length of time that it takes. The need for this aspect of fortitude to be directed by prudence rules out the kind of stubborn persistence in projects that ought never to have been begun, and the kind of quixotic ideals and actions not governed by wisdom and truth. A poster that I saw recently captures this kind of quality of persistence in the virtue of fortitude: "Courage does not always roar; sometimes it is the small voice which says, 'I'll try again tomorrow.'"

This attitude of quiet courage that resists the urge to give up or not try is obviously an important and essential part of human character, and not a marginal or occasional virtue. And it certainly cannot be reduced to a matter of will power or determination. The person who lacks confidence, or is depressed and anxious, or finds it hard to tackle challenging situations needs more than a pep talk or the challenge to "just do it."

RESILIENCE AND FORTITUDE

There is a whole range of modern psychological study of the ways in which people are able to face challenges and difficulties in life, and of the "coping" mechanisms that are helpful. Naturally, the vocabulary, starting points and methods are very different in contemporary psychology from Thomistic Scholasticism, but there are valuable points of comparison, links and similar conclusions that are useful in affirming the value and basis in truth of both the Thomistic conception of fortitude and what many contemporary psychologists call "resilience."[20]

---

[19]Titus, *Resilience*, p. 304.

[20]In *Resilience and the Virtue of Fortitude*, Craig Titus represents a thorough knowledge of Thomas Aquinas as well as a wide-ranging and fruitful survey of recent psychological literature.

Craig Titus shows how more extensive modern research does not contradict, but instead enriches, the Thomistic account of fortitude. Patience and longsuffering function in Aquinas's account as the way to bear evil without giving in to sorrow, and to hold fast to the quest for goodness, truth and happiness with a calm spirit, especially when there is a delay and a need to wait for attaining the goal. Research into resilience helps Thomistic virtue theory in showing how humans endure difficulty or suffering, hold firm in a painful struggle, resist self-destructive pressures, wait for the attainment of good, persist until the accomplishment of some goal and even express sorrow as a virtuous good. "The social and developmental lines of insight are especially strong in cognitive, evolutionary and social developmental sciences. Their insights into the three aspects of resilience that involve coping, resisting, and constructing suggest a nuanced grid through which to cull insights for the virtues of enduring."[21]

The perspective of research on resilience affirms that pain and suffering and loss can have negative or detrimental effects, as well as steeling or strengthening effects, on humans at physical, psychological and social levels. The concept of coping, especially, as formulated by cognitive psychology (with some inevitable jargon of the discipline) parallels the notions of patience and perseverance as developed by Aquinas. We can use "coping" to understand how humans develop active, passive and evasive strategies to reestablish homeostasis in the face of suffering, or even choose high levels of discomfort in order to achieve a goal. Representation-oriented and evaluation-oriented coping operations parallel the role of prudence, knowledge and wisdom in virtue theory. Some resilience research even speculates that cognitive appreciations of a moral order (e.g., a sense of solidarity or justice) can help us in bearing suffering and managing sociobiological inclinations concerning pain in altruistic perspectives.

MAGNANIMITY AND MAGNIFICENCE, ENTERPRISE AND INITIATIVE

Aristotle included in his understanding of courage the kind of person with noble ambition, capable of major achievements worthy of respect and honor.

---

[21]Titus, *Resilience*, p. 262.

Such a person was *megalopsychikos* ("great-minded"). We might think that the virtue of a person with lofty goals and desirous of great achievement and honor would conflict with the Christian virtue of humility, but Thomas Aquinas did not think so (and we will consider this point explicitly in the section on pride and humility under the virtue of temperance).

In the 1970s the journalist and Christian convert Malcolm Muggeridge traveled to Calcutta and filmed an inspiring documentary about Theresa titled "Something Beautiful for God." The foundation and leadership of the Sisters of Charity and the type of work done among the poor and dying that was initiated did not occur as the result of a committee meeting, or a foundation setting up a new nongovernmental organization; they were the response of a person to a grand vision and calling of the Holy Spirit, and a spirit that would not be kept back by obstacles and discouragement. This is the virtue of our great heroes and saints, those like Francis Xavier and Ignatius, John Wesley and the missionaries Hudson Taylor and Adoniram Judson, those who achieved something on a grand scale and inspired many others. William Carey, an Anglican who became a Baptist, made the statement "Expect great things from God, and attempt great things for God," which became the watchword in the founding of the Baptist Missionary Society in 1792.

As a moral virtue, this is not restricted to Christians, of course, and there are many explorers, inventors, writers, artists, founders of corporations, universities and other organizations who have exhibited the virtue of enterprise and achievement. The characteristic of this virtue that makes it part of fortitude is that it has to do with achieving something good and of value on a large scale, and therefore involves challenge and difficulty. It is the ability to pursue a vision successfully in spite of hardship and discouragement that gives Thomistic magnificence, better understood as enterprise or initiative, its place and character as a virtue.[22]

---

[22]Obviously, some of the challenge for a modern Christian appropriation of Aquinas's appropriation of Aristotle has to do with terminology. "Magnanimity" and "munificence" were retained in the Blackfriars translation by Ross and Walsh, while Timothy McDermott (*Summa Theologiae: A Concise Translation* [Westminster, MD: Christian Classics, 1989], p. 424], helpfully changed magnanimity to "enterprise." The term *initiative,* used by Craig Titus, is particularly applicable, since we do not regard as virtuous (Christian or otherwise) someone who "lacks initiative," thereby pointing to it as a standard quality of good human character and removing it from the aristocratic elitism implied in the Aristotelian account.

Note that as with all moral virtue, the relation to reason is crucial. We are not dealing with dreams and mistaken notions of grandeur and inflated ambitions (which would, of course, be pride). It is a matter of accurate assessment of gifts, receiving the sense of calling or mission, and the accurate understanding that by grace such a mission and vision can be fulfilled. Aquinas described this kind of confidence as an aspect of enterprise, "a certain strength of hope arising from some observation which gives one a strong opinion that one will obtain a certain good" (*ST* II-II, q. 129, a. 6).

In summarizing Thomas Aquinas on magnificence, we can see how persons not only can build their lives in the face of difficulty, but can also face the difficulty of building something grand or complex. In order to accomplish challenging endeavors, we use our emotional and intellectual dispositions or virtues and engage emotions of hope and assertiveness. We manage our desires for excellence, honor, confidence and security, and at the same time we overcome the counterforces found in insecurity, presumption, timidity, stinginess, vainglory and ambition.[23]

If we look at the modern research on resilience, we find an expansion and enhancement of Aquinas's conception, through insights into hope and optimism. Through initiative-taking virtues we mobilize hope and daring in an active and constructive resilience. These virtues are more than simple coping responses to difference types of stress, challenge or loss. They can be differentiated by their sources of motivation: the quality and finality of goals, competencies and dispositions. Social support, from family, friends and society in general, can also make us optimistic and trusting in the value of people's assistance. It is hope and motivation that underlie human actions, and our motivation increases with hopefulness, and more hopeful people are motivated to attain more challenging and fruitful goals.

FOR FURTHER READING

Thomas Aquinas, *ST* II-II, qq. 123-40.

Jennifer Herdt, *Putting on Virtue: The Legacy of the Splendid Vices* (Chicago: University of Chicago Press, 2008), chap. 3, on Aquinas's treatment of magnanimity.

Josef Pieper, *The Four Cardinal Virtues: Prudence, Justice, Fortitude, Temperance*, trans.

---

[23]Titus, *Resilience*, summarizing Thomas Aquinas, *ST* II-II, qq. 127-35.

Richard Winston et al. (Notre Dame, IN: University of Notre Dame Press, 1966).

Craig Steven Titus, *Resilience and the Virtue of Fortitude: Aquinas in Dialogue with the Psychosocial Sciences* (Washington, DC: Catholic University of America Press, 2006), chap. 3.

Lee Yearley, *Mencius and Aquinas: Theories of Virtue and Conceptions of Courage* (Albany: State University of New York Press, 1990).

13

SELF-CONTROL

TEMPERANCE, AS THOMAS AQUINAS would put it, is a disposition to be well moved "about pleasures and desires" (*ST* II-II, q. 141, a. 3). The virtue of temperance (Latin *temperantia*; in Greek there are two words: *sophrosynē* and *enkrateia*) deals with the response of a person to the desires for those things that give pleasure, such as food, drink and sexual relations. Note, however, that we must also consider the negative emotions of sadness, irritation and so on, when one is faced with the absence or deprivation of these pleasures.[1] As with justice and fortitude, choices regarding pleasure must be guided by reason to become part of the mental equipment of moral virtue.

We observe the strength of the sensual desires in ourselves and in others, and their potential for self-destruction. It has been noted that the very powers of nature that are necessary for life and survival (if not the individual, then the human race as a whole) can become easily disordered, so that they can undermine and destroy an individual's physical and mental well-being. We hardly need to be reminded of the health problems and early deaths from diabetes and heart disease caused by overeating; the physical and mental scourge of alcoholism; the diseases associated with smoking; the high price of addiction to drugs; the deaths and problems caused by AIDS and venereal disease associated with promiscuous sex.

SELF-CONTROL OR TEMPERANCE IN GENERAL

Temperance is the only virtue that is directed purely toward oneself in the

---

[1]See Thomas Aquinas, *ST* II-II, q. 141, a. 3.

moderation of desires and emotional responses. Josef Pieper distinguished between a proper form of self-love, which he called "selfless self-love," by which a person's natural desires for preservation and fulfillment in this life are channeled properly, and a "selfish self-love," where self-love is directed toward pleasure and fulfillment for its own sake and only on terms willed by the self-centered individual.[2] People who pursue the avenue of personal development/destruction involving immoderate sensual pleasure often experience unhappiness and irritation that they then mask or deal with by further temporary pleasures, a pattern often leading to addiction and loss of freedom. The Thomistic approach sees in this the fact that the selfish form of self-love and the pursuit of pleasure is something fundamentally unnatural, in the sense that our human nature, including of course our bodies, was created to function when ordered toward its proper end: in right relation to self, to other people and to God.[3] "Selfless self-love" seeks a proper measure of life's pleasures in right relationship to true reality and requires the insight, wisdom and the Holy Spirit for the fullest and most accurate understanding of the reality of our physical, psychological and spiritual world.

Temperance deals with sense appetites that are strong and accompanied by pleasurable sensations. Good judgment is needed for the moderate and reasonable satisfaction of the appetites, which will vary from person to person, and with culture and circumstances. Bodily necessity is the starting point for consumption of food and drink, recognizing that body size and level of activity are important factors. But we may broaden this beyond survival and health to what is proper or fitting in the circumstances. If your job as a CEO involves occasionally entertaining dignitaries, then providing a sumptuous meal—one that you might never have on your own, perhaps—would be proper in that context.

Temperance moderates movements of the sense appetite, in particular, by keeping them consonant with the order of reason and divine law, which may involve times of feasting as well as of fasting. This involves developing a pattern of learning to choose both to act and feel in accordance with the

---

[2]Josef Pieper, *The Four Cardinal Virtues: Prudence, Justice, Fortitude, Temperance*, trans. Richard Winston et al. (Notre Dame, IN: University of Notre Dame Press, 1966), pp. 149-50.
[3]Ibid.

mean (the moderate point) between excess and deficiency discerned by good judgment.[4]

Note that this means that a person is moved appropriately by various attractive objects. For example, while passing by a doughnut shop or a pub, a person is able to enjoy the fragrance of a honeysuckle growing outside. The Aristotelian model of habituated virtue aims not at the suppression of emotions, but rather at the education and training of emotional response so that one's sensual urges are in line with one's moral principles and framework. Thus we may distinguish Aquinas's account from Puritan or other accounts of self-control, which are based on a struggle against strong urges and temptations. Struggles there may be, of course, but the goal of developing the virtue is to develop a pattern of harmonious emotional response, so that the sense of struggle occurs less often.[5]

One can also move in the direction of vice—intemperance. If one's appetites become disordered, if one repeatedly succumbs to powerful impulses to sensations of touch in pleasing but detrimental ways, then one becomes disposed to seek what is bad under the impression that it is good.[6] The result is that one thus sinks ever further into confusion and compulsion, and, as Aquinas says, the disordered pleasures "dim the light of reason from which all the clarity and beauty of virtue arises: wherefore these pleasures are described as being most slavish" (*ST* II-II, q. 142, a. 4).[7]

EATING AND DRINKING

We find no real mystery or surprise in reflecting on gluttony and drunkenness. Both are the excessive and immoderate enjoyment of pleasures not wrong in themselves but that need to be pursued by the use of reason and in relationship to our love for God. In this respect, the abuse of alcohol is more serious (and the knowing and intentional action of drinking to become drunk is a mortal sin), because the loss of reason caused by this deprives a person of moral agency: the person who gets drunk diminishes or loses the

---

[4]See Thomas Aquinas, *ST* II-II, q. 141, aa. 2, 4; see also Diana Fritz Cates, "The Virtue of Temperance," in *The Ethics of Aquinas*, ed. Stephen Pope (Washington, DC: Georgetown University Press, 2002), pp. 321-39.

[5]Cates, "Virtue of Temperance," pp. 322-23.

[6]Ibid., pp. 323-24.

[7]Ibid., p. 324.

ability to make good judgments and choose morally good actions and thus becomes open to occasions of sinful actions.[8]

Gluttony. Thomas Aquinas writes, "Gluttony is immoderate appetite in eating and drinking, and appetite becomes immoderate when it departs from a basis in reason where moral good is to be found" (*ST* II-II, q. 148, a. 1). Gluttony is a serious matter for him because it disposes a person to eat in a way that is incommensurate and not proportionate to the end, although often it will be less serious because the person does not mean to be choosing the pleasures of the table over his or her relationship to God.[9]

Theologians who wrote on the sin of gluttony (including Aquinas and Jeremy Taylor) often cited Gregory the Great, who provided insights into various aspects of the vice in five adverbs, "hastily, sumptuously, daintily, too much, and greedily," meaning that gluttony goes far beyond simply eating too much.[10] A preoccupation with exotic and costly food and complicated recipes can be a sign of gluttony just as much as the intensity of the appetite shown in the speed and voraciousness of eating.

The problems associated with gluttony have to do with dullness and confusion: thinking becomes murky or confused, feelings unreliable, and talk and behavior become foolish.[11] In general, there is a sensual pre-occupation that tends to turn attention from God and spiritual matters, and with this focus on sensual pleasure, gluttony may result in the lowering of moral defenses in general. In the words of Thomas à Kempis, "When the belly is full to bursting with food and drink, debauchery knocks at the door."[12]

Is it possible to imagine a person with a deficient interest in the pleasures of food? This should sometimes be the case if the Aristotelian dynamic of the mean applies here, although it would seem to be rare. As an ascetic practice (and not because of disinterest in food), some have deliberately prepared simple food in unadorned, perhaps dull ways. And apparently, according to biographers, Francis of Assisi used ashes as a spice

---

[8]See Thomas Aquinas, *ST* II-II, q. 150, a. 2.

[9]Ibid., q. 148, a. 2.

[10]See Gregory, *Moralia* XXX.18 (cited in Thomas Aquinas, *ST* II-II, q. 148, a. 4); see also Jeremy Taylor, *Holy Living and Holy Dying*, ed. P. G. Stanwood, 2 vols. (Oxford: Clarendon, 1989), 1:64.

[11]See Thomas Aquinas, *ST* II-II, q. 148, a. 6.

[12]Quoted in Francine Prose, *Gluttony* (Oxford: Oxford University Press, 2003), p. 19.

with which he sprinkled his food in order to destroy any hint of taste.[13] This was probably a dramatic gesture (like going naked in the town square) rather than a consistent practice. Francis's aim may well have been to underscore Paul's point in Philippians 4:11-12 that we should learn to be content with what we have. Our happiness should not depend on having certain foods to enjoy.

Since we think of gluttony primarily as a problem of eating too much food, it is quite likely that gluttony is much more common than we realize, since it has to do with an unreasonable preoccupation with the consumption and pleasure of food. People may be average in weight and yet drive to distant places for special foods, be fascinated with new gourmet trends, insist on special ingredients or particular methods of preparation. A contemporary observer remarks, "Precisely because of our inordinate interests, our preoccupation with sampling the trendiest dishes at the costliest new restaurants, and our apparently paradoxical, obsessive horror of obesity, we have become a culture of gluttons."[14]

Fasting and abstinence. Fasting, or abstinence (with one meal in the day), is to be recommended for several reasons. There probably is a connection between all of our sensual desires, and we improve our ability to control and moderate our bodily desires in general by developing control over our desires for food. The biblical instructions regarding fasting connect the practice with the ability to devote time in contemplation of spiritual matters and to focus on repentance and amendment of life.[15]

Thomas Aquinas says that one abstains and fasts, first, in order to restrain the sensual cravings that we have and to use the experience to learn how to master other concupiscent urges; and, second, in order to loosen one's attachments to sensual pleasures in general in order "that the mind may arise more freely to the contemplation of heavenly things" (*ST* II-II, q. 147, a. 1).

Sobriety and drunkenness. Aquinas interprets the words of Jesus, "It is not what goes into the mouth that defiles a person" (Mt 15:11), as meaning that no food or drink is illicit in itself.[16] Moderation is required

---

[13]Ibid., p. 28.
[14]Ibid., p. 41.
[15]See Thomas Aquinas, *ST* II-II, q. 147, a. 1.
[16]See ibid., q. 149, a. 3.

by all, but no exact rules or quota can be set because of the great variety between people's bodies, circumstances and responsibilities.

The use of alcoholic drinks should reflect an inner peace in the soul, and usage should be consistent with maintaining health. However, those who find it difficult to drink moderately, who would be a stumbling block to others or who find that drinking hinders them in their spiritual life should avoid alcohol.[17] Aquinas thought that sobriety is to be strongly recommended for the young because of their strong desire for pleasure at their age, which of course is the opposite approach from modern culture, which tends to be indulgent to a phase of youthful excess. Aquinas also counseled abstinence for women, the elderly and weak, and those in positions of authority, especially for clergy.[18]

Drunkenness is a sin when it stems from inordinate desire, and it may be less serious if there is lack of awareness of the potency of a certain drink, for example; but when there is awareness, and the drunkenness is intended in preference to sobriety, then the sin is serious. Jeremy Taylor reminds us of some of the many evil consequences of drunkenness, among which are that it causes a tendency to lust, hinders the understanding, removes moral restraints, and "quenches the Spirit of God."[19]

SEXUAL BEHAVIOR: CHASTITY AND LUST

It is not surprising that Thomas Aquinas held to views about sexual relations shaped by Scripture, patristic tradition and natural law. The combination of these sources left no doubt in his mind (nor in the collective thought of Western Christianity before the twentieth century) about the sinfulness not only of rape and adultery, but also of fornication (and all sexual relations outside of marriage), masturbation and homosexual relations.

Aquinas recognized that to a certain extent sexual desire and arousal are not under our control; and yet the intensity and progress of desire is a kind of passion and has an intentional aspect to it. Thus it can be formed and shaped and acted on through our volition.[20] Thus the development of

---

[17]See ibid., q. 149, a. 3.
[18]See ibid., q. 149, a. 4.
[19]Taylor, *Holy Living*, 1:68-70.
[20]See Cates, "Virtue of Temperance," p. 331.

chastity, the virtue to moderate sexual desire in accordance with reason and God's will, is an important matter of moral character. The virtue of chastity governs sexual activity in different ways in relation to status: for those who are not married (single, widowed or under a vow of chastity), this means abstention from sexual relations. Even for the married there have traditionally been restrictions (as we see in Jeremy Taylor's treatment below) that many people find quaint today.

One recent and largely sympathetic treatment of the Thomistic virtue of temperance raised the question of why there is no room in it for prudent judgments in relation to sex.

> It is noteworthy that Thomas does not say in his discussion of chastity, as he does in discussions of abstinence and sobriety, that within the bounds set by general moral principles, there is room for varied, context-specific determinations of appetitive and behavioral rightness. This is because he does not allow the use of non-necessary sexual relations in the way that he allows the use of non-necessary foods and beverages. . . . He does not explore the complex particulars of personal and social circumstance that many people in the present age think they need to consider in order to exercise practical wisdom in the expression of their sexuality.[21]

One obvious factor is that sexual relations are not necessary for any individual (although, of course, they are necessary for humanity as a whole) in the same way that food and drink are. There are many differences in outlook and assumption that keep the modern Western mind from seeing the correctness of the traditional approach, not least being the inability to perceive that there are inherent purposes in human activities that need to be recognized and respected; we are not free simply to impose our individual desires and purposes as our culture trains us to. However, there is a common charge made against the Christian tradition in sexual matters—the suspicion of pleasure—that deserves some consideration here, especially as it falls directly under the virtue of temperance, which is meant to regulate human desires and pleasures.

Is there a problem with sexual pleasure in Christian thought? There was what might be considered an overreaction against the sexual license and

---

[21]Ibid., p. 333.

decadence of the late Roman Empire resulting in the celebration and ele-
vation of virginity and corresponding devaluing of normal human sexuality
and family life. In Jerome, for example, we find rather caustic attitudes
toward marriage. And in Augustine, who laid the foundation for the Western
teaching on marriage and sexuality, even Roman Catholic theologians speak
of a "dark strain" and "moral pessimism" that led him to a view of the link
between original sin and sexual desire that made the pleasures that we experience in sexual activity disordered and suspect.[22] It is a major part of the
ongoing revisionist moral project in contemporary churches to affirm the
essential goodness and naturalness of human sexual desire.

It is worth pointing out that Aquinas differed in emphasis from much of
the Augustinian tradition with respect to the pleasure of sexual activity.
Where Augustine saw the pleasure of sex as inherently disordered because of
the fall, Aquinas was able to affirm the goodness and desirability of pleasure
in the sex act, as long as sexual activity was practiced according to reason (i.e.,
in marriage). In fact, he speculated that the pleasure of sex before the fall,
with Adam and Eve in paradise, would have been even greater, since both
mind and body would have had greater awareness and sensitivity.[23]

It is not sexual pleasure per se that causes concern, and we may admit
that certain periods of Christian thought and some lines of argument were
not so clear in affirming this. The concern is for having, as with all actions
and emotions, the structure of intention for ends properly in place, and
emotional responses and actions decided on properly guided by prudence.

Coming somewhat closer to the modern period, the seventeenth century,
we take a look at Jeremy Taylor's teaching on marriage and chastity. Here is
an Anglican priest, and later bishop, married and with children, who wants
to share helpful counsel in his *Holy Living*, and he has the benefit of extensive reading in moral philosophy and theology, from the ancients to contemporary Roman Catholic and Reformed thinking. And yet some of his
"rules for married persons" (even in their abbreviated form here)[24] would
give many of us pause:

---

[22]See John Mahoney, *The Making of Moral Theology: A Study of the Roman Catholic Tradition* (Oxford: Oxford University Press, 1987), pp. 44-48.
[23]See *ST* I q. 98 a. 2 ad 3.
[24]Taylor, *Holy Living*, 1:81-83.

1. Their affection for each other should not be greater than for God.

2. They must be sure to observe the order of nature and the ends of God. "He is an ill Husband that uses his Wife as a man treats a Harlot, having no other end but pleasure."

3. They never force themselves "into high and violent lusts, with arts and misbecoming devices."

4. It is a duty of matrimonial chastity to be restrained and temperate in the use of lawful pleasures.

5. Married persons by consent are to abstain from their mutual entertainment at solemn times of devotion.

6. "It were well if married persons would in their penitential prayers . . . ask a general pardon for all their undecencies and more passionate applications."

Without going into detail about shifts in attitudes in the present century, I want to focus on the line of reasoning about pleasure in the second principle above. Taylor explained that sexual appetite should be compared to appetites for food: just as in eating and drinking there is an appetite to be satisfied, "which cannot be done without pleasing that desire," yet since that desire and satisfaction was intended by nature for other ends, they should never be separate from those ends. Taylor seems to be arguing that in eating and drinking, one's purpose must be to supply the body's needs and not merely to have pleasure.[25]

The problem here seems not so much with fear or repression of sexuality, but rather the difficulty of affirming pleasure as a valid moral purpose in itself. There seems something rather perverse or out of touch in the notion that eating a chocolate bar (and enjoying it) is morally permissible if you are on a hike and need the calories, but wrong if your only reason is the pleasure of chocolate; and presumably, since hiking has the purpose of getting us from one point to another, or to provide exercise for our bodies, then simply going out for a walk for enjoyment would be morally questionable. This does not seem to be the right way to think about these matters.

Lust: the downside of sex. One thing that our modern culture needs to

---

[25]In discussing eating and drinking, Taylor says of temperance, "It does not eat and drink for pleasure but for need" (ibid., 1:64).

be reminded of is the potential destructive tendencies of lust, the desires regarding sex that can easily become disordered and immoderate. When we talk about the dangers of immoderate sexual activity, we almost always focus on observable damage, which can be extensive and severe: fatal diseases, broken relationships and divorce, abusive relationships, unwanted pregnancies and abortions, and so on. But our culture tends to accept sexual activity between consenting adults, as long as these bad consequences are avoided or guarded against.

What we have forgotten is that with sexual thoughts and desires (with or without corresponding actions) there are spiritual consequences in the mind and will. In his discussion of the results of lust Aquinas mentions these with respect to reason: (1) a blindness of mind, where our ability to apprehend some end as good and desirable is affected by lust; (2) deliberation and taking counsel about various courses of action is affected, sometimes by hastiness and rashness under the influence of lust; (3) lust also affects the stage of judgment, causing a kind of thoughtlessness; and (4) lust keeps us from carrying out what we have decided to do, and causes inconstancy.[26]

On the part of the will, the desire for the end is affected: instead of love for God, there is inordinate self-love, and to the extent that God's will is seen in opposition to self-love, a kind of hatred of God is generated. With regard to the lesser ends and the means to the final end, there develops a love for the present pleasures of the world, with a concomitant loss of interest in spiritual pleasures. Thus, even while we want to affirm the inherent goodness of sexual desire and activity, when in accordance with God's will, we need to be aware of the strength and potential for corruption of sexual desire when it is misplaced, disordered, excessive and not directed by prudence.

MODERN CULTURE AND THE NEED FOR TEMPERANCE

Classical Christian moral theology dealt with the "desires of the flesh" in terms of sex, food and drink, and with the recognition that pride and selfishness represented desires that were misdirected and unregulated by reason.

The aspect of consumerism in the modern world (which is rapidly expanding to China, India and other countries in the process of development)

---

[26]See Thomas Aquinas, *ST* II-II, q. 153.

is obvious but difficult to comprehend. This has led to awareness of the problems of scarcity of resources, pollution and degradation of the environment under industrial and commercial pressures, growing inequalities and many other spin-off problems. Without at all downplaying the importance of this materially destructive aspect of modern consumerism, my interest here is restricted to the relationship to the virtue of temperance and the effect on the mind and heart—a question that, though highly relevant to Christian virtue, seems not to be raised very much in comparison to the obvious consequences of consumerism.

In some ways the concerns of traditional Christian moral warnings against greed, coveting and the desire to acquire are dismissed in the adoption of the good of general economic expansion: the more that people consume, the more demand there will be for production and services, and then there will be higher employment and rising economic well-being for all. But perhaps the more obvious environmental limits to world growth should prompt also a reconsideration of the moral limits and the application of right reason to our lifestyle and consumption patterns.

The typical modern suburban American family (a significant percentage of which are churchgoing Christians) lives very differently from the Puritans, whose "Protestant work ethic" and habits of saving were seen by Max Weber to have been a force in the development of capitalism. But the old Protestant work ethic also involved an avoidance of self-indulgence and an ascetic lifestyle as part of Christian discipleship, while the contemporary American Christian (whether committed or nominal) is little different from any other modern American, having a fascination for larger and better televisions, the latest electronic gadgets, new fashions in clothing and home decorating, and so on. The contradiction between traditional moral ideals and modern lifestyle, as well as the undermining of the virtue of self-control has been noted by many observers: "The emphasis on consumption in modern American society undermines the value of self-control, despite the fact that hard work and self-reliance are the cornerstones of the American dream."[27]

The point is not that because our homes are larger and our closets are

---

[27]Christopher Peterson and Martin Seligman, *Character Strengths and Virtues: A Handbook and Classification* (Washington, DC: American Psychological Association; Oxford: Oxford University Press, 2004), p. 508.

brimming we are therefore much more greedy and indulgent than our grandparents. But we are unaware of the way in which our culture shapes us, since it is happening to almost all of us, and we take it as "normal." It relates to self-image and the need to construct and display our own individual identities in modern society, and we do that through the individuality of taste and expression that the variety of car models, of interior decorating possibilities, of musical tastes, of clothing styles and so on, allows. We no longer receive our identity and self-understanding from our localities and from traditions and roles; we have to construct this identity through consumerism.[28] This is alarming enough when applied to society in general; but consider the contradiction for the Christian, who is meant to have Jesus as the definer of personal identity and worth, and who is meant to be conformed to the image of Christ, but has no interest in understanding or following Jesus in having an appropriately Christian attitude toward possessions and lifestyle.

This is only to take a few stabs at a large and complex subject, but it surely needs further thought and analysis within the context of temperance, prudence and the Christian moral life in general.

FOR FURTHER READING

Thomas Aquinas, *ST* II-II, qq. 141-70.

Diana Fritz Cates, "The Virtue of Temperance," in *The Ethics of Aquinas*, ed. Stephen Pope (Washington, DC: Georgetown University Press, 2002), pp. 321-39.

Kent Dunnington, *Addiction and Virtue: Beyond the Models of Disease and Choice* (Downers Grove, IL: IVP Academic, 2011), especially chaps. 4 and 5.

Josef Pieper, *The Four Cardinal Virtues: Prudence, Justice, Fortitude, Temperance*, trans. Richard Winston et al. (Notre Dame, IN: University of Notre Dame Press, 1966).

---

[28]See John Webster, *Holiness* (Grand Rapids: Eerdmans, 2003), especially the conclusion, pp. 99-105.

14

FAITH

FAITH, LOVE AND HOPE are three individual theological virtues, but they are united in having God as source and focus: they indicate different aspects of the relationship of the Christian to God. One way to put it (the Thomistic way) is that faith unites the believer to God, the first truth; hope unites us to God, who is the highest good for me; and love (*agapē*) to God, who is the highest good in himself.[1] It follows, then, that faith is mainly (not exclusively) a matter of the intellect, and that hope and love are centered in the will.

One danger of making faith largely an intellectual matter is that many draw the conclusion that knowledge of the church's teaching, and agreement with it, are sufficient for the virtue of faith. One central concern of the sixteenth-century Protestant Reformation was the need for a living, relational faith built on trust in Christ, not just an intellectual concurrence with the articles of faith (or worse, "unformed" faith, referring to actual ignorance of doctrines but an implied general consent to what the church teaches). Karl Barth pointed out that a mere willingness to believe a series of doctrinal points is not yet faith; faith is not at heart a belief "that" but a belief "in" the God of the gospel.[2]

To bring out this attitudinal dimension, qualities of trust, commitment, following Christ and union with Christ were added to or even replaced the notion of faith as the contents or articles of faith. This has been a

---

[1]Romanus Cessario, *The Moral Virtues and Theological Ethics*, 2nd ed. (Notre Dame, IN: University of Notre Dame Press, 2009), p. 95.
[2]Karl Barth, *Evangelical Theology: An Introduction*, trans. Grover Foley (New York: Holt, Rinehart & Winston, 1963), p. 103.

central note of the Lutheran tradition, taken perhaps to its extreme point in the existential focus of Søren Kierkegaard, who so stressed the aspect of affirmation and commitment in the face of doubt that the famous "leap of faith" became a matter of the will's nearly blind commitment in the face of uncertainty.

When the volitional side of faith is emphasized in its definition, then faith begins to take on the characteristics of hope and love, and the essence of faith as a distinct virtue begins to disappear. The need to correct an intellectualized faith lacking in genuine Christian discipleship—what concerned the Protestant Reformers and the reform movements of Pietism, Methodism and Pentecostalism, against an orthodoxy "correct" in its teaching but dead in its Christian fruit—is understandable; however, the result can be that faith, hope and love become one composite virtue. This underlies the concern expressed by Kenneth Kirk: "Unless we define faith with primary reference to its intellectual character, it becomes almost indistinguishable from hope and love."[3]

On the other hand, one of the traditional expositors of Anglican moral theology, R. C. Mortimer, offers a chapter on the virtue of faith that is preoccupied mostly with the intellectual side of faith: the objectivity of faith, its relation to doubt, the nature of heresy and blasphemy, and the unforgiveable sin.[4] These same topics are to be found in Thomas Aquinas's treatment in the *Summa Theologiae*, but the reader wonders, where is the moral dimension, the link to human action and character that objective faith is meant to lead to?

Herbert Waddams criticized Mortimer for not recognizing the wider dimensions of faith; he pointed out that Mortimer seems to equate the "faith delivered to the saints" (faithfulness to intellectual content) with "justification by faith" (personal trust in God).[5] There is a misconception that faith is concerned with a mere "intellectual recognition of the facts," and that is a restriction not found in Aquinas, who stressed the insufficiency of faith

---

[3]Kenneth Kirk, *Some Principles of Moral Theology and Their Application* (London: Longmans, Green, 1934), p. 81.

[4]R. C. Mortimer, *The Elements of Moral Theology*, rev. ed. (London: Adam & Charles Black, 1953), chap. 7.

[5]Herbert Waddams, *A New Introduction to Moral Theology*, rev. ed. (London: SCM Press, 1972), p. 111.

unless completed by love.[6] Much more important than intellectual assent, said Waddams, is the personal relationship between the Christian and Jesus;[7] faith, then, is the act of trust and surrender that restores the right relationship between a person and God. Mortimer's limited view of faith reflects a kind of historical and institutional bias, according to Waddams:

> When . . . the theological virtue of faith is discussed, the fulness of its meaning must be remembered and in particular the implications which it carries of full surrender to God without any merit or standing on our part. The Lutheran insistence on this aspect is an essential part of true Christianity. Unhappily Roman and Anglican criticisms of Lutheran views have often misrepresented what they really meant.[8]

In the description that follows I will use the Thomistic account as a basis but will stress the relationship to action and character (rather than the matters of doubt, apostasy and heresy, which preoccupied the older Roman and Anglican handbook tradition). I will incorporate what Luther and Calvin considered essential to faith and conclude that the balance found in Jeremy Taylor's *Holy Living* provides a usable synthesis.

THE PRIORITY OF FAITH TO LOVE

Thomistic understanding of faith is based on the inherent relation of intellect and will. As established above in the early chapters on practical reasoning, the will does not operate without an object presented by the intellect, because the will does not move toward an object that is not understood (i.e., interpreted by reason) as attractive in some way.

The relationship between faith and love has the same basis. If the final goal is the underlying motivation for our actions, then this goal or ultimate end must be perceived or apprehended in the intellect. The ultimate end is in the will through the virtues of hope and love, and in the intellect through faith.[9]

Thus without some basic concept in the mind of the nature of God as the ultimate end, God simply will not be the object of our love. Thus faith in certain basic aspects of the revealed nature of God (involving both

---

[6]Ibid., p. 110, with reference to Thomas Aquinas, *ST* I-II, q. 65, a. 4.
[7]Ibid., p. 111.
[8]Ibid.
[9]See Thomas Aquinas, *ST* II-II, q. 4, a. 7.

knowledge and commitment) comes before, both logically and temporally, the actual response of love to God. We have Augustine's summary: "Wherefore there is no love without hope, no hope without love, and neither love nor hope without faith" (*Enchiridion de Fide, Spe, et Caritate* VIII).

The Bible makes this sequence clear: "We love him because he first loved us" (1 Jn 4:19). Aquinas reminded us that the response of God's people to the Decalogue is based first on the character of God as revealed in relationships of love and care: "I am the LORD your God, who brought you out of the land of Egypt, out of the house of slavery" (Ex 20:2).[10] The command and the expectation to love the Lord God above all else are based on faith in his love and promise of salvation.

There are historical reasons for confusion about the relation of faith to love: in the Roman Catholic tradition the Franciscan theologians emphasized love and freedom of the will without intellectual limitation.[11] In the Protestant tradition the collapse of Calvinism in Anglican theology led to the divorce of ethical motivation from systematic theology, and in moral philosophy the moral sense theories of Francis Hutcheson and others implied a theory of the human person whose natural sentiment was "benevolent." This provided a watered-down secularized version of love that could function without involving theological controversies.

More recently, the "situation ethics" of Joseph Fletcher, influential in the 1960s and 1970s, represented the slimmest vestige of the Christian tradition of love, where the one binding principle is "Do the loving thing." The lack of the virtue of faith is apparent in the complete neglect of the development of the true objects of love: God and neighbor. The command to love God above all else disappears into thin air without faith, and the command to love others degenerates into a principle to do what seems to be the most loving thing, judged mostly by a vague consequentialism.

Aquinas, in his discussion of the gift of understanding as part of faith (*ST* II-II, q. 8), emphasizes that correctness (*rectitudo*) of the will requires a corresponding grasp of truth. The object of the will is not just what is good

---

[10]Cited by Thomas Aquinas on the old law, *ST* II-II, q. 16, a. 1.

[11]See Servais Pinckaers, *The Sources of Christian Ethics*, trans. Mary Thomas Noble (Washington, DC: Catholic University of America Press, 1995), chap. 14, on late medieval developments in relating the will to morality.

without qualification, but things "interpreted as good." In other words, people may easily be mistaken about the qualities of what they are attracted to, and if the will is to be on the right track, this requires a "certain pre-existing knowledge of truth" (*ST* II-II, q. 8, a. 4).

The role of the Holy Spirit is crucial for both love and faith. "Just as the Holy Spirit orders the human will through the gifts of charity so that it may be moved toward a supernatural good, so through a gift of understanding the Holy Spirit illumines the human mind so that it may know certain supernatural truth towards which a right will should tend" (*ST* II-II, q. 8, a. 4). Here we note that not only are both faith and love dependent on the work of the Holy Spirit, but also love is dependent on faith for its correct direction.

The truth of this is either obscured or entirely ignored when love is thought to function without the virtue of faith. This is partly due to the disagreement on doctrinal matters, to the Enlightenment assumption that Jesus the moral teacher could be conveniently separated from belief in the Trinity, incarnation, atonement, miracles and other dogma. Upon reflection, we can see that the kind of God we believe in makes a difference to both the content of our visions of the goods to which we are directed and also to our motivations. In a world created by God but spoiled by sin, rather than a world produced haphazardly or by a competing source different from God, the need for atonement and the coming of Christ to judge the living and dead and whose kingdom will never end are appropriate morally and theologically. The unpopularity of the concepts of sin, judgment and hell point not just to the difficulties in the doctrines themselves, but to their sometimes unwelcome implications for moral reasoning, choice and action. The freedom to determine action and judge reasons and consequences without reference to accountability before God seems standard in the world of the twenty-first century.

We cannot return to the kind of thirteenth-century Thomistic Christian world when unity of doctrine was under ecclesiastical monopoly, and delineations of heresy and apostasy could be made and enforced. But if love does depend on faith, then a summary of a basic faith in creed or catechism as the core of Christian faith serves as a basis not only for a Christian worldview, but also for loving Christian action in the world.

THE ORIGIN OF FAITH

Herbert Waddams has written that faith is within the grasp of all of us: "There is no man who cannot have faith if he wills, unless he be mentally incompetent."[12] It is true that the potential for faith is there, but Waddams places too much emphasis on the ability and responsibility of the human will—that we stand before the entrance to the promised land, and all we have to do is decide whether to cross over there, or refuse to do so. Waddams makes clear his view of the volitional nature of faith: "Faith is the act of will which takes Jesus as a man's saviour and Lord. It is the decision which recognizes the truth of the claim of Jesus, 'I am the way, the truth and the life.'"[13] It is true that there is an element of the will in the assent that is a necessary part of faith,[14] but to reduce the generation of faith to a decision of the will is an oversimplification.

First, because faith is a virtue of the intellect, there is an attraction or drawing to the truth that needs to take place. The Gospel—the good news about God's triumphant love in Christ—should be presented to us as the most important truth that we will encounter. Faith, then, is what unites the believer to God as the "first truth," the reality behind all other realities, the truth that makes every other reality true. The decision to believe this is based on a kind of persuasion, a conviction, a realization, that the gospel is true, rather than on a decision of the will. Or, rather, there is a difference between the development of faith and the stark, infrequent decision (or affirmation of a previous decision) that confronts the believer as a choice between nonbelief and faith, between faithfulness to God and denial of him, such as Christian martyrs had to face and is implied in the challenge issued by Joshua: "Choose this day whom you will serve" (Josh 24:15). In those rare crisis points of life it is the resolute confident type of faith that is required; but in the ordinary development of faith, what is mainly required is a kind of humility, an openness, a recognition of the claims of truth.

This points, second, to the most important omission on the part of Waddams: the work of the Holy Spirit in the formation of faith. As Aquinas put it, in the assent that is essential to faith there is a supernatural prin-

---

[12]Waddams, *Moral Theology*, p. 111.
[13]Ibid.
[14]See Thomas Aquinas, *ST* II-II, q. 2, a. 1.

ciple at work. To put the generation of faith in human free choice is to make the mistake of the Pelagians.[15] When we assent to matters of faith, we are going above the natural areas of reality and evidence, and we need God to move us inwardly by his grace. This is a fundamental point reinforced by the Reformers.[16]

With that said, there is certainly room to talk about the means of encouraging or developing faith, or even recovering faith in the life of the believer. Here Jeremy Taylor has some helpful advice. Among his eight points here are the following helpful ingredients:[17]

- To have a humble, willing mind, with a desire to be instructed in the way of God;

- To remove all prejudice and love for things contradictory to faith;

- Prayer, both when sensing the need for wisdom and encouragement, and in times of temptation;

- To make a list of the reasons for belief in times of confidence to use as reminders in times when faith is challenged;

- The observation of the church's feast days (such as Easter and Ascension) as a great aid to our assent.[18]

FAITH, FEAR AND TRUST

The character of the God whom we believe in has something do with the framework for our decisions and actions. It is obvious that the doctrines of creation, providence, redemption and eschatology have a direct bearing on the attitudes making up part of the framework that we use for choosing our paths in life.

What Richard Hays describes as the "symbolic world" is generated by the

---

[15]See ibid., q. 6, a. 1. Note that the common translation "man's free will" does not accurately translate *liberum arbitrium*; it should be "free choice."

[16]See John Calvin, *Institutes* III.1.4.

[17]Jeremy Taylor, *Holy Living and Holy Dying*, ed. P. G. Stanwood, 2 vols. (Oxford: Clarendon, 1989), 1:178-79.

[18]While Jeremy Taylor offers practical and unexceptionable advice here, we note that there has been criticism directed at Taylor's tendency toward Pelagianism, shown in the reaction to Taylor's treatise on sin and redemption, *Unum Necessarium*. See C. FitzSimons Allison, *The Rise of Moralism: The Proclamation of the Gospel from Hooker to Baxter* (Wilton, CT: Morehouse Barlow, 1966), p. 63.

whole scriptural narrative and has to do with the human condition and the character of God.[19] Hays points to the analysis by Paul in Romans 1 of the fallen human condition, and to the characterization of God in Matthew 5:43-48 (God providing sun and rain for the unjust as well as the just), for example, as part of the mental framework for discipleship.[20]

The example used by Thomas Aquinas of faith's appropriation of a symbolic world and the character of God is the punishment for sins. Through faith, says Aquinas, we have a kind of apprehension of certain penal evils (*mala poenalia*) that are brought about by divine judgment. In this way, a certain level of faith (knowledge of God) is the cause of the kind of fear "by which one fears being punished by God."[21] This type of fear, called "servile" fear, is of course an immature or inadequate phase of relating to God. Lack of faith (i.e., lack of knowing the true God), in an uninstructed person, or in a secularist or post-Christian view of God, often hopes, or simply assumes, that judgment by God is simply not part of the picture that we as humans need to worry about, and that it probably is incompatible with the loving character of God.

Rather than removing judgment entirely, it ought to be put in the context of justification in Christ, and the relationship to God still has a kind of fear, but motivation and appraisal are quite different: by faith one fears to be separated from God, so sins are avoided for fear of losing the closeness to God. Aquinas writes, "Through faith we have this appraisal of God as an immense and highest good, to be separated from which would be the worst thing, and to desire to be equal to whom is an evil" (*ST* II-II, q. 7, a. 1).

This filial fear is based on faith in God as the great good not to be lost, and it results in a person's adherence to God and in obedience through love. Formally, the object of faith is prime truth (*veritas prima*), while materially, there are certain evils: sinners will sustain evil punishments from God, and it is an evil thing to be separated from God or not to be subject to him.[22] The contemporary preacher or theologian may perhaps be guilty of watering

---

[19]Richard Hays, *The Moral Vision of the New Testament: Community, Cross, New Creation; A Contemporary Introduction to New Testament Ethics* (San Francisco: HarperSanFrancisco, 1996), chap. 11.
[20]Ibid., p. 209.
[21]See Thomas Aquinas, *ST* II-II, q. 7, a. 1.
[22]See ibid., q. 7, a. 1.

down the faith to the extent that consideration of God's love excludes a judgment about sin.

A contribution of the Protestant Reformers was the insistence on the certainty of faith. Aquinas, for example, in his treatment of justification, left the question about whether a Christian might know that he or she has grace somewhat ambiguous.[23] It may be that what occupied Aquinas most at this point was the fact that there is no certainty corresponding to the knowledge of mathematical or scientific facts available to us, and that there is a kind of contingency attaching to our status as pilgrims on the way. But what we miss is the clear New Testament affirmation that "the Spirit himself testifies with our spirit that we are God's children" (Rom 8:16 NIV).

John Calvin was rightly critical of the hesitancy or ambiguity of the Scholastic theologians at this point, and he made sure to incorporate the aspect of assurance in his basic definition of faith, that it is "a firm and certain knowledge of God's benevolence towards us, founded upon the truth of the freely given promise in Christ, both revealed to our minds and sealed upon our hearts through the Holy Spirit" (*Institutes* III.2.7).

FAITH, ACTION AND SIN

Faith is concerned not just with the primary or foundational principles—the doctrines of God—but with all things that are connected to faith. One can apply theological principles to a wide range of matters, of course, but human actions are an especially important area. Aquinas reminds us of Paul's famous phrase "faith working through love" (Gal 5:6), which specifically links the actions of the Christian shaped by *agapē* love to the underlying theological vision. Actions are measured by a rule, for which we need both human reason and the gift of understanding to bring to bear the eternal law.[24]

As actions are brought into a relationship with eternal principle, they gain in meaning. Aquinas refers to the Augustinian doctrine of "eternal reasons" as the framework for judging, and to the role of the eternal law.[25] The character of God, as divine beatitude, is the ultimate foundation for the purpose and character of human acts, and to judge actions in that light requires the

---

[23]See Thomas Aquinas, *ST* I-II, q. 112, a. 5.

[24]See Thomas Aquinas, *ST* II-II, q. 8, a. 3.

[25]See ibid., q. 8, a. 3.

illumination of the Holy Spirit in the gift of understanding.

Examples will clarify the point. An act of generosity, getting married or attending a funeral are perfectly understandable and good moral actions on a human level because these actions are so integral to our common life, and because kindness, marital friendship and raising a family, and showing respect to the dead are commendable. But the additional perspective that comes from Christ's examples of kindness and generosity, or seeing marriage in the light of Christ's love for the church, or combining grief at a friend's death with confidence in the resurrection adds a much deeper dimension to our actions.

Enduring an unjust punishment may be done in a variety of different ways. One can endure with sullenness, with a vow to exact revenge or with simple acquiescence and resignation (as the sheep before the shearer in Is 53:7). But the character of Christ's patience is different; and when we follow Christ, the motivations are not masochism or resignation, but rather are connected to the example of Christ and to the character of God himself. Then the nature of the action of endurance has an altogether different character.

On the vexed and mysterious question of sin against the Holy Spirit, Aquinas, following Richard of Saint Victor, considers sin against the Holy Spirit in relation to sins against the Father and the Son. The Father may be associated with power, the Son with wisdom and the Holy Spirit with goodness. Thus, to sin from weakness would be sinning against the Father; to sin from ignorance, sinning against the Logos; and to sin against the Holy Spirit, sinning with a certain evil motive (*ex malitia*), explained by Aquinas as the very choosing of an evil.[26]

How might such an evil happen? First, it may arise from the inclination provided by a habitual vice; this kind of malice, however, is not sin directly against the Holy Spirit. But, second, one may have a kind of contempt that rejects or removes the thing which might have impeded the choice of sin. These impediments are things such as fear (of punishment) and hope, which are effects of the Holy Spirit in us, and to deliberately overrule their role in steering us away from sin is to impugn and blaspheme the Spirit.

This may be expanded into six different types of sin against the Holy

---

[26]See ibid., q. 14, a. 1.

Spirit, analyzed according to the complete removal of, or attitude of contempt for, the impediments meant to discourage us from sinful choices: (1) the judgment by God; (2) the very gifts of the Holy Spirit; and (3) on the part of the sin itself.[27]

First, the role that divine judgment plays in the consideration of sin is nullified either by a kind of despair that removes the hope that considers God's mercy in remitting sin and offering good gifts, or by the opposite, a certain presumption that ignores God's judgment on sin and consequent punishment that might generate a proper fear. Presumption is the false confidence that one may attain glory and reward without much effort or may receive pardon with no repentance.

Second, the gifts of God in the form of knowledge of the truth and interior grace can be resisted. The truth concerning sin is ignored or attacked in order to pursue sin and vice, while envy of others can work against the help available through grace.

Third, with regard to sinful action itself, two things might hinder the choice of sin. First, there is a consideration of the shame or disordered nature of the action. There ought to be a built-in reluctance against crimes and a recognition of the horror or sinfulness of it; unfortunately, this can be overpowered by a strong pattern of impenitence, resistant to what might otherwise draw us back from the brink of sinful action. Second, there ought to be a consideration of the limited results of the good to be found in the sin (pleasure), but this consideration can be overpowered by obstinacy. This becomes a kind of "pigheaded" determination to pursue the disastrous course of action in spite of the marginal benefits, the costs, the punishment and inconvenience, not to mention God's disapproval.

SIGNS OF FAITH

With a more strict focus on the consideration of faith as spiritual knowing, the concern in the *Summa Theologiae* is on the sharpness, accuracy and illumination of faith. With a more affective picture of the virtue of faith, then, the visible results or "signs" of faith have a broader scope. Kenneth Kirk, for example, set down these things as the visible fruits of a growing faith: (a) an

---

[27]See ibid., q. 14, a. 2.

equable temper in the vicissitudes of life, marked by "an unswerving optimism as to the supremacy at all times, of the providence of God"; (b) a
quality that, were it not founded upon God but on self, we would call self-
confidence or self-reliance; (c) a decline in impulsiveness before action, and
patience and perseverance in action; (d) "a certain simplicity and directness"
that is less interested in tact and goes straight to the point; (e) a spirit of
contentment and even joy in believing; and (f) an ardor for an ever-
increasing knowledge of the truth.[28]

The two qualities here that would clearly be associated with a Thomistic
virtue of faith are confidence in God's providence (a), and a desire to grow
in God's truth (f). The qualities of self-confidence (b), and directness (d),
seem to be individual characteristics, the product of the interaction of faith
with different temperaments (a person shy and retiring by temperament
could nevertheless have vibrant faith). Decline in impulsiveness, and growth
in perseverance (c), and contentment and joy (e), are qualities of other
virtues: prudence, courage and love, respectively (and thus indirectly reflective of faith, of course).

Jeremy Taylor's "signs of true faith" seem to be more directly connected
to the biblical model of faith:[29]

1. "Earnest and vehement prayer." Taylor's reasoning is that if we "heartily
   believe" the things of God and the glories of the gospel, it follows that
   we will desire and pray for what is promised from God.

2. "To do nothing for vain glory." We will be acting not for human glory,
   but for the praise of God.

3. "To be content with God for our judge, for our patron, for our Lord, for
   our friend; desiring God to be all in all to us, as we are in our understanding and affections wholly his."

4. "To be a stranger upon earth in our affections," by which Taylor means
   that if we truly believe that our inheritance is in heaven, we will not set
   our hearts on wealth or be upset by changes in worldly circumstances.

5. The best sign is found in the Epistle of James: "Show me your faith by

---

[28]Kenneth Kirk, *Some Principles of Moral Theology and Their Application* (London: Longmans,
Green, 1934), p. 104.
[29]Taylor, *Holy Living*, 1:176-78.

your works." True faith will reveal itself in corresponding behavior. Understanding and believing that one's sins are forgiven, for example, must result in readiness to forgive others.

6. The believer waits patiently until the times of refreshment come and dares to trust God for the morrow. If you dare trust to God when the case, to human reason, seems impossible, and trust out of choice, not because you have nothing else to trust to, "then you give a good testimony of your faith."

7. "True faith is confident, and will venture all the world upon the strength of its persuasion." People who fear the reactions of others more than God trust in human beings more than they believe in God.

8. Faith, if "true, living, and justifying," cannot be separated from a good life. This faith works the kind of miracle where a drunkard becomes sober, a lascivious person becomes chaste, and a covetous person becomes generous. In other words, faith truly "overcomes the world" (1 Jn 5:4) and makes us diligently to do, and cheerfully to endure, whatever God places in our way toward heaven.

SUMMARY

Thomas Aquinas has a sound foundation for the reality of faith, that it is connected to knowing the truths about God—indeed, it centers on God as the source of all truth—and needs enrichment with gifts of the Holy Spirit. True faith, as the Reformers pointed out, and as we see clearly in Jeremy Taylor, involves trust and stakes the whole of human life on God's care and providence, the truths of the gospel and the promise of salvation in Christ.

THE CHANGE IN THE MORAL VIRTUES

The structure provided by faith creates a set of reasons for acting, ultimate purposes and a network of new objects for intention in the framework of practical reasoning. "Seek first the kingdom of God" becomes a reason for acting for certain goals, but also for relativizing the importance of mundane goals involving, say, pension plans or mortgages. Not that they become unimportant, but that trust in God means that, as Jesus promised his disciples, "all these things will be given to you as well" (see Mt 6:33).

Faith in God is confidence in the cause, plan and purposes of God. When evil temporarily has the upper hand (e.g., in civil wars or unjust totalitarian regimes), the believer in God, like Aleksandr Solzhenitsyn in his years in the gulag, is able to have spiritual realities and God himself as a purpose for difficult actions beyond mere self-preservation (which, of course, is a powerful natural motivation that has kept many people going in severe circumstances).

If we turn to the key "focal images" identified by Richard Hays as the lenses by which we should look at our place and theater of action in the world, we have the new community, the cross and the new creation. These are concrete realities that inform our minds when we judge the significance and meaning of our actions, and they are added to us by our faith in Christ and his kingdom. The community that captures our allegiance is the body of Christ, the church, which is the bride of Christ. The cross symbolizes the reality of death to self, a sacrificial attitude, the acceptance of suffering and the resurrection in light of which the cross has its place. Together and with the power of the Spirit, we have the new creation that God is bringing about.

The devotion to God's kingdom and actual faith in the coming of Christ and the resurrection of the dead and the eradication of sin and death provide the focus for organizing an otherwise diffuse life and an ability to face death. Thus faith has a direct impact on the development of fortitude as well as the expansion of practical wisdom and the sharpening of self-control. The encouragement at the beginning of the Epistle of James provides a fitting conclusion: "My brothers and sisters, whenever you face trials of any kind, consider it nothing but joy, because you know that the testing of your faith produces endurance [*hypomonē*]; and let endurance have its full effect, so that you may be mature and complete, lacking in nothing" (Jas 1:2-4).

FOR FURTHER READING

Thomas Aquinas, *ST* II-II, qq. 1-16.

Romanus Cessario, *Christian Faith and the Theological Life* (Washington, DC: Catholic University of America Press, 1996).

Brian Davies, *The Thought of Thomas Aquinas* (Oxford: Clarendon, 1992), pp. 274-85.

John Jenkins, *Knowledge and Faith in Thomas Aquinas* (Cambridge: Cambridge University Press, 1997).

William Mattison III, *Introducing Moral Theology: True Happiness and the Virtues* (Grand Rapids: Brazos Press, 2008), chap. 11.

15

LOVE

IN THIS CHAPTER (and throughout this book) the terms *agapē*, "charity," "Christian love" and *caritas* are treated as synonyms for the virtue described by Paul in 1 Corinthians 13 and referred to by Jesus when reminding us that the two great commandments are to love God completely and to love one's neighbor as oneself.

At first, the description of *caritas* by Thomas Aquinas, at the start of his treatment of love in the *Summa Theologiae* (II-II, q. 23, a. 1), as essentially a kind of friendship seems questionable; but I hope to demonstrate here not only the legitimacy but also the wisdom of that bold approach by Aquinas. The most significant adjustment required on the part of many readers, especially those who have heard the usual range of sermons and teaching on Christian love, is to change the central definition of *agapē* from self-sacrificial love to the concept of friendship or union with God.

If we consider a couple of well-known biblical texts referring to God's love (*agapē*) for us in Christ, the self-sacrificial dimension seems central: "God proves his love for us in that while we still were sinners Christ died for us" (Rom 5:8); "We know love by this, that he laid down his life for us" (1 Jn 3:16). But we will see below that support for Aquinas's view of love as friendship rests not just on philosophical or theological principles, but on the Bible as well.

DIVINE AND HUMAN LOVE

God gives without needing anything in return. In creation and redemption, the self-giving and unconditional character of God's love can be highlighted so as to provide a model for human love that is centered on the object of love. On the cross the Son of God is the supreme example of self-sacrifice, and in the midst of the passion, more mindful of others than of himself, he says "Father, forgive them; for they do not know what they are doing" (Lk 23:34). The qualities of character exhibited by Jesus on the cross are the supreme instance of *agapē*, the distinctive Christian form of love. There is no thought of self, no thought for personal benefit. Further, there is no partiality or favoritism; Jesus' love was not just for the twelve whom he chose and for other close disciples, nor just for the chosen people, but for all who would receive him. The sacrifice upon the cross takes away the sins of the whole world—past, present and future, near and far.

If Jesus' love on the cross is the example par excellence for Christian love, then it seems to exclude friendship and other forms of love where there was mutuality and preferential relationships. This crucicentric basis for an understanding of love as totally free from any self-reference has been strengthened by various developments in theology and philosophy in the Western church, especially in Protestant circles.

Martin Luther, in his zeal to attack religion based on human "works," was suspicious of the Catholic doctrine (based on Augustine) of love seeking fellowship with God on God's own level by a Godward ascent of the soul inspired by spiritual desire. Justification by faith meant that God and humans meet only "on the level of sin," where God meets the sinner in Christ.[1]

Søren Kierkegaard, with his Danish Lutheran background, contrasted Christian love with the kind of love between friends or between husband and wife, which by definition is preferential, partial and limited, focused upon someone particular to the exclusion of others. The basis for this love is something loveable—that is, the presence of certain attractive qualities in the object of love. For Kierkegaard, this represented a disguised form of self-love, as well as a kind of love subject to change, depending on changes in the object of love.[2] Real Christian love, *agapē*, does not choose its object, but instead goes to help the neighbor, whoever that might be; and because such love is accepted as a duty, in obedience to the command to love our

---

[1]See John Burnaby, "Love," in *Dictionary of Christian Ethics*, ed. John Macquarrie (Philadelphia: Westminster, 1967), p. 199.
[2]See especially Kierkegaard's *Works of Love*, first published in 1847.

neighbor, it is independent of the qualities, good or bad, present in the other person and thus secure from change.

Another Lutheran theologian, Anders Nygren, had an enormous influence on twentieth-century theological reflection on love through his book *Agape and Eros*, published (and translated) in the 1930s. Nygren depicted Christian love in contrast to egocentric love as a contrast between *agapē* and *eros*. Love inspired by *eros* is the kind of love depicted by the Catholic tradition as the pursuit of good for oneself, and even though set on spiritual things and on God, it is still an earthly, acquisitive, selfish type of love. In contrast, *agapē* is entirely unselfish, seeking only the good of others, exemplified in the outgoing love of God, which loves irrespective of the qualities in the object of love. Since *eros* is the wrong kind of love, and *agapē* is divine love, the Christian's love for neighbor must be the *agapē* kind of love, poured into our hearts through grace and channeled toward others.[3]

Understanding the nature of Christian love as nonpreferential and a matter of the will obeying the command to love the neighbor harmonized well with principles articulated in the philosophical ethics of Immanuel Kant, himself influenced by the Lutheran tradition. Truly moral actions cannot be determined on the basis of personal attachment or affection, because that would be an unreliable foundation; there must be no self-regard, no preferential treatment. The divorce of morality from affection and from relationships of friendship was meant to secure an impartial, other-regarding benevolence in action.

A rather large body of theological ethics (including Reinhold Niebuhr) followed this approach, supported as it was by Kantian ethics and by the self-offering of Christ on the cross as the main exemplar.[4] In the mid-twentieth century it also seemed validated by the experience of the civil rights movement: many white people, when they were open and honest, realized that on the natural and cultural level of family, friends and social relationships, their natural inclination was not to associate with people of other races; while on the moral level there was an imperative to expand the

---

[3]Anders Nygren, *Agape and Eros*, trans. Philip Watson, 2 vols. (London: SPCK, 1938-1939).

[4]For recent surveys, see Bernard Brady, "Christian Love Is Sacrificial Love," in *Christian Love* (Washington, DC: Georgetown University Press, 2003), pp. 194-209; Werner Jeanrond, "Love as Agape," in *A Theology of Love* (London: T & T Clark, 2010), pp. 105-34.

circle of concern, to show the kind of love based on principles of equality, respect and nonpreferential regard.

If the understanding of love as totally other-regarding and unselfish was the result of a confluence of premises and principles from Kantian ethics, Lutheran theology, selective New Testament texts and elevating *agapē* above *philia*, then one can see the return or revival of mutuality and preferential aspects connected with divine love and Christian love for neighbor as similarly reflecting influences from different sources. We can point to philosophical traditions strongly critical of Kantianism (such as certain lines of feminist critique); the revival of Aristotelian ethics, especially the analysis of friendship; a closer analysis of the uses of *agapē* and *philia* in biblical texts; and a focus on other aspects of love in the New Testament, which have helped to provide a wide range of material for countering the view of *agapē* as essentially self-sacrifice.

We begin with Scripture and God. If *agapē* is the only virtue or quality directly affirmed to be equivalent to God's nature ("God is love" [1 Jn 4:16]), then love is associated with the very being or essence of God, even before revealing his love in creation and salvation. The relations between the persons of the Trinity enable God to be understood as multipersonal, able to give and receive love. There is a mutuality to the love within the Godhead that is much easier to explain with the concept of friendship than with a view of love as essentially self-sacrifice.

Leading up to the passion and death of Christ was the love that Jesus showed for the twelve disciples (in preference to others) and a kind of inner circle, with the disciple John singled out as the disciple "whom Jesus loved." And in the relationship Jesus had with Lazarus, Mary and Martha there is obviously a special affection for the women, and for Lazarus a deep sense of loss at his death in Bethany. Important too as a guide for the kind of love we are to return to Christ, Martha has often been seen as the self-sacrificing woman, thinking only of serving others (thus acting in a more "*agapē*-like" way), while Mary is talking with and listening to Jesus, engaging in friendship love, for which Jesus commends her to us.

Further, a close look at the use of *philia* and *agapē* in the New Testament does not support a clear difference between friendship and self-giving. In fact, sometimes *agapē* is used to describe improper, selfish love, such as the desire of the Pharisees for the praises of men (Jn 12:43), or for Demas, whose love "with this present world" caused him to desert Paul (2 Tim 4:10).[5]

The use of *agapē* is rare in much of the Synoptic material, and it is in the Gospel of John that love develops into a central Christian virtue. But it is precisely in the Johannine material where there is a large overlap between *agapē* and *philia* such that they are nearly synonymous. The attempt to distinguish *phileō* and *agapaō* in the dialogue of Jesus with Peter in John 21:15-17 is misguided in trying to establish that Jesus meant something different when switching from *agapaō* to *phileō* when the question was posed the third time: Peter was hurt not so much by the choice of wording, but because Jesus felt the need to ask him three times.[6]

Criticism of the nonpreferential, equal-regard mode of defining *agapē* or the highest form of love received impetus from a line of feminist reflection that questioned the assumptions of Kantian ethics and the transfer into Lawrence Kohlberg's model of moral maturity. Rather than understanding the ideal of love as a generalized, universal love without any special regard for particular individuals, Carol Gilligan and others pointed to the kind of love a mother shows in caring for a child. The love of a parent is largely other-regarding and self-sacrificial in many instances, and maternal caring is not contingent on the return of affection or love. But it is preferential, directed to specific objects of care.[7]

Stephen Post has helpfully developed an ethic based on this kind of parental nurturing love as the model for our understanding of the nature of *agapē*.[8] Post argues against the tendency to "idealize selfless love at the expense of mutuality" and contends that the desire for reciprocity and return of love actually reflects and is grounded in the nature of God's love. Rather

---

[5]For a helpful study, including the background of *agapaō* in the Septuagint, see James Barr, "Words for Love in Biblical Greek," in *The Glory of Christ in the New Testament: Studies in Christology in Memory of George Bradford Caird*, ed. L. D. Hurst and N. T. Wright (Oxford: Clarendon, 1987), pp. 3-18.

[6]See Gustav Stählin, "φιλέω, κτλ.," in *Theological Dictionary of the New Testament*, ed. Gerhard Kittel and Gerhard Friedrich, trans. Geoffrey Bromiley, 10 vols. (Grand Rapids: Eerdmans, 1964–1976), 9:113-71.

[7]Carol Gilligan, *In a Different Voice: Psychological Theory and Women's Development* (Cambridge, MA: Harvard University Press, 1993).

[8]Stephen Post, *A Theory of Agape: On the Meaning of Love* (Lewisburg, PA: Bucknell University Press, 1990); idem, *Spheres of Love: Toward a New Ethic of the Family* (Dallas: Southern Methodist University Press, 1994).

than try to exclude completely any self-regarding dimension to love under a concept of "selflessness," Post suggests that we aim at "unselfishness."[9]

A powerful challenge to nonpreferential love is the Aristotelian doctrine of friendship, in which the highest form of love for a friend is based on a mutual desire for the good of the other. The focus is completely on the good of the other, but there is a return, if you like, to each friend in the mutuality of the relationship. This kind of relationship, in the Aristotelian analysis, usually depends on similarity or equality of class, status and background.

LOVE, FRIENDSHIP AND GOD

Thomas Aquinas began his description of *agapē* (*caritas*) with the point that charity is essentially a form of friendship with God: there is a sharing of humankind with God by his sharing his happiness with us, and it is on this that a friendship is based. Aquinas refers to Paul's words in 1 Corinthians 1:9: "God is faithful; by him you were called into the fellowship of his Son." It is based on the relationship of love between the person of the Trinity, and it is the sharing of this love through Jesus Christ's incarnation that makes possible the participation of human beings in this love.[10]

This definition unites both the Aristotelian and biblical teaching on friendship and love, although there are strong prima facie objections to incorporating both sources. The Aristotelian definition of the highest form of love for the good of the other assumes a relationship of equality, and this of course seems impossible to apply to divine-human friendship, where the gap in level of being is immense, not to say infinite. But it is here we see the centrality of grace: the Holy Spirit and the work of grace in us create the possibility of a relationship that according to nature would be impossible, "astonishing" and "almost blasphemous."[11] It can be argued, in fact, that

---

[9]Post, *Theory of Agape*, pp. 11-12.

[10]On the originality and daring of Thomas Aquinas in using Aristotle to develop Christian love as friendship, see Fergus Kerr, "Charity as Friendship," in *Language, Meaning and God: Essays in Honour of Herbert McCabe, OP*, ed. Brian Davies (London: Geoffrey Chapman, 1987), pp. 1-23. Kerr provides a more recent and helpful reflection on the nature of the ethics of Thomas Aquinas in "Doctrine of God and Theological Ethics according to Thomas Aquinas," in *The Doctrine of God and Theological Ethics*, ed. Alan Torrance and Michael Banner (London: T & T Clark, 2006), pp. 71-84.

[11]See Paul Wadell, *The Primacy of Love: An Introduction to the Ethics of Thomas Aquinas* (New York: Paulist Press, 1992), pp. 63-64.

Aquinas is really following the teaching and example of Christ in the Gospels rather than being influenced by Aristotle.[12]

Agapē love is focused on the goodness of God. A friendship of the deepest sort is sharing in the mutual desire for the good of the other. For the person of faith, who knows God to be the greatest and ultimate good—the *summum bonum*—the love for God is a love of both the goodness of God and one's own good. The element of contradiction or "self-regard" involved in this is firmly set aside by reflecting on the role of grace: it is the *sharing* of God's eternal beatitude that must be given by God through grace, so that the human being brings nothing but the self to the sharing, as he or she would in a marriage or other deep human friendship. The intentional basis of *agapē* is not just benevolence or selflessness; it is directed to the goodness and glory of God.

The discussion by Jennifer Herdt of the doctrine of love in Augustine provides a helpful summary. When we truly love ourselves, she points out,

> we seek to enjoy the Supreme Good, but this means that we love God more than self, that we surrender ourselves to God. It is not the case, then, that the eudaimonistic framework requires that all other loves are in fact subordinated to love of self. I am not my own supreme good; my end is not self-enjoyment but enjoyment of God.[13]

Can someone have virtue without Christian love? Can someone act well, habitually, and yet not have God as final end? These are important questions both practically and theoretically. What are we to make of the discipline, generosity, fairness, patience and courage (not to mention sacrificial love) of many non-Christians who have no relationship to God or Jesus Christ?

In the *Summa Theologiae* Thomas Aquinas points out that there are human actions that have ends that are intrinsically good, capable of being ordered to the right final end: raising families, fulfilling work, play, conver-

---

[12]Anthony Keaty argues that John 15:15 is the primary authority for Thomas's discussion of charity, "since the love which is charity is revealed in and made possible for the disciples only through Christ's own love for his disciples. While Aristotle's categories of benevolence and communication are used to construct a definition of charity, the content for the benevolence and the communication that define charity are displayed paradigmatically only in Christ's friendship love for the disciples described in John 15:15" ("Thomas's Authority for Identifying Charity as Friendship: Aristotle or John 15?" *Thomist* 62 [1998]: 594).

[13]Jennifer Herdt, *Putting On Virtue: The Legacy of the Splendid Vices* (Chicago: University of Chicago Press, 2008), p. 55.

sation with friends and so on. Other actions have ends that are apparent goods (not actual or genuine goods) such as power over others, certain pleasures and so on, which cannot be brought into line with a proper ordering to the final end. In 1 Corinthians 13 Paul talks about the patience, skill, wisdom, self-sacrifice, immense generosity, fidelity and so on that a person might have, but that all of these come to nothing unless there is *agapē*.

Aquinas gives a more philosophical explanation in the *Summa Theologiae*. All the other virtues are given their form and ordering by *agapē*. This is because an action has its essential nature given to it by the end or final purpose. The will, which is the principle of moral actions, is moral by the end it is moving toward. Thus *agapē*, by its orientation to God as ultimate goodness, provides the proper ordering for all the other virtues (*ST* II-II, q. 23, a. 8).

The sharing in the divine goodness is something beyond our natural abilities, of course; it is something that must be given to us in grace, by the Holy Spirit. It is the Holy Spirit, who is the bond of love between Father and Son,[14] who becomes the actual principle of our sharing in the divine friendship (*ST* II-II, q. 24, a. 2).

This means that unlike the patterns of ordinary virtues, there can be no question of the increase or growth in the virtue of *agapē* by mere repetition of actions and building up a disposition as we do with moral virtues (*ST* II-II, q. 24, a. 6). *Agapē* is purely the result of grace.

This explains why *agapē* is lost with serious sin, and modern theologians have found this a troubling teaching. But seen in relational terms, the bond of love created by the Holy Spirit is bound to be affected by sin; as Aquinas put it when describing the dynamic motivation of sin, it is a case in which "man prefers sin to divine friendship" (*ST* II-II, q. 24, a. 12).

Every mortal sin is contrary to charity. Thus Christian love can be lost (*ST* II-II, q. 24, a. 11), because in this life the very essence of God, the essence of goodness, can be lost. Addressing the specific question of the loss of *caritas* through one mortal sin, Aquinas says that an act of mortal sin is corruptive of the very rationale of *agapē*, which is that God is to be loved above all things (*ST* II-II, q. 24, a. 12).

Human beings are to be totally subject to God, and everything is to be

---

[14]See Thomas Aquinas, *ST* I, q. 37.

referred to him (God being one's highest end not just in name but in reality). This means that we are to be subject to God in everything, and to follow the rule of his precepts in all things. Therefore, whatever is contrary to God's precepts is contrary to *caritas*. If Christian love were acquired by building up actions, then a single action would not result in its loss; but since charity is "infused," or shared with us by the Holy Spirit, then divine friendship is lost when a person prefers the sin to divine friendship. The analogy that Aquinas used was that the light of the sun disappears when an obstacle comes in between it and what it shines upon.

THE OBJECTS AND PRIORITIES OF LOVE

It is because of the incarnation of God in Christ that we know the love of God for us. Thus our knowledge of God's love and our own love for God begin in Christ and are centered in him; and this in turn provides the basis for our love for other people and all other beings. As Oliver O'Donovan has put it,

> Love of Christ has priority over all other obligation because it is the love of Jesus as the Christ, the acceptance of him as the one whom the Father has sent. From it there follows that we are given to love the whole of reality in its due order: God, the neighbor, self and the world. And from it there follows obedience to the authoritative teaching and life which interpret what is given us in reality, "if you love me, you will keep my commandments" (Jn 14.15). It is a love which springs from faith, and which therefore loves the universal in the particular, finding in Jesus the head in whom every neighbor is summoned to appear before God and in whom the non-human creation awaits its redemption.[15]

The love for neighbor is based on love for God. This is not just the motivation for love, but the object of love. If love in general is for the good of the other person, then the supreme good for the other person is to be in God, to have union with God, and that is precisely what we desire for the other. All the rest of the good things that we desire for another—security, fulfilling relationships, success in work and so on—are secondary and included in wanting what God wants to provide.

Are animals to be loved in the same way? If Christian love is a form of

---

[15]Oliver O'Donovan, *Resurrection and Moral Order: An Outline for Evangelical Ethics*, 2nd ed. (Grand Rapids: Eerdmans, 1994), p. 243.

friendship, then we cannot will the good for our friends in the animal kingdom, at least not in the same way. Since animals cannot experience "good" in a rational way, it is only in a limited way that we can love them. Since animals have no free choice, this is the basic factor of distinction. It is not rationality per se (e.g., the ability to understand a recipe or newspaper article), but the ability to have purpose in action. Animals show affection and loyalty, but in a trained or programmed sense. When a friend makes a telephone call or a visit or sends a letter of condolence, this represents an *act* of kindness, concern, a choice to show friendship, that an animal is incapable of. Fundamentally, animals cannot be a part of the human community; more profoundly, divine friendship shares in eternal beatitude, and animals are not capable of sharing in this, and thus we cannot properly extend Christian love to animals in this way.

What about love for self? Love of self would seem to be just as impossible (in a logical, formal sense) for a theory of love defined in terms of friendship as it is for self-sacrificial love. There is, first, an apparent contradiction in conceiving of mutuality or exchange in the notion of love for self. We also have a couple of verses (among others) in Scripture that undermine this notion of self-love. As Thomas Aquinas noted, "Love . . . does not seek its own" (1 Cor 13:4-5 NASB), and there is a verse describing people in a degenerate age who, besides possessing many other bad qualities, were primarily "lovers of themselves" (2 Tim 3:2).[16]

It is possible to distinguish here between self-love that is directed toward the wrong goods—pleasure, power, money, abuse and so on—and in the context of an aversion from God and true good (which is clearly spelled out in 2 Tim 3), and self-love that seeks what is truly good in accordance with our nature as created by God.[17] But if you take *agapē* as friendship love for God primarily, including whatever belongs to God, then a person can certainly include love for self under the framework of love for all that concerns the heart of God.

When we consider other sinful people, we make a distinction between their natures—who they are created to be—and the blemishes and distortions that occur because of sin. To the extent that others, even very sinful

---

[16]See Thomas Aquinas, *ST* II-II, q. 25, a. 4.
[17]See ibid., q. 25, a. 4.

people, have natures that are capable of transcendence and the enjoyment of God's presence (to which faith and hope direct us), then we affirm and love them in the light of our love for God. But we regard sins and moral faults as obstacles to their enjoyment and capacity for beatitude, so *in that respect* we cannot love them. We cannot both desire the kind of love that would bind them to fellowship with God and also look kindly on the very qualities of character that constitute a barrier to that fellowship.

What about love for enemies? Is there not too deep a contradiction between enmity on the natural level and the attempt to show Christian love? If a Christian disciple were to take our Lord's injunctions in Matthew 5 to love one's enemies and to turn the other cheek, would this not imply that we could not resist with violence? It would seem either that we have to recognize that some people put themselves (at least temporarily, such as the Nazis during World War II) beyond the operating range of Christian love, or that if we truly love all people, including our enemies, then we must follow those who find that pacifism is the genuine implication of the teaching of Jesus and a requirement for the Christian disciple.

The distinction, following Aquinas, is analogous to love for the sinner. To the extent that a person is indeed our enemy (and not merely perceived to be), we cannot love that person in that regard. But as human beings, and as genuine objects of God's love, our love for God must extend to enemies in that they have been created and have potential for fellowship with God, even if there is no sense of affection for them.[18] Further, an attitude of *agapē* toward all people in general should lead us to be prepared to show acts of kindness to particular enemies if the occasion arises.

Are there certain priorities in our loving? There is a sense in which we ought to universalize love, when we step back and understand the world, with all its individuals, as the object of God's love and beneficence. In Christ, God loved the entire world. Our love for God implies that we need to understand that general benevolence with which God views the entire universe,

---

[18]Gilbert Meilaender thought that Aquinas has not explained very well love for an enemy, because unless there is a union on the level of affection, there is no real friendship (*Friendship: A Study in Theological Ethics* [Notre Dame, IN: University of Notre Dame Press, 1981], p. 48). But Aquinas's category of loving (or trying to love) what our friend cares for is much more like trying to "be nice" to a rather threatening dog owned and loved by our friend: we have no affection for the dog directly, but we behave as if we do, knowing how much our friend cares for the dog.

the world and humanity in connection with the kingdom of God.

Since we are embodied creatures in time and place, including geographical location and culture, living in families and close relationships with relatives, neighbors and friends, there is an important sense in which we have priorities and different degrees of love. It will not do to divide up these relationships in categories of familial affection (*storgē*), marital love (*eros*), close friendships (*philia*), and then leave *agapē* or Christian love for the "real" project of loving the needy, the members of the church and humankind in general. If we are following Aquinas in extending *agapē* to be a form of friendship, this implies a partial reordering here; a good marriage must be seen as encompassing all four forms of love, since Ephesians 5, with its comparison to the relation between Christ and the church, links the affectionate, erotic and friendship aspects of love in a context where faithfulness, self-giving and the eschatological union (heavenly banquet) are part of the connection of *agapē* with married love.

Clearly, we ought to love God more than our neighbor, because God is the source of the ultimate good that we desire for our neighbor. The highest form of love for our neighbor is that we can share with them the happiness of the presence of God.

What is the relationship between love for oneself and love for neighbor? The answer from Thomas Aquinas will be surprising and counterintuitive at first, especially if one is approaching Christian love from self-sacrificial assumptions. He uses a philosophical consideration of the distinction between union and unity. With oneself, there is a fundamental sense of oneness, more intimate of course but also more important than the relationship with another person based on a union of association (whether kinship, ordinary friendship or *agapē*). Thus in our love for God, the fact that we ourselves participate in it directly makes it more direct and fundamental than our desire to share that with another. The proof or "clincher" of this view is that we are not permitted to commit a sin even in order to help another person, even if our sin helps to free someone from a sinful situation in order to be joined with God. We may not attack our own union with God and eternal beatitude even for the purpose of enabling someone else to experience it (*ST* II-II, q. 26, a. 4).

In comparing our neighbor relationships, we might say that we have the same concern ("interior affection") for all people, but not the outward demonstrations of affection (*ST* II-II, q. 26, a. 6). There is a principle of closeness that operates with people as with God: the nearer the object of love is to God and to the person loving, the dearer it is.

In respect to the good that we wish for people, there is a kind of equality, because the absolute good, eternal beatitude, is the best that we can desire for all; but in terms of the intensity of affection, we are not going to be loving everyone equally (*ST* II-II, q. 26, a. 6 ad 1).

Relatives are more closely connected, and there are more reasons for loving them, including the sharing of common background and community solidarity. But because these relationships are something given rather than chosen, they are different from friendships formed by choice and affinity, which can be stronger than the affection of kinship.

Can one compare the kind of love we should show to parents and to children? Aquinas pointed out the principles involved here: (1) in terms of the *object*, in which case the degree of closeness to God and what represents the greatest good would be the principle of ordering; or (2) in terms of the *one who loves*, and here it is the degree of intimacy that is the controlling factor. Parents rank highest with the first criteria, because they have a quasi-divine status in relationship to us: they gave us being, and we simply would not exist without them. As a parent of children, however, there is a greater bond of love, because children represent something of the parents themselves (both through nature and nurture) and constitute a living continuation of the parents' lives. And the affection for a child begins at birth and often before.

Can we compare the love between husband and wife with the love between children and parents? This also has some of the tricky complication of competing principles involved, and this complexity offers insight into the difficulties that many married couples experience with competing loyalties and the degree to which leaving father and mother and becoming one flesh changes these relationships with parents. Parents are to be preferred over spouse in terms of representing principles of existence and nurture; however, in terms of closeness of relationships and intimacy, a spouse is to be loved more. Aquinas cannot solve, of course, the many practical dilemmas that couples face (e.g., in planning the frequency of visits home) when he summarizes: "A man loves his wife more intensely, but should show greater reverence for his parents" (*ST* II-II, q. 26, a. 11).

These relationships are based on natural relationships, geography and conditions on earth. As such, these principles of ordering involving neighbors, friends and relatives and marriage partners will come to an end in heaven. We know from the teaching of Jesus that the kingdom of God has a higher reality and loyalty than familial ties, and that marital bonds will not have the same meaning or even existence in heaven (Mt 22:30). The basic principle in heaven, of course, will be the degree of closeness to God, and our love for those (such as the most devoted saints) who were closest to God will be greater than for others. And there will no longer be a need for people to prioritize their care and concern as there is on earth.

THE EFFECTS OF LOVE

The results of union with God and living in that love are evident to us and to others, since they involve feelings and attitudes as well as actions and behavior. Joy, peace and mercy are the attitudes generated by friendship with God, which may be seen as the "interior" effects, while the "exterior" effects are good deeds, generosity to the poor, and fraternal correction. Of course, no rigid boundary can be drawn here, since relationships to others and style of behavior certainly will be affected by the degree of joy and peace in our hearts. Mercy crosses the boundary, since it would be a defective form of mercy that resulted only in a feeling of pity for others and not in concrete action.

Joy. The presence of God is closely associated with joy. "In your presence there is fullness of joy; in your right hand are pleasures for evermore" (Ps 16:11). In Jesus' discourse to the disciples about abiding in God as branches are united to a vine, we have this close link between union with Christ, discipleship and behavior, and joy: "If you keep my commandments, you will abide in my love. . . . I have said these things to you so that my joy may be in you, and that your joy may be complete" (Jn 15:10-11).

Even on the more pedestrian level of philosophical ethics, a key theme in Aristotle's depiction of human action and virtue is that pleasure and happiness are associated with finishing a task, performing something well and developing excellence. There is greater pleasure in becoming accomplished at an activity, such as playing the flute, becoming good at rock climbing or dancing the tango. And the happiness associated with the development of moral virtues, self-control, courage, wisdom and so on, is of a higher order.

If we approach the matter in this way, we can see the importance and centrality for Thomas Aquinas of the link between joy and Christian love. There is the strong biblical emphasis on the joy of knowing and serving God; there is the pleasure that humans are meant to find in human excellence; and then understanding *caritas* fundamentally as the deepest possible kind of friendship and union unites these strands in a powerful source of profound joy: God, the object of our love, is not only the most faithful and devoted friend, but also is the truth for our contemplation, the good for our deepest desire, the inexhaustible source of grace that makes it possible to be united to him and supplies the power and gifts for developing virtues beyond our capacities. God supplies us grace so that we are enabled to develop more Christlike virtues and deepen the quality of our relationship with the Trinity; thus joy comes not only from the union itself, but also from the increasing capability of friendship and from the actions and behavior that belong to a more Christlike life.

We will see shortly how important the connection between *caritas* and *gaudium* ("joy") was for Thomas Aquinas. There is hardly a hint of this in the entire post-Thomistic moral tradition on charity and love. R. C. Mortimer and Herbert Waddams deal with love but not joy; neither did Kenneth Kirk, who should have made this connection, at least in the treatment of the links between moral and ascetical theology in *The Vision of God*.[19] Taking Henry Davis as typical of the Roman Catholic handbook tradition, we see the relics of the Thomistic analysis of charity, and discussion of self, neighbor and the order of love, but only a strange little bit on pity, and no treatment of joy or peace.[20] A popular concise edition of the *Summa Theologiae* includes only a little snippet of reference to joy,[21] and perhaps more tellingly, one of the key pre-Vatican II books in moral theology that pointed away

---

[19]Kenneth Kirk, *The Vision of God: The Christian Doctrine of the Summum Bonum* (London: Longmans, Green, 1931).

[20]Henry Davis, *Moral and Pastoral Theology*, vol. 1, *Human Acts, Law, Sin, Virtue*, 2nd ed. (London: Sheed & Ward, 1941).

[21]See Timothy McDermott, *Summa Theologiae: A Concise Translation* (Westminster, MD: Christian Classics, 1989).

from the emphasis on law to the central role of love in the theology of Thomas Aquinas has no treatment at all of the important connection to joy.[22] Whether or not the influence of Kant is part of the explanation, it seemed logical to separate the topics of joy and union to Christ from ethics and relegate them to ascetical or spiritual theology.

Love causes joy in two ways: either because the object of love is present, or because what we love is in possession of what is good.[23] In other words, when we are in the presence of people we love, we are happy; but we can also experience joy when we hear good news (e.g., a new job or wedding engagement) about someone we care about. In the case of God, however, who is his own goodness, joy comes from the love of abiding in him (1 Jn 4:16).

This theme of the enjoyment of the presence of God, while clearly biblical and prominent in spirituality both Catholic and Protestant, is made more prominent by Aquinas than his predecessors, clearly buttressed as it is by the strong category of friendship. Though Augustine may be the premier theologian of love, his view of love has a stronger element of hope and less emphasis on present joy. As Michael Sherwin has argued,

> Augustine's theology of love is primarily a theology of hope. . . . When Augustine in *On Christian Doctrine* defines charity as a *motion toward* enjoying God instead of as simply the enjoyment of God, he underlines an aspect of charity that exists only in this life. . . . This is understandable in Augustine's concern to show that perfect happiness (and thus also the perfect enjoyment of God) is possible only in heaven. As a consequence, however, Augustine underemphasizes charity's other aspects, especially its proper act of benevolent well-wishing.[24]

Our joy in God is often qualified to the extent that our participation in the goodness of God is limited by something that is contrary to it, and there is a sense of sorrow, perhaps, in recognizing the limitation or barrier to potential joy.

Peace. Peace is sometimes associated with joy, as in Romans 14:17: "The

---

[22]Gérard Gilleman, *The Primacy of Charity in Moral Theology*, trans. William Ryan and André Vachon (Westminster, MD: Newman, 1959).

[23]See Thomas Aquinas, *ST* II-II, q. 28, a. 1.

[24]Michael Sherwin, "Aquinas, Augustine, and the Medieval Scholastic Crisis Concerning Charity," in *Aquinas the Augustinian*, ed. Michael Dauphinais, Barry David and Matthew Levering (Washington, DC: Catholic University of American Press, 2007), p. 203.

kingdom of God is not food and drink but righteousness and peace and joy in the Holy Spirit." Peace is not a separate virtue, but, like joy, is caused directly by *agapē* for God and for neighbor. There is no other virtue to which we can say that peace is related so directly.[25]

Following Augustine (in *The City of God*), we extend the notion of peace to cover not only relationships among people, but also the unifying of different aspects of the human personality, so that a person is at peace when there is no discord between emotion, will, reason, imagination or any other aspect of the soul or psyche. One needs to remember, as well, that though all things seek peace in a generic fashion, there can be a false or illusory peace, just as many seek only what is apparently good. True peace can be achieved only by unified focus on what is truly and actually good.

Thus peace in a person's life comes about when heart, soul, mind and strength are centered on God as the true good above all; and peace among people is realized when they are united in what is good for each other. This does not mean that people who are, as the *Book of Common Prayer* puts it, "in love and charity with their neighbor" will share the same opinions about things; but what is important is that they have a common agreement on what constitutes moral good.[26] Members of a church fellowship will disagree about which films are best, what music to include in worship, and which political party to support, but their shared faith expressed in the creed and their participation in the new life in Christ are what provide the basis for Christian love.

Mercy. Following Augustine, Thomas Aquinas can define mercy as "heartfelt compassion for another's misery, a compassion which drives us to do what we can to help him" (*ST* II-II, q. 30, a. 1, citing Augustine, *The City of God* IX.5). We feel a kind of sadness when people encounter disasters and evils that cause them harm. When such people are dear to us, or are special friends, then the misfortune is felt even more keenly, because the misfortunes are felt as closer to one's own.

Both philosophy and Scripture can be referred to here. Aristotle made one of the functions of friendship to sorrow with one's friends (*NE* IX.4), and Paul tells us, "Rejoice with those who rejoice, weep with those who

---

[25]See Thomas Aquinas, *ST* II-II, q. 28, a. 4.
[26]See ibid.

weep" (Rom 12:15). Thomas Aquinas adds that older people and those with more experience in society often are better able to be sympathetic because they realize the real possibility of misfortune for themselves, in contrast to the attitude common among young people of being immune to disaster, seeing misfortune as abstract or as something that happens to other people elsewhere.

The narrow horizons of premodern society must be modified, of course, to take into account the ability of modern media to bring home to us disasters such as famine, floods and earthquakes, which may happen anywhere in the world, but whose occurrence impinges on us. We need to be moved to pity by the presentation of urgent needs. Nevertheless, just as it is not wrong to show more love and care to those in our family or congregation than to people we do not know, so it is not wrong to be sometimes more concerned with a lesser misfortune suffered by a relative (e.g., the loss of a job) than with a family on the other side of the world who have lost their home.

Mercy is an excellent quality, especially in those who are in a superior position of command or responsibility. God, who of course has no superior, is especially associated with mercy and kindness. For human beings, mercy probably is the most important feature in terms of our relationships to others and love of neighbor, because it is what leads us to actually be involved in the relief of other people's needs. But overall, of course, *agapē* toward God, which unites us to him, is more fundamental.

Doing good in a general sense can be seen as an attitude of kindness associated with Christian love. Thinking of *agapē* in the sense of friendship focuses on willing the good for our friend. Of course, in our love for God it is not our part to "do good" to God, but rather to honor him with our submission, and it is for him to be gracious to us out of his love for us.[27]

There is an ordering to charity based on closeness of relationship and the various bonds that we share: in kinship, we have biological ties; with fellow citizens, a shared civil community; and with fellow Christians, a bond of fellowship in Christ. It is not wrong to take these linkages into account, and other things being equal, our kindness naturally reflects these relational bonds. But when we reflect on kindness, we need, in principle, to be open

---

[27]See ibid., q. 31, a. 1.

to showing kindness to all whom we may come in contact with, as the parable of the good Samaritan so powerfully teaches. Even though "charity begins at home" in ordinary circumstances, we need to be prepared for the possibility of showing kindness to those beyond these circles who are in need, especially if there is a major or urgent need requiring help. An important form of concern and help is to pray for all, whether Christians or not, and this is a form of kindness that we ought to practice.[28]

In a kind of triage situation, where a choice might have to be made in an emergency between rescuing a parent or a child, or between helping a close friend or an important official, there probably can be no general rule. There are too many variables in circumstances and degrees of need and relationship, and this points to the need for the development of discernment and practical wisdom.[29]

Just as *charity* by its narrow frame of reference in contemporary English misrepresents the virtue by extreme limitation, so the term *almsgiving* is an even worse misfit, conjuring up in our minds little Victorian alms boxes with a slot for a sixpence or a shilling perhaps. This misleading and constricting term is retained, unfortunately, in the most recent translations of the *Summa Theologiae*. "Generous and loving involvement in the lives of others" would be much more apt, as what is envisioned and described is a fairly complete range of helpful actions for the physical and spiritual needs of the neighbor. This kind of generous concern includes the efforts to provide food and sustenance, clothing, shelter, in addition to visiting the sick and caring for those in prison; but there is also concern for a person's spiritual welfare, including forgiveness, reproof if necessary, living with the consequences of an evil act of someone else, sharing others' burdens and, as an act of love, putting up with people whose behavior is strange or disordered. We are not used to the spelling out of this range of action as a manifestation of the generosity of Christian love, but it certainly accords with Paul's description that *agapē* is not rude or irritable, but rather bears and endures all things (1 Cor 13:5-7).

Fraternal correction. Fraternal correction ought to be considered as an effect or expression of *agapē*, although it would strike many contemporary

---

[28]See ibid., q. 31, a. 2.
[29]See ibid., q. 31, a. 3; see also chap. 10 above, "Wisdom in Action."

Christians as "judgmentalism." Appropriate correction has two aims in mind in addressing a sinful act: the hurt to the sinner, and the injury or scandal that may affect the community.

Attempts to evangelize or bring people into a relationship with God are seen in many Christian circles as coercive or even unloving; instead, they should be seen as an expression of love for God. It simply means "that there is, in our love for the neighbor, a recognition of his calling and destiny to fellowship with God and a desire to further that destiny in the context of concern for his welfare."[30]

Since love is what directs our will to the well-being of our brother or sister (in Christ), then helping to ward off the harm caused by sin is really more important than dealing with sickness or poverty, since sin undermines the moral virtue that is close to the essence of Christian love itself.[31] Of course, correction that stems from jumping to conclusions about someone's motives, that expresses one's own animus toward the other person or that is not proportionate may make the situation worse and will not be a genuine expression of charity.

One need not be perfect to provide correction, of course, for otherwise it would be impossible. Appropriate correction requires good judgment, which a person can retain even though he or she may have committed serious sins as well. As a member of a monastic community, Thomas Aquinas would have had relevant experience here to provide some caution. Since the whole point of correcting a brother or sister is for that person's recovery (of spiritual health), we should not feel obliged to supply correction whenever something wrong is done, but only when it is necessary for the purpose of healing. Circumstances, time, place and manner need to be handled with wise care.

THE VICES OPPOSED TO LOVE

Thomas Aquinas rounds out his discussion of Christian love by considering outward manifestations and actions contrary to charity, including schism, war, sedition and scandal, which are manifestly opposed to and destructive of charity. It is important to note the wide scope of the virtue of love in

---

[30]O'Donovan, *Resurrection and Moral Order*, p. 229.
[31]See Thomas Aquinas, *ST* II-II, q. 33, a. 1.

Aquinas's schema, even if we have to draw limits to any detailed consider-ations here.[32] But what seems clearly relevant in this section of the *Summa Theologiae* is the treatment of hate, sloth and envy as contrary to *caritas*.

Hatred. Hatred of God, obviously, is directly opposed to Christian love. But is that even possible? For if the will is, by its nature, drawn to what is good or interpreted as good, then would we not love God? Strictly speaking— and Aquinas is consistent with his principles—it is indeed impossible to hate the goodness of God; but in this life we do not directly encounter God in his goodness. Thus there is room for lack of clarity or doubt about the goodness of God, which does not furnish a basis for hatred, but it does ex-plain the freedom that we have as human beings not to love God if we are not persuaded or drawn by the Holy Spirit.

If people consider God in his role as the enemy and punisher of sin, then those who are attached to sin—a sign of disordered will—may well perceive God as an object of hatred.[33] This makes the hatred of God an especially "sinful sin" in the sense that all sin involves a turning away from God, but in other sins the turning away is an indirect turning, where here we are speaking about a direct and intentional aversion from God.

What about hatred for our neighbor? Here it is apt to apply the slogan "Hate the sin but love the sinner" because, as we noted in considering fra-ternal correction, it is part of our love for someone to be concerned about the effect of sin in that person's life. If our *agapē* for someone means that we desire what is good for that person, then correspondingly we hate the evil present in his or her life that undermines the good.

How does hatred arise? Hatred is unnatural to us, in the same sense that sin is unnatural (to our prefallen, created natures). Because living in com-munity is part of what it is to be human, our natures direct us to be affable and cooperative. Aquinas discussed both envy and anger, but he considered envy the primary factor. Love in general, called *amor*, is related to pleasure, and dislike and hatred are related to what gives us unhappiness (we talk about "hating" certain foods, types of music, unwelcome chores and so on,

---

[32]For extended treatment of the topics of discord, schism, war and scandal in relation to love, see Matthew Levering, *The Betrayal of Charity: The Sins That Sabotage Divine Love* (Waco, TX: Bay-lor University Press, 2011), chaps. 5-8.

[33]See Thomas Aquinas, *ST* II-II, q. 34, a. 1.

as well as serious sources of moral evil such as terrorists). When we feel envy, it is a kind of sorrow or unhappiness over the blessings that our neighbor enjoys. Anger, on the other hand, can generate hatred, but indirectly. Because the initial phase of anger is the feeling of getting back at our neighbor, a kind of distorted justice, if not dealt with it can become a settled hatred for the neighbor. Thus, as Aquinas notes, "hatred comes from envy directly as a result of the objective situation; it comes from anger as a result of a subjective disposition" (*ST* II-II, q. 34, a. 6).

Spiritual depression (**acedia**). Directly opposed to the joy and energy for living the Christian life that ought to come from *agapē* and union with God, a person may experience a profound spiritual depression and lethargy. This is when activity, and especially Christian activity, seems altogether tedious.[34]

This is bad both in itself and in the effects caused by it. There is a kind of perverse falsification involved in the persistent reversal of good and evil: what is actually and supremely good (divine good) is seen by the person as something bad and unattractive, something causing unhappiness and boredom.[35] Every vice involves a kind of dislike of virtue and good, but spiritual apathy as a vice focuses on the divine good itself and sees it as a source of unhappiness rather than the object of joy associated with *agapē*.[36] As Matthew Levering puts it, "Rather than taking joy in the relationship with God that charity enables, we turn away from such a relationship."[37]

Prolonged spiritual apathy is highly destructive. The soul that no longer takes delight in spiritual goods will naturally turn to the things that do bring happiness, which will most likely include bodily pleasures. Despair, lack of fortitude, resistance to spiritual discipline and eventual hatred and malice are then generated.

If we move from the individual and consider societies and cultures as a whole, it is worth considering to what extent in modern society the strong and insistent attachment to the pleasures of sex, food, drink and sensual experience

---

[34]For Thomas Aquinas's treatment, see ibid., q. 35. This vice was brought into Anglican discussion by Francis Paget in his introduction to *The Spirit of Discipline* (1891). For historical treatment, see Siegfried Wenzel, *The Sin of Sloth: Acedia in Medieval Thought and Literature* (Chapel Hill: University of North Carolina Press, 1967); for an evangelical treatment, see D. Martyn Lloyd-Jones, *Spiritual Depression: Its Causes and Cures* (Grand Rapids: Eerdmans, 1965).

[35]See Thomas Aquinas, *ST* II-II, q. 35, a. 1.

[36]See ibid., q. 35, a. 2.

[37]Levering, *Betrayal of Charity*, p. 61.

in general are linked to post-Christendom secularism. In many Christian circles there is a certain pride at having moved away from world-denying attitudes and puritanical mores of the previous generation; but instead of indicating cultural sophistication or wholesome maturity, this may simply be evidence of a culture that now has turned its back on a Christian view of reality, finds spiritual things, including prayer and reading Scripture, to be unattractive and boring, and then fills the vacuum with hedonistic pursuit.

Envy. We noted above that envy is the central element shaping the vice of hatred. Thomas Aquinas gives a rather sophisticated treatment with insight into the nature of envy, and an instance where he clearly overrules Aristotle with Scripture (*ST* II-II, q. 36).

If envy is taken, in general, as the discontent caused by good things happening to someone else, then we can make a four-part refinement. First, there is the kind of unhappiness or concern when someone else comes into sudden wealth (perhaps through an inheritance or a lottery prize), and you are worried about its corrosive effect on yourself or others. Second, you may be upset by another's possession of some good not because he or she has it, but because you do not. This is not necessarily envy, if what he has is something good (perhaps an award for civic service) and it leads to greater effort on our part to be zealous for similar achievements.

Third, there is another kind of discontent that arises from considering that awards, and especially financial remuneration, go to people who are undeserving. Aristotle regarded this as a kind of "righteous indignation" and compatible with the moral life, but Thomas Aquinas explicitly disagreed, pointing out that this kind of discontent is understandable if mortal life on earth is one's entire framework (as it was for Aristotle); but if we take an eternal perspective, and that the rewards in this life pale in significance and value compared to what is laid up for us in heaven, then this kind of discontent and envy is misplaced for a Christian. The Scriptures clearly tell us not to be envious of evildoers: "Do not fret because of the wicked; do not be envious of wrongdoers" (*ST* II-II, q. 36, a. 2, citing Ps 37:1).

Fourth, there is the kind of envy based on discontent about someone else's good while being aware that it surpasses our own. This is pure envy, and it always wrong because it is contrary to the kind of Christian love for our neighbor that ought to be able to rejoice in his or her good. We are reminded in 1 John 3:14, "We know that we have passed from death to life because we love one another." In this light, we can see envy and *agapē* as similar in both referring to our neighbor's good, but as entirely contradictory movements of the will, *agapē* taking joy in the good, and envy being upset and resentful.

To conclude his extensive treatment of charity, Aquinas made the link between Christian love and wisdom (*sapientia*) as a gift of the Spirit. Divine wisdom, given to us by the Holy Spirit, enables us to know God as the highest cause and provides both the overall basis for love and its need for wise discernment. Aquinas points out the correspondence of wisdom with the beatitude that he associated with charity, "Blessed are the peacemakers" (*ST* II-II, q. 45, a. 6). We are directed then to the wonderful vision of Augustine in *The City of God* XIX, where the "tranquility of order," which applies to the individual soul, to the family and community, to our relationships with God and the whole created universe, requires the proper ordering of all objects of our love, accomplished by the wisdom that comes from the Holy Spirit.

FOR FURTHER READING

Thomas Aquinas, *ST* II-II, qq. 23-44.

Stephen Post, *A Theory of Agape: On the Meaning of Love* (Lewisburg, PA: Bucknell University Press, 1990).

Michael Sherwin, *By Knowledge and by Love: Charity and Knowledge in the Moral Theology of St. Thomas Aquinas* (Washington, DC: Catholic University of America Press, 2005), pp. 147-203.

Glen Stassen and David Gushee, *Kingdom Ethics: Following Jesus in Contemporary Context* (Downers Grove, IL: InterVarsity Press, 2003), ch. 16.

Paul Wadell, *Friendship and the Moral Life* (Notre Dame, IN: Notre Dame University Press, 1989), pp. 120-41.

16

HOPE

THE OBJECT OF CHRISTIAN HOPE is eternal life and God himself. The virtue comes to us through grace, linked to the virtues of faith and love. Just as love, a virtue of the will, depends on the relationship of faith that develops and perfects knowledge, so hope perfects the will by directing our desire to what God offers us in the age to come.

Hope (Latin *spes*, Greek *elpis*) as a theological virtue is related to the human emotion of hope, since both are directed to obtaining some good thing in the future. In this life we face uncertainty and other obstacles, and we use the word *hope* when we refer to good things or events in the future that may be difficult but possible to attain.[1] When we get into the car to take a trip, it would ordinarily be strange to say, "I hope we get there all right," unless the weather and road conditions or a possible defect in the car made things potentially hazardous. Likewise, the statement "I hope that there will be a decent harvest this year" means one thing in Iowa (where bad harvests are rare) and something very different in Darfur or any other area where people have few resources and famine is common. In most Western countries a full supermarket six months from now is taken for granted and does not involve hope, but where the difficulties are real and substantial, and good outcomes in the future are uncertain, hope is very relevant.

We need to note that there is a point of possibility beyond which hope becomes wishful thinking, that what we desire is simply unattainable, and there are no legitimate grounds for actual hope. For nearly all of us, be-

[1]See Thomas Aquinas, *ST* II-II, q. 17, a. 1.

coming an Olympic athlete or a concert pianist is material for daydreams rather than for hope.

On this natural level there is really no need to speak of a "virtue" of hope. There is an "emotion" of hope (e.g., on the level of feeling or in the sense of a more remote and rational aspiration for a fulfilling career), but the corresponding virtues that are relevant to the difficulties and dangers attaching to the things that we hope for are covered by fortitude and related subvirtues such as patience.

THE THEOLOGICAL VIRTUE OF HOPE

It is really only as a theological virtue, something given us through grace by the Holy Spirit, in association with faith and love, that there is genuine hope. The theological virtues are similar to each other in that they all have God as their object, a unique object who can be described in technical terms as first and final cause, and a divine person whom one trusts, loves, worships and lives for. The differences arise from the different aspects of relationship. *Agapē* love brings about a personal union to God for his own sake, binding the soul to God in the affection of love. Faith and hope bring about a relationship with God as the source from which other good things come to us.[2]

In relation to love and hope, faith precedes. The virtue of hope requires an object to hope in and for, and this is provided by faith. *Agapē* has the same relationship to faith, based on the general manner of relating the will to the intellect: in Thomistic terms, a totally unspecified object cannot move the will, or, in Augustinian terms, we cannot love what is unknown. But when we consider the saints in heaven, enjoying the presence of God, there will no longer be any need for faith or hope: God is no longer unseen, and the perfect happiness is no longer something in the future.[3]

The virtue of hope is thus coordinated with faith. Faith in God and in Christ establishes the basic core of the gospel: in God there is eternal life, not available by our own efforts, but made possible by the grace offered to us in Christ through the cross and resurrection. This good news of God's kingdom

---

[2]See ibid., q. 17, a. 6.
[3]See ibid., q. 18, a. 2.

is worth centering one's life on; it is worth sacrificing or subordinating all other goals for the sake of the pearl of great price (see Mt 13:45-46). To have hope, then, is to believe in eternal life with God as the supreme goal of life, and then to live one's life by that goal. This involves believing that the goal is attainable, which implies that we have faith and trust in God providing the grace that is required to attain the goal.

One may take a modern materialist view that eternal life is mythical or psychological projection, and that there is no eternal spiritual realm; or again, that such a beatitude may well exist, as the church teaches, but that one is ineligible, too sinful, not among the elect or for some other reason that this will not be personally possible. Thomas Aquinas quoted Hebrews 11:6 in this context: by faith a person believes that God exists, and that God rewards those who seek him.

In the twenty-first century, at least in the post-Christian West, it is no longer very common (as it was, for example, in Puritan Massachusetts) to have the fear of losing salvation, the guilty fear of having been too sinful for God's forgiveness or the fear of not being among the elect; rather, there is skepticism concerning the reality of beatitude—heaven is perhaps only a symbolic ideal—and in most liberal church circles there is the confident assumption that there is nothing arduous or difficult in attaining it. On the basis of a modern liberal view of the love and justice of God, all should receive eternal life, and none will be excluded. There is some biblical and theological basis for trusting in the generosity of God, but there is also the possibility of the sin of presumption (see below). Here we can make the point that a faith that makes universal salvation a starting point for these matters makes biblical hope unnecessary. If the future good is assumed to be the automatic inheritance of all human beings, then it no longer represents anything difficult to achieve, nor is its possible fulfillment in doubt.

There are two lines of analysis that criticize this Thomistic and traditional understanding of hope: the first deals with the emphasis on personal fulfillment as a selfish motivation, while the second questions the individualistic nature of the traditional virtue of hope.

The object of hope is beatitude, the eternal life with God, with which we began. This, of course, has been true for the Protestant tradition as well. As the Westminster Shorter Catechism puts it, "The chief end of man is to glorify God and enjoy him forever." Hope is centered on God as the fulfillment of our need for truth, life and being. Is this not a selfish motivation? If hope is seen as some kind of prize or reward in heaven for following Christ in this life, then is it not the case that perhaps we are making difficult choices and actions simply to gain the advantages that we will have in the next life?

This line of critique carries more weight to those under the influence of Kantian ethics, where the right basis for action is seen as whatever is inherently right to unprejudiced reason, based on universal principles and not contingent factors, and not under the influence of reward or punishment.

But even before Kant and the Enlightenment's attack on traditional Christianity, there were schools of thought in Roman Catholic circles where such a self-regarding view of a relationship with God was seen as questionable. François Fénelon, Madame Guyon and others in the seventeenth-century movement known as Quietism proposed that the kind of hope that seeks fulfillment in God has an element of egotism. We need to aspire to "disinterestedness" in our relationship to God, focused purely on himself and his goodness rather than on any benefit that we derive.[4]

A complete answer to this would be lengthy and complex, involving as it does explaining and contrasting a number of fundamental points in the ethics of Augustine and Thomas Aquinas, on the one hand, and the later tradition of nominalism and voluntarism, on the other. One key point to keep in mind, however, is that acting for our own happiness and fulfillment is fundamental and natural; it is not a matter of choice. The key is to make sure that our notion of fulfillment is centered on God above all else, and that is precisely the virtue of hope. This relates also to the discussion in the chapter on love, where there has been a running critique of a theological love that has any kind of self-regarding element.

Another line of critique is directed to the object of hope being personal fulfillment in a heavenly dimension, removed from earthly concerns and

---

[4]See the brief treatment of Quietism by William Hill in appendix 2 of the Blackfriars edition of the *Summa Theologiae*, vol. 33, pp. 136-38. See the helpful study of Jesuits and Jansenists in Jennifer Herdt, *Putting On Virtue: The Legacy of the Splendid Vices* (Chicago: University of Chicago Press, 2008), chap. 8, and note her point that the error of this and other similar movements was to see divine grace and human agency as mutually exclusive (p. 238).

not including hope for earthly justice. As Nicholas Wolterstorff has described the teaching of Aquinas,

> Christian hope is hope for consummation—consummation here being understood as a supernatural mode of union with God. Christian hope is not hope for what might transpire in history but hope for a state of *eudaimonia* that transcends history. Hence it has nothing to do with the struggle for justice within history.[5]

Wolterstorff goes on to argue that what we as Christians should hope for is God's new creation, a "transformed mode of existence" brought about by God, and also deliverance in this created order, within history, especially deliverance from injustice.[6]

The main problem here is a category confusion. Since Wolterstorff is concerned about the rectification of injustice, the relevant virtue is justice and righteousness, which is directed to establishing justice, insofar as it is to be accomplished by human action and institutions. This is not simply a human moral virtue, but one that is spiritually formed—that is, coordinated with the virtues of faith, hope and love, and enriched with the gifts of the Holy Spirit. There will be a need for wisdom and discernment in connection with the right means and the timing, plus fortitude and patience in working for goals that may be remote and not able to be fulfilled within one's own lifetime.

There is, however, an aspect of consummation in Thomistic teaching that seems truncated, and that has to do with the inclusion of the neighbor—friends and community—in the beatific vision. In the *Summa Theologiae*, in the section on the final end and happiness at the beginning of the *prima secundae partis*, Aquinas proposes for discussion the argument that since charity includes the love of God and neighbor, then the fellowship of friends is necessary for happiness.[7] In his reply to this argument Aquinas says that if there were only one soul enjoying God, it would be happy, even with no neighbor to love. And if there were a neighbor present, love for that person would be a result of love for God. Thus friendship is not an expansion, but

---

[5]Nicholas Wolterstorff, "Seeking Justice in Hope," in *The Future of Hope: Christian Tradition amid Modernity and Postmodernity*, ed. Miroslav Volf and William Katerberg (Grand Rapids: Eerdmans, 2004), p. 79.
[6]Ibid., p. 87.
[7]See Thomas Aquinas, *ST* I-II, q. 4, a. 8.

a kind of concomitant with perfect happiness. This seems to rule out having one's family and friends as directly part of the hope one has in God's consummation, unless seen as implied and included in hope in God.

This line of critique receives further strength by considering Aquinas's treatment of the question of the existence of the virtue of hope in Christ. There is an important reason—the union of the Son with the Father in the divine nature—why it is inappropriate to talk about Christ having faith, or hope, as Jesus would have already enjoyed the fruits of that divine relationship (to which ordinary faith and hope point). But, adds Aquinas, Jesus would have had hope regarding "things which he did not yet possess" (*ST* III, q. 7, a. 4), things that would come to him in the future. These would pertain to his perfection, such as immortality and the glorification of the body, which he could hope for as things yet to come.

These objects of hope, however, pertain to his individual perfection and leave out the corporate dimension of the church, the sharing of glory with the rest of the body. The prayer of our Lord in John 17 seems to point to these specific, corporate matters of hope and desire: "That they may be one, as we are one" (Jn 17:11), "That they . . . may be sanctified in the truth" (Jn 17:19), and especially the concluding verses of the chapter:

> Father, I desire that those also, whom you have given me, may be with me where I am, to see my glory, which you have given me because you loved me before the foundation of the world. . . . I made your name known to them, and I will make it known, so that the love with which you have loved me may be in them, and I in them. (Jn 17:24-26)

It is hard to understand why, among those future matters that Jesus was looking forward to as things to come but not yet possessed, there would not also be the fulfillment of his brothers and sisters, their perfection in truth, and their sharing in the unity and love of the Trinity.

LACK OF HOPE: DESPAIR AND PRESUMPTION

There is a proper fear of God (fear of offending the Father); then despair can be seen as excessive fear, while presumption is a deficiency of the proper fear of God. Despair and presumption in a way collapse the eschatological or future dimension of God's work in us and in the world by anticipating an unwarranted conclusion. As Josef Pieper put it, "Against all reality, they transform the 'not yet' of hope into either the 'not' or the 'already' of fulfillment."[8]

To despair, in theological terms, is not so much to be very depressed about life in general and to lose all optimism, but rather to lose the specific hope of eternal life, beatitude and union with God. The loss occurs when a person thinks that forgiveness of sins for him or her is impossible, that following the way of Christ is simply too difficult, or that God will not supply the grace and strength necessary.

Just as the virtue of hope depends on faith and a correct appreciation of God's character, so the vice of despair relates to a false understanding of God. Thomas Aquinas points to the evidence in Ezekiel 18:23 of God's desire: "Have I any pleasure in the death of the wicked, says the Lord GOD, and not rather that they should turn from their ways and live?" Thus to think that God does not turn sinners to himself is a false opinion.[9] Despair is not just an attitude or psychological depression, but an attitude based on a falsehood. Despair is not so much a mood into which one falls, but rather a decision of the intellect: "Both he who hopes and he who despairs choose these attitudes with their will and lets them determine their conduct."[10] Thus in a very real sense, despair in a Christian is a decision against Christ. It is a denial of the redemption. Despair becomes a denial of the way of fulfillment, and this "before the very eyes of him who is preeminently 'the way' to eternal life."[11]

It is possible, of course, to be well acquainted with the Scriptures and to have theological knowledge about the grace of God but not be able to apply this effectively to one's own situation and relationship to God. This corresponds, according to Aquinas, to the gap between universal knowledge and particular judgment, which is one way of explaining the phenomenon of sin (as we see in the chapter on that above): just as a person may choose fornication in a particular instance even though knowing that it is wrong in general, so a person may know that God wants sinners to be saved in general and yet despair of that in his or her own particular situation.[12]

---

[8]Josef Pieper, *On Hope*, trans. Mary McCarthy (San Francisco: Ignatius Press, 1986), p. 47.
[9]See Thomas Aquinas, *ST* II-II, q. 20, a. 1.
[10]Pieper, *On Hope*, p. 49.
[11]Ibid., pp. 50-51.
[12]See Thomas Aquinas, *ST* II-II, q. 20, a. 2

In R. C. Mortimer's treatment, Aquinas is said to have held that despair was the greatest of all sins, worse than not believing in God at all, even than hating God, because when we despair, we give up all efforts to serve God, and we sink into torpor or indulge recklessly in sin.[13] Despair is more serious from our point of view, says Aquinas, but in itself despair is less grave than infidelity and hatred of God, since despair is not aimed at God so directly.[14] Despair can be linked to *acedia*, or spiritual dejection, the loss of interest in spiritual things, because despair is connected to a loss of confidence that the difficulties of the Christian life can be overcome or that the struggle is worth the effort.[15]

Presumption is the counterpart to despair on the opposite side, but it similarly fails to see the situation of a person's relationship to God accurately. It minimizes the obstacles on the path to eternal life and exaggerates the ease of attainment.

As Aquinas explained it, an action or way of life may be possible through the appropriate virtue, which a person may develop, or may be possible only through the help of divine power. There can be presumption about both one's abilities and God's grace. One may overestimate one's abilities or capacities and thus think something possible of performance when it in fact is beyond our capabilities. Or in the area of grace, one may think that God's grace will be forthcoming automatically, as though God "gives pardon to those who persist in their sins or leads those to glory who shirk from an upright life" (*ST* II-II, q. 21, a. 2). Both kinds of error are prevalent. Many have a Pelagian kind of confidence in human nature's moral capacities. Likewise, many falsely view God's mercy in forgiveness as something automatic. As the German writer Heinrich Heine is famously reported to have put it on his deathbed, "God will forgive me; that's his job."

There is always a kind of misunderstanding associated with a falsely ordered love. Just as some have difficulty believing that God is indeed lenient to sinners or actually enables them to repent, so presumption is based on obviously false notions about God. Where this is the case, then this is a sin

---

[13]R. C. Mortimer, *The Elements of Moral Theology*, rev. ed. (London: Adam & Charles Black, 1953), p. 133.
[14]See Thomas Aquinas, *ST* II-II, q. 20, a .3.
[15]See ibid., q. 20, a. 4.

against the virtue of faith. There is definitely an element of pride in the generation of presumption, involving the assumption (false hope) that God will not, after all, punish impenitent sinners or exclude them from his glory.[16]

PROPER HOPE: REPENTANCE AND CONVERSION

A common moral theology textbook in many Anglican seminaries in the mid-twentieth century was *Some Principles of Moral Theology*, by Kenneth Kirk.[17] One merit of Kirk's approach was his recognition of the overlap with ascetical theology, with which he tried to take account of contemporary psychology, as it was developing in the early twentieth century. While generally within the Anglo-Catholic Thomist tradition, he was, more than most, willing to modify the Scholastic terms and be flexible, perhaps even radical at times, with the inherited terminology and structure.

With the theological virtues, for example, he was not content to leave them as the traditional inherited triad of faith, hope and love. According to Kirk,

> We can conclude that the inward dispositions, without which progress in the Christian life is impossible, involve the dedication, purification, or right orientation, of intellect, desire and will. The first of these may be called faith, the second penitence or hope, the third the zeal of love. These inward dispositions are the gift of the Holy Spirit, though even in his natural state man is not altogether without them. For . . . it is impossible not to recognize in every man, however little touched by religion, a tendency to progress towards a higher condition.[18]

Kirk was on shaky ground in assigning hope to "desire" rather than the will, and on even shakier footing in eroding the distinction between theological and moral virtues by suggesting that the Pauline theological virtues can be seen to overlap with moral idealism.

With these reservations, and with the observation that we should not follow Kirk in his reductionist strategy of calling hope "repentance" (because it leaves out too much), we can point to a great insight on his part: the

---

[16]See ibid., q. 21, a. 4.
[17]Kenneth Kirk, *Some Principles of Moral Theology and Their Application* (London: Longmans, Green, 1920) (with many reprints).
[18]Ibid., pp. 46-47.

central dynamic feature of hope is grounded in the character of God depicted in Scripture:

> The purpose of contrition, of repentance, is to be the gateway to a new life;
> and a new life is only possible in the light of hope. Mere regret for the past
> can never produce a change of character, if unaccompanied by a guarantee of
> a better future. Such a guarantee, foreshadowed in the Old Testament, is given
> in the New: God has commended His love to us, in that while we were yet
> sinners Christ died for us. In this we know ourselves loved with a love that is
> able to overcome all impediments in ourselves; and shame for the past and
> hope for the future spring to life together.[19]

Kirk has indeed grasped something here. He recognized that in the notion
of repentance the emotion of sorrow for sin is not the most important or
crucial feature;[20] rather, it is the change of life to which we turn. He affirms
that "repentance is idle unless it is the gateway of the new life,"[21] and that
this appeal to turn from sin to the new life is a constant theme throughout
the Bible, summarized in Isaiah 1:16-17: "Cease to do evil, learn to do good."

Further, Kirk's fastening on repentance ties in well with guiding a passage
between the antitheses of despair and presumption. Despair gives up on the
possibility of receiving God's gift of grace and wholeness, while presumption
sees God's grace as unnecessary, redundant or automatic. Repentance expresses that element of hope that change is possible, by God's grace, and precisely by facing sin in the light of the cross and salvation in Christ renews hope.

However, *conversion* would be the better term for what Kirk had grasped
(but actually failed to follow through with), since *repentance* in modern
English (whatever the Latin etymology) means primarily "to feel remorse,
contrition and self-reproach, to feel regret." Though Kirk acknowledged
that the emotional aspect of contrition should not be the dominant note,
his choice of the term *repentance* was unfortunate. Even more revealing
is the way in which he develops and concludes this chapter: he notes the
three parts of confession, reparation and amendment, but he focuses on
the duration and signs of growing penitence. What has unfortunately
dropped out of Kirk's account is the confidence in the new life in Christ that

---

[19]Ibid., pp. 72-73.
[20]Ibid., p. 66.
[21]Ibid., p. 73.

he identified as hope, and that he might have developed under the category of amendment.

More profoundly, however, hope must be centered not on the possibility of improvement, or on progress, or even on grace, but on God, the reality of the coming kingdom, and the new life in Christ, only partly available to us now. God and the inevitable triumph of his purposes for the universe are our ultimate hope; that the opposition to God, and the disorder so evident now, will yield to the peaceable kingdom; and that, as the Gospel and Epistles of John emphasize so well, this new life in Christ is something that begins in us now.[22]

The community as well as the individual context of hope can be seen in the phrase from Colossians, "Christ in you, the hope of glory" (Col 1:27). About the phrase "Christ in you" (*Christos en hymin*), Eduard Lohse was categorical in saying, "Doubtless this does not mean the pneumatic indwelling of the Lord in the hearts of the believers, but rather the Christ preached among the nations, the Lord proclaimed in the community's midst."[23] In this reading, the object of hope is the glory of Christ proclaimed throughout the world.

Rather than follow Lohse in this, we can take the broader set of meanings, both corporate and individual, that Christ as our hope is both "among you"—that is, among groups of Gentiles like the Colossians—and within us as individual Christians.[24] The Spirit dwelling within us (the indwelling Christ and indwelling Spirit are pretty much interchangeable in Paul's thought) is a key part of our confidence and hope for our future relationship with God, the beatific vision, the fullness of glory yet to be revealed (Rom 8:18-21). By including both the individual and community dimensions in our hope in Christ, we point to our personal consummation in Christ and that our hope also includes the whole redeemed community.

---

[22]See N. T. Wright, *Surprised by Hope: Rethinking Heaven, the Resurrection, and the Mission of the Church* (San Francisco: HarperOne, 2008), especially pp. 93-186.

[23]Eduard Lohse, *Colossians and Philemon*, trans. William Poehlmann and Robert Karris, ed. Helmut Koester (Philadelphia: Fortress, 1971), p. 76.

[24]F. F. Bruce remarks, "The phrase 'in you' might mean 'in your midst' (as a community) or 'within you' (as individuals). Neither sense should be excluded, but the thought of Christ as indwelling individual believers is completely in line with Pauline thought" (*The Epistle to the Colossians* [Grand Rapids: Eerdmans, 1984], p. 86).

HOPE AND THE MORAL VIRTUES

Hope directed to the kingdom of God and a new heaven and new earth provides a basis for wisdom in acting that both respects the integrity of this world now and anticipates its renewal in the coming kingdom. Although death and destruction are still all too real and confront Christians with challenges in the form of allocations of resources, involvement in wars, and so on, such difficulties can be faced more clearly with the informed Christian view of God's ultimate triumph and renewal of heaven and earth.

As a virtue of the will, hope is especially related to the moral virtue of justice. As a cardinal virtue, justice, as we have seen, relates to the ordering of the person's psyche and overall being, including the body, mind and spirit. The virtue is especially extended to proper relationships with people and other external relations. With a firm belief in the resurrection of our Lord and in the new heaven and earth to be ushered in, we can work for appropriate goals in the right away. As N. T. Wright observes, proper Christian hope will enable us to work for a justice that avoids both a liberal activism that emphasizes human responsibility and a quietism that avoids confronting injustice and flees to individualist escapism.[25] As for specific issues of justice, it is hard to disagree with Wright's concern for economic imbalance in the world and the problem of Third World debt.[26] There is an excellent biblical basis in the concepts of jubilee and the shared well-being of shalom for reducing inequality and enabling the poor in the Third World to ease the burden of debt.

There is a parallel in Christian hope between personal holiness and social justice. Just as we would not accept the argument that any attempt at developing a holy life will be frustrated by human imperfections and lingering sinfulness, and that therefore we should simply wait for the transformation after our resurrection, so we should not allow Christians to argue that it is too difficult and frustrating to work for social improvements, and that we can simply wait for the eschaton's fulfillment. Both attitudes are contrary to the New Testament, especially Paul's message in Romans.[27]

Scripture links the virtue of hope with patience (and thus fortitude) in

---

[25]Wright, *Surprised by Hope*, pp. 215-20.
[26]Ibid., pp. 216-17.
[27]Ibid., p. 221.

several different places. In Romans 5 Paul offers this marvelous assurance: "Since we are justified through faith, we have peace with God through our Lord Jesus Christ, through whom we have obtained access to this grace in which we stand; and we boast in our hope of sharing the glory of God" (Rom 5:1-2). And Paul commends the Thessalonian Christians for their "steadfastness of hope in our Lord Jesus Christ" (1 Thess 1:3).

A prayer by the theologian John Baillie puts hope in close connection with faith and love:

> Help thou mine unbelief, O God, give me greater patience in my hope, and make me more constant in my love. In loving let me believe and in believing let me love; and in loving and in believing let me hope for a more perfect love and a more unwavering faith, through Jesus Christ my Lord. Amen.[28]

FOR FURTHER READING

Thomas Aquinas, *ST* II-II, qq. 17-22.

Romanus Cessario, "The Theological Virtue of Hope," in *The Ethics of Aquinas*, ed. Stephen Pope (Washington, DC: Georgetown University Press, 2002), pp. 232-43.

Oliver O'Donovan, *Self, World, and Time*, vol. 1, *Ethics as Theology: An Induction* (Grand Rapids: Eerdmans, 2013), pp. 99-133.

Josef Pieper, *On Hope*, trans. Mary McCarthy (San Francisco: Ignatius Press, 1986).

N. T. Wright, *Surprised by Hope: Rethinking Heaven, the Resurrection, and the Mission of the Church* (San Francisco: HarperOne, 2008), chap. 6.

---

[28]John Baillie, *A Diary of Private Prayer* (New York: Scribner, 1949), p. 97.

Name Index

Subject Index

SCRIPTURE INDEX

Finding the Textbook You Need

The IVP Academic Textbook Selector
is an online tool for instantly finding the IVP books
suitable for over 250 courses across 24 disciplines.

ivpacademic.com